Rav Dovber Pinson

ILLUMINATED

SOUND

THE BAAL SHEM TOV
ON PRAYER

Rav Dovber Pinson

ILLUMINATED SOUND

THE BAAL SHEM TOV
ON PRAYER

IYYUN PUBLISHING

Published by IYYUN Publishing
232 Bergen Street
Brooklyn, NY 11217

http:/www.iyyun.com

Iyyun Publishing books may be purchased for educational, business or sales promotional use. For information please contact: contact@IYYUN.com

Cover and Book Design: Rochie Pinson
Cover Art: "Transcendence" by Sandra Encaoua / www.encaweb.com

pb ISBN 978-1-7367026-1-1

Pinson, DovBer 1971-
Illuminated Sound: The Baal Shem Tov on Prayer
1.Judaism 2. Spirituality 3. Philosophy

This book was made possible by

THE NAGEL JEWISH ACADEMY

CONTENTS

Note to the Reader

Parts of this text are taken from previously published works, such as *Inner World of Jewish Prayer*, *Breathing and Quieting the Mind*, and *The Power of Sound and Vibration*. In the present text, these ideas are enhanced and expanded upon.

OPENING

To pray, or in Yiddish to 'Daven', is to dream, to yearn, to long, to reach out and connect to the Infinite. Conversely, life devoid of Davening is a dreamless, disconnected wasteland. Without prayer, a little something within us dies, as it is an intrinsic part of being human to dream, to imagine, to aspire, and to create.

The Hebrew word *Adam* / human is rooted in the word *Dimyon* / imagination. We are created in the Divine imagination, as it were, and we, in turn, create our reality through the prism of our own imagination. We are not merely 'Homo Sapiens'; we are more accurately *Homo Imaginus*. Part of what makes us human is our ability to completely reimagine our lives, or even the entire world, at any given moment. Hence, when we lose touch with our *Dimyon* and stop dreaming, praying, or yearning, we cease being fully human.

The Torah relates the shocking tale of the sale of Yoseph, the beloved son of Yaakov. Yoseph has aroused tremendous animosity in his brothers; one day a tipping point is reached and the brothers perform the horrifying act of selling their little brother into slavery. When Yaakov inquires of the whereabouts of Yoseph, they lie and tell him that he has been killed. After years of mourning and never being fully consoled, the truth is revealed that Yoseph is still alive. Yaakov then gathers up the whole family and descends to Egypt where Yoseph is now the vizier, and reunites with his beloved child. At the end of Yaakov's life, Yoseph goes to his father to receive blessings for his own children, and Yaakov, overwhelmed with emotion, declares: "I never פללתי / *Philalti* that I would ever see your face again, and Hashem has granted me to even see the face of your children!" (*Bereishis*, 48:11). *Philalti*, says Rashi, means 'filled my heart'; Yaakov is saying: "I was so devastated by your absence that I never 'filled my heart' with the thought that I would ever see your face again."

The word for prayer in Hebrew is *Tefilah*, and thus 'to pray' is *l'Hispalel*. The word *l'Hispalel* comes from the same root as *Philalti*, implying that 'prayer' fills our hearts and minds with dreams and visions of what we most deeply desire for ourselves and for the world.

In this sense, to pray is to fill our hearts with the 'impossible' dreams and prophetic visions of an ideal future. Despite all the suffering and brokenness we may see in the world in its present state of concealment, to pray means to live prophetically, as it were — to long, hope, dream, envision, and strive for a better tomorrow. Prayer is therefore intricately bound up with prophetic consciousness.

In fact, the very first time a variation of the word *Tefilah* appears in the Torah, it appears in relation to a *Navi* / prophet. Hashem appears to Avimelech, the king of Gerar, who somewhat innocently took Sarah, the wife of Avraham, into his home, and tells the king in a dream, "You are to die because of the woman that you have taken, for she is a married woman...." "O G-d," he responds, "Will You slay people even though innocent? He (Avraham) himself said to me, 'She is my sister!'"...And Hashem said to him, "I know that you did this with a blameless heart...And now, restore the man's wife כי-נביא הוא ויתפלל בעדך / for he is a prophet, and he will pray for you" (*Bereishis*, 20:3-7). In other words: Avraham will pray for you *because* he is a prophet and knows the truth of your predicament and purity in relation to Sarah. The juxtaposition of these fundamental ideas expresses a profound relationship between prayer and prophecy, which we will continue to explore.

Tefilah, like prophecy and dreaming, is a spiritual practice or state of mind which helps us to avoid getting stuck in what *appears* to be, and instead focuses our awareness on the infinite possibility of what *can* be. And when we are struggling to even see the possibility of our hopes and dreams manifesting, whether for ourselves, our loved ones, all of Klal Yisrael or the entire world, then we need to pray to be able to pray.

When we live with hope, and an overarching awareness of the positive development and momentum of the world, understanding deep in our being that we are getting closer and closer to the ultimate prophecy of worldwide Redemption, then we are effectively living our Tefilah. To never despair, and to always cultivate a mindset of hope, this in itself is a vital aspect of Tefilah. Chazal tell us, ולואי יתפלל אדם כל היום כולו / "If only a person would pray throughout the entire day" (*Berachos*, 21a). In its depth, this statement means, 'If only we would live our entire lives in constant connection with the Infinite Source of blessing!'

Prayer enhances the quality of the human spirit. It is the eternal moment in which we renew our commitments to ourselves, to our family and friends, and to the Creator as well as Creation. It is how we formulate and express our deepest yearnings and aspirations, our highest hopes and dreams. During the act of Davening, we remind ourselves of what we truly want and need in life, what really matters, rather than what all the advertisers work so hard to convince us we should want.

Deeper still, our life is meant to be a living prayer because, in fact, we were created by prayer. The Torah tells us at the beginning of creation that rain only came down to the earth through the participation of man, as it did not rain until Adam Davened for rain (מלמד שיצאו דשאים ועמדו על פתח קרקע עד שבא אדם הראשון ובקש עליהם רחמים וירדו גשמים וצמחו: *Chulin*, 60b). On the other hand, the Torah states, ואד יעלה מן־הארץ / "A flow welled up from the ground." This means, as Rashi writes, "Hashem caused the deeps to rise and fill the clouds with water (and thus rain) in order to moisten the dust; man was then created [from the moist clay]" (*Medrash Rabbah*, Bereishis, 14:1). As such, our very existence is dependent on rain, and the very existence of rain, in turn, is dependent on us and our prayers. We are birthed through the very rain that paradoxically has been drawn down through our Davening. We are thus created through our own Tefilos, as it were, making prayer a constituent element of our being human. We are created through prayer and our lives are prayer. An allusion to this idea is that the 'filling' or 'hidden' letters of the name *Adam*, the primordial human being, spell the word מתפלל / praying (אדם / *Adam* is spelled אלף דלת מם, the hidden letters of *Adam* spell the word מתפלל: *Ben Yehoyada*, Berachos, 5b). The very essence, the sap of our existence, is Tefilah.

Tefilah is a process that distills truth. Through the act of prayer, we reveal to ourselves what truly matters to us. In a focused and transparent state of mind, we are able to see that whatever comes up for us and whatever we end up praying for is a sign and indicator of what is troubling us and which areas in our life that we truly wish to improve. Balancing expression and reflection, Davening is a sifter that separates nonsense from sense. Sometimes, what we think we really yearn for may be, in fact, utter foolishness. Yet, through the act of verbalizing (crystalizing) our desires with a heightened awareness and open heart, we are able to more objectively assess what wants are nonsense and foolishness, and which are truly needed or necessary.

Through our Davening, we are able to confirm and establish דעת / *Da'as* / integrated understanding in our life. In prayer, a holistic awareness of what is important, and what is not, is clarified (*Moreh Nevuchim*, 3:44).

And, interestingly, while Davening gives us the clarity of Da'as, we also need Da'as to Daven: אם אין דיעה תפלה מניין / "If there is no Da'as how can there be Tefilah?" (Yerushalmi, *Berachos*, 5:2). It is only through Da'as that a person can really know what they are praying for, and to then take the proper approach to Davening. In other words: We need self-knowledge to Daven, and we gain even more self-knowledge through Davening.

Indeed, Davening is an intimate encounter with one's essential self. Prayer is an opportunity to enter a time and place in which we can cleave to Truth and ask ourselves, "What do I actually want?" This practice of 'active opening' allows us to peel and strip away the externalities of our personal narrative, thereby revealing our real desires.

The word *Tefilah* shares the same root-letters as the word *Yefalel*, which means 'judgment', from *Pallel* / to judge. *L'hispalel* / to pray, thus means to assess or judge oneself.[*]

---

* *Tehilim*, 106:30. ויעמד פינחס ויפלל :Sanhedrin, 44a. ויתפלל לא נאמר אלא ויפלל מלמד שעשה / פלילות עם קונו / "'And he prayed' is not stated; rather, 'and he executed judgment' is stated, which teaches that he entered into a judgment together with his Creator": Rav Hirsch, *Bereishis*, 20:7.

Tefilah is simultaneously an act of self-reflection and soul-expression. It is a time to attain proper perspective concerning our own personality and our duties towards Hashem, the world and humanity. To pray is to self-reflect in order to see where we have come from, and envision where we would like to go.

In a moment or mode of prayer, we are filled with an overwhelming awareness that we are in the Divine Presence, and thus in a time of revealed truth and clarity.

As a result, our egoic walls of self-deception and delusion come tumbling down. Who we are and what we truly desire become increasingly clear when the garments of our superficial schemes and desires simply evaporate.

We may at first seek prayer as a means to petition the Creator of the Universe to give us things we think we need. Yet, as we move deeper into prayer, through the very act of verbalizing our dreams and yearnings, we are able to become more aware of what we really do want and need. Through the lens of our beseeching and pleading, we gain access to a self-reflective awareness of our own desires.

To stand in front of the Creator of the Universe is to stand in your deepest truth and purpose. One cannot say, 'I am standing in front of my Creator and the Creator of all life, and I don't care about my life or the world.' That would be an obvious contradiction in terms. To stand in front of *HaKadosh Baruch Hu* / The Holy One, blessed be He, is to align oneself with the 'vision' *Kaviyachol* / so-to-speak, of The Creator of all Life. When we pray, we are able to see the world through G-d's eyes.

As we step into Tefilah, we need to ask ourselves: What do I stand for? What does HaKadosh Baruch Hu want from human lives in general, and what does He want from my life in particular? Where is my own life heading? What do I need to dream and pray for? Where is the world heading? What should I pray for on behalf of the world? In this way, through honest prayer, we strengthen and reaffirm our positive convictions and healthy attachment to our highest ideals. Through Tefilah, every deeper truth that we have learned and experienced becomes integrated deeper into our psyche and into our very being. In prayer, we learn to stand in our truth while standing before the Absolute Truth.

Davening is a process of inner transformation, where ideas and ideals are converted into real life. Accordingly, Tefilah is called *Avodah* / work or service, since it is through the inner alchemy of prayer that we can turn ourselves over and elevate every aspect of our lives for the better. Prayer is a practice of opening ourselves up to examine, experience and express our authentic self.

Davening is a time to turn inward in reflection; it is a time for quietness, contemplation and being still, amid a world dominated by noise and movement. And yet, Tefilah is specifically referred to by the sages as the 'work of the heart' (*Ta'anis*, 2a). The work of prayer is rooted in rousing and refining our dreams and emotions, not in pondering abstract ideas. In the language of the Gemara, זמן תורה לחוד וזמן תפילה לחוד / "The time of Torah (intellectual pursuit) is distinct, and the time of Tefilah is distinct" (*Shabbos*, 10a). Davening demands *Kavanas HaLev* / focus of the heart, which is different than *Kavanah Iyyunis* / focus of the mind (*She'eiris Yisrael*, Sha'ar Hiskashrus, 1. The Rebbe, *Sha'ar Halacha uMinhag*. Tefilah includes sensing and feeling the Divinity in what one learned previously: *HaYom Yom*, 20th of Tamuz).

When we Daven honestly, with Kavanas HaLev, there is a deep inward movement, connecting us to our deepest, most vulnerable selves. Paradoxically, this is also the path of deepest connection to that which is beyond ourselves. The root of the word *Tefilah* is *Tofel* / to bind or to connect.* In Tefilah, we reach deep within and connect to our deepest self and, simultaneously, we reach out and connect to a power beyond ourselves, the Creator of all life.

There are two general perspectives or paradigms of reality: הנהגת המשפט / *Hanhagas HaMishpat* / the ways of justice, and הנהגת היחוד / *Hanhagas HaYichud* / the ways of unity. *Hanhagas*

HaMishpat refers to the world of linear causality, otherwise known as cause and effect. From this perspective, what was put into motion in the past cannot be transformed or redeemed, only redressed. This is the world of strict *Din* / Justice. In *Hanhagas HaYichud*, however, there is no past or future, as it were, and everything exists right now, in the eternal present. Tefilah is a portal through which we can access the deeper dimensions of perfection and unification present in the prayerful moment, including all past and future possibilities. From this perspective of unity, we can access the eternal 'now' and alter the imprints and effects of our past upon the future.

By moving 'inward' during prayer, we simultaneously travel upward, connecting with the Ultimate Unity beyond all duality. From within this timeless moment of intimate connection to the Infinite, Unmanifest Source of all Life, we openly express all of our deepest dreams and highest ideals, our yearnings and hopes, our needs and desires for our own lives and for the good of the world. From this place of integral expansion, we are able to not only transform ourselves, but positively affect the world around us.

---

* See *Targum Onkelus*, Bereishis, 30:8. Note, *Mishnah Kelim*, 3:5. הטופל כלי חרם. The Alter Rebbe cites this Mishnah with a Tav (not a Tes), התופל כלי חרם as a cognate of the word *Tefilah*: *Torah Ohr*, Terumah, 79d. See *Tikunei Zohar*, Tikkun 49. The Rebbe's Ha'ara on *Sefer HaMaamorim Tav/Shin/Tes*, p. 79. *Likutei Sichos* 24, p. 29.

The deepest of all of our hopes and yearnings is the yearning to be consciously connected with the Source of All Life. All creations, from humans to animals, plants and minerals, share this yearning in some form. In this sense, all beings and all phenomena are essentially always in a state of prayer. This idea is explored and expressed beautifully by the sages in an ancient text called *Perek Shira* / Chapters of Song, a poetic montage of Torah quotes attributed to various animals, plants, and landscapes. Its underlying, and even overt, message is that *Nishmas Kol Chai t'Varech* / the Breath of All Life Shall Praise You!

All states of consciousness, as well, are essentially states of prayer. Even when we are frustrated, fearful, stressed or broken-hearted, expressing these feelings to HaKadosh Baruch Hu in Davening is healing and hopeful, as we are offering them up, as it were, or placing them into Hashem's hands. They are no longer just 'ours', and turning them over to HaKadosh Baruch Hu allows us to feel unburdened.

Davening imbues us with a sense of lightness; we realize that our lives are not a series of random coincidences or an inescapable chain of events. We are never alone, rather the Master of the Universe is listening to every word and every feeling and thought we express. In this way, prayer is its own reward. In truth, all our prayers are always heard and answered, although sometimes not immediately or in the ways that we had expected. We come to recognize that our lives are lived within the Divine Presence. We are thus enabled to make Divine Reality our reality.

While Davening is the main Yiddish term for 'prayer', its origin is uncertain. Perhaps it is derived from the Aramaic of Chazal, *Da Avuhon* / "This is (from) our ancestors," meaning that this methodology comes from our forefathers and foremothers. (*Da Avuhon* is not a recorded expression of Chazal, rather it is how they most likely would have said, "This is from our ancestors.") Or perhaps it is related to the English word 'Divine', implying that Davenen is a process of 'Divine-ing' or 'becoming more Divine-like'. When we Daven, we are indeed communing and unifying with the Divine, and tapping into the transformational practices of our *Avos* / ancestors, as well.

Although we are always in essence bonded with HaKadosh Baruch Hu, we are not always conscious of this fact. By Davening, we nurture and develop this intrinsic bond. More than just aligning our lives with the Creator of Life, in prayer we come to experience a revelation of our inherent unity with the Divine. Such revelatory experience elevates us to a peak of sensitivity, a sense of potential, an awareness that all and everything around us is one and unified with the Infinite One.

Perhaps we begin our Davening by expressing our wants, desires, needs, hopes and dreams. However, as we move deeper into more elevated states of Davening, it becomes less about what we want or think we want, and more about opening ourselves to Hashem's blessings that are always already present. The deeper the prayer, the more it is about being a transparent channel, a conduit for the Divine flow to move into and through us — thereby refining both our lives as well as the world around us.

This understanding of the world-repairing function of prayer is illustrated beautifully in a classic Chasidic story. When the young brilliant scholar, Rebbe Schneur Zalman of Liadi (later to be known affectionately as the *Alter Rebbe* / the Old Rebbe), was pondering his next move in life, he said to himself, "I know I need to go travel to a center of Torah, and I have two options, Vilna or Mezeritch." In Eastern Europe at that time, there were two great capitals of Jewish life: Vilna, the seat of the famed Gaon of Vilna, and Mezeritch, the town where Rebbe DovBer the Magid, the prime disciple of the Baal Shem Tov, resided. "I know that in Vilna students are taught how to learn Torah, and that in Mezeritch one can learn how to Daven. I already know a little how to learn, but how to truly Daven, I know very little, so I will go to Mezeritch." In Mezeritch he became the youngest and most erudite student of the Magid and went on to be a great Tzadik, teacher and Rebbe in his own right. Ultimately, R. Shnuer Zalman became the greatest expounder of the teachings of the Baal Shem Tov and the Magid; the author of the 'Written Torah' of Chasidus, the *Tanya*.

In addition to being a Mitzvah and a mode of connection with HaKadosh Baruch Hu, Davening also serves to gather together what a person has studied and turns it inwards, making it more real and tangible in their life (בכל יום צריך להיות בבחי' תשובה למקורא דכולא ושרשה העליון והוא בשעת התפלה בק"ש. וזהו שמע ישראל שמע לשון אסיפה וקיבוץ :*Likutei Torah*, Hazinu, 72b). We can study brilliant revelatory texts about the Presence of HaKadosh Baruch Hu and the Oneness of Hashem, but it is only through Davening that our learning becomes alive and begins pulsing within us. In Davening, we can take an abstract intellectual understanding of what HaKadosh Baruch Hu is and is not, and render Hashem as *Elokim Chayim* / Living G-d, arousing a visceral experience of truth and a vivid personal relationship with the Source of All Life.

Tefilah is the laboratory where learned ideas become lived ideals. It is the place where lofty concepts such as the Oneness of Hashem, Divine Providence, as well as love and awe of Hashem become experiential realities. Davening cultivates *Emunah* / faith and *Bitachon* / trust, as well as clarity, expanded consciousness and deep inner certainty.

Davening is the focal point of the Baal Shem Tov's teachings. The Baal Shem was once told (by his "soul," a manifestation of *Ru'ach HaKodesh* / the prophetic spirit) that all of his spiritual achievements were attained not through his scholarship in learning Torah, but through his great devotion in Davening (*Keser Shem Tov*, 197. *Tzava'as HaRivash*, 41). For the Baal Shem, Davening is not just another discipline to be learned or just another tool to be acquired in a life of *Avodah* / spiritual work. It is *the* discipline and tool; it is the *Ikar* / main thing. (The Alter Rebbe writes, in the name of Rebbe Chayim Vital, that the *Ikar Avodah* today is Tefilah: *Tanya*, Kuntres Acharon, p. 162.)

Beginning with the example set by the Baal Shem Tov, Tefilah is in fact the Ikar of Chasidus in general, for Chasidus turns all teachings 'inward,' toward personal Avodah, and so does Tefilah. Whereas the earlier *Mekubalim* / Kabbalists and teachers taught in terms of 'higher lights' and cosmic structures, the Baal Shem Tov explained how these are all reflected in this world below, as an aspect of human consciousness and activity (Rebbe Rashab, *Sefer haSichos*, Toras Shalom, p. 185).

It is for this reason, and certainly not mere coincidence (of course, nothing is mere coincidence), that most of the known teachings of the Baal Shem Tov revolve around the theory and practice of Davening.

The Rambam rules that there is a Mitzvah to Daven each day (*Sefer HaMitzvos*, Mitzvah 5. *Hilchos Tefilah*, 1:1. *Sefer HaMitzvos*, Rasag, Esei 2), and even those who argue that there is no Mitzvah to Daven every day agree that when one is in need there is a Mitzvah to pray (Ramban on *Sefer HaMitzvos*, 5. *Sefer HaMitzvos Katan*, 11). Additionally, there is a separate Mitzvah connected with Davening, and that is the Mitzvah of דביקות / *Deveikus* / cleaving: "And cleave to Him" (*Devarim*, 13:5). "Cleaving to Him" can mean many different things, such as 'walking in the ways of Hashem' (*Sotah*, 14a), or 'associating with Torah scholars' (*Kesuvos*, 111b), but the simple meaning is that there is a Mitzvah — or the essence of all Mitzvos — to cleave to Hashem, to experience and consciously be in a state of attachment or unity with HaKadosh Baruch Hu, and to think about Him always (Ramban, *Devarim*, 11:22. *Chayei Adam*, Klal 1:1. See also *Moreh Nevuchim*, 3:53. Rama, *Orach Chayim*, 1).

In the teachings of the Baal Shem Tov, these two Mitzvos, Tefilah and Deveikus, are inextricably linked; Davening is the path of Deveikus. But what exactly is Deveikus? And how, exactly, can we achieve it through Davening? These essential questions will be explored in great detail throughout the rest of this book.

For now, suffice it to say that in the teachings of the Baal Shem Tov, everything in life is about Deveikus. Even the deep, complex, contemplative *Kavanos* / intentions in prayer from the earlier Mekubalim are all about Deveikus. A student of the Baal Shem Tov writes, regarding the Kavanos of the holy Arizal (Rebbe Yitzchak Luria), "The main purpose of the *Kavanos* / intentions… is solely to cleave and connect oneself to Hashem, to experience Deveikus (*Toldos Yaakov Yoseph*, Parshas Vaera).

To illustrate this idea, the following metaphor is offered in the name of the Baal Shem Tov (*Ohr HaMeir*, Haftarah of Vayera). Imagine a person is desperately hungry and desires to eat certain delicious foods. Suddenly, as he is dreaming of these foods, he looks up and actually sees them before him. They are just beyond his reach, and so he has 'intention' as if to eat them, but of course, as he cannot reach them, he remains hungry. Similarly, says the Baal Shem Tov, having a mental and intellectual understanding of the deeper Kavanos of Davening is like seeing enticing foods from a distance; they look good but have no nourishing effect. Only by actually grabbing the foods — feeling and experiencing the *Ohr* / light of the Kavanos — can we be spiritually nourished. This is achieved through Deveikus. The path of the Baal Shem can thus be summarized as including and transcending the earlier paths of Kavanah, following the rivers back to their source—a life lived in perpetual Deveikus and prayer.

Chapter 1

THE BAAL SHEM TOV

R EBBE YISRAEL BEN ELIEZER, KNOWN AS THE BAAL SHEM TOV, 'MASTER OF THE GOOD (DIVINE) NAME', WAS THE MOST IMPORTANT AND INNOVATIVE SPIRITUAL TEACHER OF HIS TIME AND IN FACT, ONE OF THE GREATEST RABBIS AND TEACHERS OF ALL TIME. TODAY, MORE THAN HALF OF ALL TORAH-COMMITTED JEWS COUNT THEMSELVES AMONG HIS FOLLOWERS, AND ALL OF JEWRY IS EITHER DIRECTLY OR INDIRECTLY AFFECTED BY HIS LIFE AND TEACHINGS.

Before delving more deeply into the Baal Shem Tov's unique path in Davening, it behooves us to dwell a few moments on the person, his major teachings and basic spiritual foundations.

Yisrael was the Baal Shem Tov's given name when he was born in Okop, a small village in the Ukraine, on the Polish-Russian border, in the year 1698. His elderly parents, Reb Eliezer and Sarah, both passed away when he was still a very young boy. Before leaving this world, his father told him, "My son, have no fear. Fear nothing other than the Master of the Universe."

Beyond this short, albeit very significant episode, much of Yisrael's early life is unfortunately shrouded in mystery and lost to history. We do, however, know that the young orphan was cared for by the community. During his youth, perhaps lacking a true place to call home, he found solace wandering alone in the fields and the majestic Carpathian Mountains. He would spend hours on end immersed in nature, pouring out his heart to HaKadosh Baruch Hu in boundless love and overwhelming awe. Being physically alone, yet feeling utterly embraced by Hashem, he came to realize that no person is ever alone; Hashem, the Creator of All Life, is always present and forever near; closer than anything close (קרוב אתה ה'. *Tehilim*, 119:151. Says the *Even Ezra*, קרוב אתה - יותר מכל קרוב).

We also know that as a teenager, the Baal Shem Tov supported himself as a teacher's assistant. Later on in life, he showed a tremendous fascination with the Aleph-Beis, drawing great mystical insight and inspiration from the simple sounds and shapes of the holy letters, as we will soon touch upon. This fascination with the Aleph-Beis, perhaps, can be traced to his years spent with children who were learning the sacred letters of the Aleph-Beis with unbridled excitement for the very first time.

Throughout his younger years, even as he was spiritually evolving and developing into a great mystic and healer of the body and soul, the Baal Shem Tov maintained an image of unassuming simplicity. He dressed, walked and talked like any other simple villager. It was during these formative years that he developed a close relationship with other *Tzadikim*

Nistarim / hidden righteous spiritual adepts. Most importantly, he became close with Rebbe Adam Baal Shem, who would become his living teacher.

When Reb Yisrael was thirty-six years old, he received a message from Heaven to reveal himself to the world. Indeed, and perhaps as a confirmation of this revelation, within a very short period of time, his fame as a healer of both body and soul grew swiftly and he became known as Rebbe Yisrael Baal Shem Tov. 'Baal Shem' was a title given to many holy men who were miracle workers, as was his teacher Rebbe Adam Baal Shem. However, the addition of *Tov* / good was unique to Yisrael Baal Shem Tov.

He eventually settled in the small town of Medzebuz in Western Ukraine, and sources tell us he chose this town, which was near a body of water, so he would always have fresh fish for Shabbos. In Medzebuz he was supported by the community as their local healer, and many noted scholars and Rabbis became the Baal Shem Tov's disciples. It was there in Medzebuz that the foundation of the Chasidic movement was established, and would continue to flourish even after his passing in the spring of 1760.

The holy Baal Shem Tov himself did not write down his teachings, and therefore left us no writings of his own. What he did leave us were his students; examples and embodiments of his teachings, 'living, breathing, books of holy fire'. These students did eventually write down some of their Rebbe's teachings, and it is from them that we get a glimpse into this revolutionary, profound yet 'simple' Rebbe. Finally, it is worth noting that the Baal Shem spoke in Yiddish, the lingua franca of the masses, and his teachings were written in Hebrew, the *Lashon* / language of the educated elite, so one needs a fine-tuned eye to discern when perhaps a nuance was lost in translation (Alter Rebbe, *Igeres HaKodesh* 25).

Nothing Else Besides Hashem

Here is the fundamental teaching of the Baal Shem Tov on one foot: "There is nothing else besides Hashem." This is not a philosophical construct, nor a theological idea. The Baal Shem is not interested in abstract philosophy or theology, rather he is committed to actual life and human consciousness. In his teachings, this maxim is an epistemological truth. HaKadosh Baruch Hu is present and revealed in each place and every situation we choose to see Hashem's Presence. We can thus 'see' Hashem and *be with* Hashem, if we so choose. We can serve Hashem in all aspects of life, not only in prescribed rituals. If we experience Hashem as present, then Hashem is actually present. This is the bedrock foundation of the Baal Shem Tov's worldview.

According to the Baal Shem: "You are where our thoughts are." If we actively perceive and truly understand that Hashem is present in every situation, then we are actually with Hashem in every situation. And if we don't have this presence of mind, and we perceive darkness or an absence or void of Divinity, then that too becomes our reality. It is as if Hashem is not present there, indeed.

Cosmically, and objectively speaking as well, Hashem is actually already present everywhere, throughout all dimensions of space, time, and consciousness, and beyond. From the Creator's perspective, there is only Himself. However, what exists for us depends on our perception. In this sense, our perception creates what 'exists' in our lives.

"Where can Hashem be found?" Rebbe Mendel of Kotzk once asked. "Wherever you let Him in," he proclaimed. Hashem exists wherever we perceive Him. If some object or aspect of life seems devoid of Divinity, it is because we are choosing, consciously or subconsciously, to perceive reality as devoid of Hashem's Presence. This is a spiritual path of radical responsibility.

This profound teaching of the Baal Shem Tov, that Hashem is everywhere so long as we choose to see it as so, is predicated on the principle that the *Tzimtzum* / contraction of the Infinite Light of Hashem to create the finite world is *Lo k'Pesheshuto* / not literal, and everything is therefore an expression of, and contained within, the Creator's Infinite Light. The body, as well as the physical world, are in essence sacred in themselves, not merely as utilitarian vehicles to serve the soul.

For if the Tzimtzum were a *literal* reality, the body would be just a created thing, infinitely removed from the Creator. But with no literal separation, there is literally no separate body. What we call physicality is simply an extension and expression of the Infinite Light of Hashem revealed within finitude. Again, these ideas are not to be confused with abstract philosophy or theology; they are arrows pointing us inward to real experience and tangible action, to 'Know Him in all your ways'.

In All Your Ways, Know Him

The Sages of the Gemara (*Berachos*, 63a) highlight a small passage upon which the entirety of the Torah is dependent: בכל דרכיך דעהו והוא יישר אורחותיך / *B'chol D'rachecha Da'eihu v'Hu Yiyasheir Or'chosecha* / "In all your ways know Him, and He will straighten your paths" (*Mishlei*, 3:6). Simply put, we should internalize and live with the awareness of Hashem's Presence at all times and in everything we do, as this will bring one to the ultimate clarity of meaning and direction in their lives.

The word, דעהו / *Da'eihu* / "...know Him," used in this all-important phrase, implies Deveikus. The Torah uses the word, דע / *Da* / know. as a euphemism for intimate relations. *Da'ei-Hu* thus means "knowing Him" by passionately cleaving to, and unifying with, HaKadosh Baruch Hu.

In the words of the Baal Shem Tov: "In all your ways know Him — this is a great principle. דעהו / know Him, comes from a term that means 'connection'; therefore you can read the word as saying, דע / connect the ה׳ו, the ה / Hei to the ו / Vav. And you must connect them in all your 'ways', in all your actions, even within the physical tasks that you do" (*Tzava'as HaRivash*, 94).

These two letters, Vav and Hei, are the two final letters of the Four-Letter-Name of Hashem, the Yud-Hei-Vav-Hei (י - ה - ו - ה). Inwardly, the letter Vav in this Name represents the world of transcendence and attachment to what is higher and deeper, while the final Hei represents the world of action and manifestation. Reading the verse this way suggests that we should connect (Vav) every one of our actions (Hei) to Hashem, the Transcendent One. Every experience is but a means to enter into an intimate relationship with HaKadosh Baruch Hu. Every moment of life presents itself as an opportunity for *Yichud* / unification, through impassioned dialogue with the Creator of Life.

According to the Baal Shem Tov, we need to connect to both the Transcendence *and* the Immanence of HaKadosh Baruch Hu at every moment and through every physical activity we do. We can no longer reserve this connection only for prayer, study, contemplation, or any of the other refined spiritual works. Everything now needs to be included in our *Avodah* / spiritual service.

Everything we do, not only sacred pursuits such as Davening or learning Torah, is an opportunity to connect and unify with the One Above, and thus every action may be transformed into a sacred action. This is a

Chidush / novel idea of the Baal Shem Tov. Our 'mundane' actions are not merely means to an end, such as eating, sleeping or working so that we will have the strength or resources to learn Torah or do another Mitzvah (as the Rambam, *Hilchos De'os*, 2:3, and others learn. Tur, *Orach Chayim*, 231), rather, these acts can be ends in themselves. In every action we do, and indeed within every moment, there is another opportunity to become aware of and connect with the living presence of HaKadosh Baruch Hu.

Eating, for example, can be spiritually transformative if done with proper *Kavanah* / intention. This and other bodily acts are therefore not only valuable as precursors to some future Mitzvah, but, through our elevated awareness, we can turn these bodily acts into 'spiritual' activities themselves. Then we are not just 'eating in order to connect,' but rather we are 'eating as an act of connection.' This means that, not only can actions be *L'sheim Shamayim* / For the *Sake of* Heaven, i.e., means toward a higher end, but they can actually be part of *B'Chol D'rachecha Da'eihu* / "In all your ways know Him" — the deeds themselves are thus experiential ways to "know Him" (*Likutei Sichos*, 3. 907. The Sefas Emes speaks about this type of *Avodah* / spiritual work and mindset as an Avodah for Tzadikim: *Sefas Emes*, Shavuos, Tav/Reish/Nun/Vav. Yet, the Rebbe (*ibid*, and in many places) explains that this *Atzmiyus* / Essential Avodah is one that is applicable to and possible by all. See also *Toldos Yaakov Yoseph*, Mishpatim. *Degel Machaneh Ephrayim*, Kedoshim).

Perhaps the only 'fundamental principle' in the teachings of the Baal Shem is that Hashem's Presence can be found within everyone and everything. Wherever you are standing, whatever you are doing, however you are feeling, you can, if you so choose, connect with HaKadosh Baruch Hu. If you have the presence of mind to behold Hashem's Presence within whatever you are doing, feeling or experiencing, then indeed Hashem's Presence is there, revealed to you exactly where and as you are.

A person who desires to connect with the Source, to lead a deeper and higher life, should not eat, sleep, work, and perform the mundane functions of their life merely for gaining the strength or financial ability to later on dedicate his time to matters of the spirit. We should not limit our spiritual connection by seeking it exclusively in Davening or studying Torah. Rather, we should "know Him in all [our] ways."

Indeed, eating, sleeping, working, even using the restroom, are all opportunities for Divine connection. Accordingly, the Baal Shem Tov teaches that using the restroom is a phenomenon of *Birurim* / sifting, removing the toxic and unusable from the good and purposeful: "Even when going to the restroom, have in mind, 'I am separating the bad from the good,' with the good remaining for Divine service" (*Tzava'as HaRivash*, 22). In fact, all human activities can and should be ways of "knowing Him." Even our most basic human drives can be transformed into acts of *Yichud* / unification with Hashem. The Baal Shem Tov's life was dedicated to showing and teaching us how.

Elevating Sparks

There are Divine Sparks and shards of holiness scattered throughout all of Creation. Our task in life is to 'elevate' these sparks to their original source in holiness. According to the path of the Arizal, Rebbe Yitzchak Luria (1534–1572), the primary means to elevate these sparks is through *Kavanah* / intellectual or spiritual intention. For example, before one recites a blessing over a glass of water, in order to elevate the sparks of the Divine within the water, one should meditate on a specific *Yichud* / letter- or Sefirotic-formula of unification while aspiring to draw down and connect the spiritual realm with the physical world. We can surmise, since this is for the most part an inner mental practice, that only the inner qualities of Creation, the 'souls' and perhaps 'angels,' can be elevated by it. This is in line with the Arizal's own thought, which was that the elevation of the outer, physical world itself will only occur in the future; in the times of Moshiach (*Sha'ar HaKavanos* 2, Seder Shabbos).

The Baal Shem's path of elevation, on the other hand, is very different in that, a) it can elevate the entirety of Creation; it is not merely sifting out the latent Divine Sparks that exist within the physical world, and b) the transformation and elevation occurs not merely intellectually, but through the engagement of the actual physical world itself, as well as through the words of Davening, themselves.

A Basic Distinction between the Paths of the Arizal and Baal Shem Tov in Tefilah

According to the Arizal, the movement from pure Infinite *Ohr* / light to a defined, concretized *Kli* / vessel evolves in five stages: *Ohros* / lights, *Mochin* / mind, *Tzelamim* / shadows, *Levushim* / garments, and finally *Kelim* / vessels. (The acronym for these five levels is כ-ל צ-מ-א – כלים, לבושים, צלמים, מוחין, אורות.) Mochin is where the pure Ohr begins to generate vitality and form. What the Arizal calls *Mochin* / mind, the Baal Shem calls *Chayus* / life or vitality. While this may seem like mere semantics, it does in fact allude to a profound distinction between the Arizal and the Baal Shem Tov and their focus in Davening.

The Arizal explains the process of Davening as drawing down new Mochin / intellect from Above into the below, which affects a more subtle shift in this world, as the focus of one's Tefilos is on a more inward dimension of reality. The Baal Shem Tov, who lived one step closer to the revelation of Moshiach, reveals to us a deeper level of *Elokus* / Divinity that is present in the outer world, whereby we can actually affect the physical dimensions of reality through our Davening. The Baal Shem's approach is centered on the actual enunciation of the words themselves as they are said in a state of Deveikus, rather than the intellectual meanings or abstract intentions behind them, thus transforming physical reality by way of Davening's physical vibrations, as will be explained at length.

A fundamental principle in the teachings of the Arizal with regards to Tefilah and *Berachos* / blessings specifically, as well as all Mitzvos in general, is that their intention should be to draw down new and higher Mochin (Chochmah, Binah) into the more transcendent aspect of *ZA* / *Zeir Anpin* / the six 'masculine' attributes (Chesed thru Yesod), so that it can eventually enter into Malchus, the immanence of Hashem's light within this world, thus elevating the world (Malchus) to a more G-dly state. The physical world (Malchus, the lower feminine, the 'daughter', the receiver) is sustained by the Mochin that flows into it from the higher level of ZA, and ZA (the lower masculine, the 'son', the transmitter) receives its Mochin from the *Yichud* / unity between the higher *Ima* / Mother (Binah), and the higher *Aba* / Father (Chochmah). This Yichud gives birth to Mochin, and ZA becomes empowered and alive to transmit the Mochin to Malchus.

This Yichud of Aba and Ima is a יחוד תמידי / *Yichud Temidi* / constant connection and thus it is a Yichud that is *Achor b'Achor* / back-to-back. Because they are always together, it is like these two Sefiros are attached at the hip; although they are connected, it is not with real intimacy, so to speak. This Yichud is also called יחוד חיצוני / *Yichud Chitzoni* / external or superficial unification.

This is the way the world comes into existence. Hashem creates the Yichud Temidi of Aba and Ima, and then the resultant Shefa of Mochin reaches ZA. ZA then gives life and transmits Mochin to Malchus, whereby the world receives its quality of existence. In this way, the *existence* of the world is not dependent on our actions or intentions, rather it is the *quality* of the world's existence that is for the most part dependent on us. The existence of the world itself is due to HaKadosh Baruch Hu's will and desire. But how it exists, what type of Shefa, and how much מים דוכרין / *Mayim Duchrin* / masculine waters flow downwards or outwards into the world is contingent on the *Mayim Nukvin* / feminine waters that we cause to rise upward through our actions.

This is one reason that we need to 'speak' and not just 'think' or 'meditate' our prayers: audible words are the feminine waters (actions) that rise up to affect the Divine flow coming down into this world. As the Alter Rebbe writes in Tanya: "Mere thought accomplishes nothing, for without elevating Mayim Nukvin...it is impossible to draw forth drops from Above to affect the union..." (Tanya, *Kuntres Acharon*, 2, p. 154. Although the Zohar mentions that praise offered in the heart does indeed reach the Ein Sof [*Zohar*, 3, 244b]. This is because sometimes the person, living with total Mesiras Nefesh, is *himself* the Mayim Nukvin. *Tanya*, ibid).

In other words: Our actions, not only our intentions, matter tremendously. Through our Tefilos, our Berachos, and our general performance of Mitzvos, we elevate the מים נוקבין / *Mayim Nukvin* / Feminine Waters (our Avodah), thus transforming the union of Aba and Ima from *Achor b'Achor* / back-to-back, to *Panim el Panim* / face to face, and from a *Yichud Chitzoni* / external or superficial unification to a יחוד פנימי / *Yichud Penimi* / internal or deep unification. When Aba and Ima are in such a Yichud, the child that is 'born' from this deeper unity, referred to as ZA (the son, masculine), is also on a much deeper level. When the Mochin of this level of ZA flows into Malchus, a revealed Divine desire to create is then manifest, and the Presence of Hashem is felt accordingly.

All of this affects the subtle energy fields, so to speak, within Creation. Instead of the world functioning from a place of *Zivug Temidi*, which is merely *Achor b'Achor*, through our Davening and Avodah everything reorients into a posture of *Panim el Panim*.

Alluding to this dynamic, the first word of the Torah, בְּרֵאשִׁית, has three *Nikudos* / vowels: 1) a Sh'va, one dot on top of another dot, 2) a Tzeirei, two dots side by side, and finally 3) a Chirik, a singular dot. These Nikudos reflect three possible levels of relationship with HaKadosh Baruch Hu. One begins with a hierarchical, back-to-back relationship; one dot above the other. Then one matures into a horizontal, face-to-face relationship; two dots facing each other, or even deeper, sitting next to each other and facing the same direction. Finally, this mutual relationship matures until the two merge into One; a single dot, representing a state of *Yichud* / singularity.

Ohr, Ahavah, and Simchah — Light, Love, and Joy

Before we delve further into the path of the Baal Shem Tov, it is important to understand that all of the Baal Shem's teachings are founded on the single principle that there is nothing devoid of Hashem, and thus if we so choose, we can become conscious of the fact that Hashem is present within everyone, at all times, and in all places. In other words: Hashem is in an infinitely loving relationship with all, always. As such, everything that occurs is *b'Hashgacha* / with Divine providence. The body, and every action we do, presents us with the deepest opportunity to recognize this integral relationship and Divine connection underpinning all reality, for it is here in the physical world that Hashem is most manifestly present as well as metaphysically occluded.

These teachings of the Baal Shem Tov are consistently populated by three key words: *Ohr* / light, *Simchah* / joy and *Ahavah* / love. *Ohr* refers to the recognition that the whole world is filled with Hashem's Light; every-thing, every person, and every situation is filled with Hashem's Hashgacha and Presence, albeit oftentimes in a hidden and concealed manner. *Simchah* refers to knowing and trusting deeply that Hashem is with us always, whenever and wherever we are; this faith moves one to joy. *Ahavah* is the foundation of one's very life. Hashem's love for us is, by extension, a love for all of Creation. As we recognize that Hashem's love permeates all existence, both our love for Hashem and our love for others also is able to permeate all dimensions of space, time and consciousness.

In these teachings, Hashem's 'Immanence' or Presence in this world is radically pronounced and highlighted as the center point out of which all Avodas Hashem emerges and expresses itself. Hashem's love toward us and our love toward Hashem is thus the macro-context behind every idea and action. Whereas the quality of *Yirah* / holy fear, a visceral sense of Hashem's Ineffability and Transcendence, is certainly present in these teachings, it is not often understood as 'fear', per se, as will be explained further on.

The Master Key

With regard to Davening, the earlier Mekubalim and sages gave us the individual keys and combinations to unlock the doors of the inner workings of Creation and connect us with Hashem's *Shefa* / Divine flow; these keys were presented in the form of the various *Yechudim* / sacred name combinations. When the Baal Shem Tov arrived, he gave to the world the one master key that unlocks all doors (*Likutim Yekarim*, Likutim Chadashim, 197). This master key is in fact not a highly esoteric or abstract system, but rather the letters and words of Davening themselves. The physical sounds of the letters and words are the most potent spiritual tools available, and the Baal Shem taught us how to access, harness, and utilize them to reach the highest and deepest levels of Deveikus with HaKadosh Baruch Hu.

A story is told of the Chasidic Rebbe, Rebbe Hirsch of Rimanov, who was a young simpleton when he first met his great Rebbe, Rebbe Mendel of Rimanov. After he saw Reb Mendel Davening for the first time, he too began Davening with tremendous excitement, passion, and fervor. When the other students of Reb Mendel saw the lad Davening with such *Hislahavus* / fervor and excitement, they questioned him, "How do you Daven with such enthusiasm and passion when you do not even know the proper meanings of the words you are saying?" He humbly replied, "Who needs the meanings when you have the holy words themselves!"

When the words of Tefilah are uttered with love and fervor, even a simple understanding of their meanings is sufficient for a person to Daven with the greatest Deveikus and to effect considerable change in themselves and in the world.

Once, before Rosh Hashanah, the Baal Shem Tov summoned his student Reb Ze'ev Kitzes and instructed him to study the deep *Kavanos* / Kabbalistic intentions, so that he could blow the Shofar for everyone in *Shul* / synagogue. With excitement and focus, Reb Ze'ev dedicated every waking hour to delving into the mystical teachings and Divine names connected with the Shofar. In order to remember everything he was learning, he wrote notes for himself and kept them in his *Machzor* / High Holy Days prayer book. On the morning of Rosh Hashanah, as Reb Ze'ev was walking to Shul, his Machzor opened and all of his notes slipped out without his knowing. When the time came to blow the Shofar, Reb Ze'ev opened his Machzor and to his disbelief the notes were nowhere to be found. Overcome with grief, as he saw everyone in Shul was looking at him and waiting for him to start blowing the Shofar, he broke down and began weeping. With a broken heart, he gripped the Shofar, recited the blessings, and managed through a sea of tears to blow the required sounds. After Davening, the Baal Shem Tov came over to him and complimented him for the most wonderful and awe-inspiring Shofar blowing he had ever heard. He explained, "In the palace of the King there are many chambers, each has its own door and each door has its own unique key. The deeper Kavanos are the keys to the rooms. There is, however, a master key that opens all doors, and that is a broken heart. A broken heart smashes all locks and opens the gates of Heaven" (see also *Yosher Divrei Emes*, 42).

The Baal Shem Tov teaches that even after Rebbe Nachunya ben HaKana, the famous First Century sage, had mastered all the deeper intentions connected with Tefilah, he would still pray with the intention and simplicity of a little child.* Even those who have meditated on the Kavanos of the Arizal**, or spent many hours learning Chasidus and pondering the finer details of the cosmic effects of Davening, eventually come to understand that all their esoteric learning only serves as an introduction and initiation into a deeper and higher state of consciousness so they can begin to sense the Ohr that is available when they Daven, and then to really Daven with their 'hearts'.

There is a time to learn, and a time to Daven. Ideally, one's Davening flows naturally out of their learning; but one must work to shift their consciousness from a focused mind-state to an open heart-space. Contemplating Chasidus can and should be engaged before Davening — and even

---

* *Kesones Pasim*, p. 43b. Perhaps there was a mix-up in the name of the sage, and this statement is regarding Rav Shamshin of Kinon. מה יפה כח של רבי שמשון מקינון אחר שלמד סתרי הקבלה אמר שהוא מתפלל כתינוק בן יומו. *Teshuvas Maharshal*, Siman 98. See what the Mahara M'panu writes on this. *Sh'ut Mahara M'Panu*, Siman 108. See also *Sh'ut Rav Poalim* (Ben Ish Chai) Pesichah.

** According to many Poskim, the Kavanos of the Arizal are meant to be studied before Davening (not meditated on during Davening), so that the person will know the effects of their Davening: Rav Yaakov Emden, *Mitpachas Sefarim* (Levav) p. 112. Nodah B'Yehuda, *Derushei Tzlach*, Derush 25. Parenthetically, the Nodah B'Yehuda's famous Teshuvah against saying *L'Sheim Yichud* (*Yoreh De'ah*, Siman 93) is not directed against the righteous Chasidim of the Baal Shem Tov (at least not specifically), but rather against the known heretical groups of that age. See *Derushei HaTzlach*, 40:1.

during Davening, one may pause and contemplate a point of Chasidus, and then continue Davening. However, when we are actually Davening, we are advised to *only* Daven, much like a child beseeching and connecting with his Father in Heaven, without any intellectual or conceptual gymnastics.

This approach of the holy Baal Shem Tov is consistent with an older teaching that names many great scholars who said that they too would Daven "with the intention of a child."* But what does it actually mean, to Daven like a child?

To pray like a child means to Daven with simple faith and openness; to allow the words to flow from a heart-space, not a mind-space. It is to feel absolutely free to converse, in innocence, vulnerability and trust, with the Master of the Universe.

Indeed, the gift of Tefilah is the very fact that we can pray at all — not so much that our prayers are 'fulfilled'** Prayer itself *is* the answer. We are blessed to be able to use our simple physical senses and faculties to create sounds which are 'heard' in a way that is beyond what we can sense or know. The Mitzvah to speak to HaKadosh Baruch Hu is truly a gift.

---

* *Teshuvas HaRivash*, Siman 157: גם שמעתי מפיו שהרב רבי שמשון מקינון ז"ל שהיה רב גדול מכל. See also בני דורו וגם אני זכור ממנו ואם לא ראיתיו בעיני והוא היה אומר אני מתפלל לדעת זה התינוק. Ramak, *Elimah Rabbasi*, Eyn Kol, 1:2. Rav Yoseph Ergas, *Shomer Emunim*, HaKadmon, 2:65. Although the Ramak, in *Ohr Ne'erav*, Cheilek 4:2, argues that if you Daven like a child you will receive like a child (see also *Shulchan HaTahor* [Komarna], Siman 98:1). A counter argument is that a child prays to the Essence of Hashem – since he does not know of the Sefiros and inner worlds – and thus he draws down blessings from the Source of All Life: the Rebbe, *Toras Menachem*, Tav-Shin-Nun-Beis 1, p. 314.

** Although HaKadosh Baruch Hu in fact wants all our prayers to be answered. Hashem is the Giver; the one thing we absolutely know about Hashem, so to speak, is that Hashem is the Creator and Giver of Life. Thus, Hashem's 'desire' is fulfilled when our Tefilos are answered. This is a teaching of the Baal Shem Tov as recorded by R. Moshe Yechiel Epshtein, *Rispei Eish Das*, Sha'ar HaTefilah, p. 92.

A student of the Baal Shem Tov told the following parable. Once there was a mighty king who made a proclamation throughout his domain. All his subjects would have an opportunity to come to the palace, enter the throne room, and request whatever they wished. Anything and everything requested would be granted. Some people came to ask for gold, some asked for silver, while others requested to be promoted to high-ranking positions. Each person came to the king with another personal request to be fulfilled. One humble, poor individual came in front of this mighty and benevolent king and requested only to be granted the opportunity to come speak to the king three times a day. He was so moved by the king's generosity and kindness, that all he wanted was the ability to see the king and speak with him every day. Upon hearing this man's request, and realizing that the humble man felt that conversation with the king was of greater value than any jewels or ranks of honor, the king decreed that access to the inner chamber should be granted. And, as a token, the humble person could also pass through any chamber of the palace on his way to the throne room and take whatever he liked (*Toldos Yaakov Yoseph*, Parshas Vaeschanan).

This parable is related to what Dovid HaMelech / King David express-es in Tehilim (102), תפלה לעני כי יעטוף ולפני ה׳ ישפוך שיחו / "A Tefilah of a poor person when he languishes and pours out his soul before Hashem..." The 'poor person' in this case does not desire anything; he is 'poor' in terms of personal requests. His prayer is only that he be able to "pour out his soul before Hashem." The 'rich' come before Hashem and ask for more riches, the powerful come and ask for more power, the wise for more wisdom. The 'poor' person is humble; he does not seek any riches, wisdom, or power. All he seeks is to see the King Himself, to be in the King's Presence (see *Keser Shem Tov*, 1:97).

Davening is the greatest gift of all, and along with it comes the promise which the King gives the poor person. Namely, that we are all able to lift our eyes, turn inward and know that Hashem is always right there, patiently waiting and attentively listening. Tefilah is the path we travel through the wilderness, into the courtyard of the castle, through the winding maze-like hallways, past the decadent ballrooms and into the Holy of Holies — the inner chamber. In heartfelt prayer, we are granted the privilege of entering the private throne room, where we stand in humble awe before the King, pouring out our soul to Him without any hint of inhibition.

Chapter 2

PRAYING FROM WHERE YOU ARE

"And Sometimes the Opposite"

WE ARE BEINGS IN A CONSTANT STATE OF BECOMING. AT VARYING TIMES WE FEEL EXPANSIVE OR REFLECTIVE, EXCITED OR SUBDUED, CONTEMPLATIVE OR AROUSED. THE TEACHINGS OF THE BAAL SHEM TOV PRESENT A CLEAR UNDERSTANDING OF THE CONSTANTLY FLUCTUATING NATURE OF LIFE, AND HOW OUR MIND AND HEART ARE FOREVER CHANGING AND SHIFTING.

When it comes to Avodas Hashem, this dynamic must be taken into account. We need to tailor our own spiritual practice to the state we are in presently as well as to the state we desire to be. There is in fact no דווקא / *Davka* / specific, fixed or regimented way of performing the Davening day in and day out. The only real 'Davka' is לאו דווקא / not *Davka* — the only fixed rule is that there is no fixed rule. The only 'qualification' we need in the Baal Shem Tov's way is to admit that Hashem can be found by everyone and within everything. The only 'disqualification' is then to say, 'No, Hashem is not present; I cannot find Hashem in any given situation.'

No moment is alike, and no two days are the same. Life is in constant change and we need to connect to Hashem from the place where we are at every moment. Just as we are constantly in flux, our Avodas Hashem has to dynamically harness these changes. "You shall love Hashem your G-d בכל־לבבך / b'Chol Levav'cha." בכל־לבבך is normally translated as 'with all your heart', although לבבך literally means 'your *hearts*', meaning in all our feelings, emotions and states. We need to become aware that all our feelings ultimately come from Hashem, and thus they need to be directed to, or offered back to, Hashem. Every emotion is potentially holy and noble, and ought to be guided into a higher, deeper orientation. This is the inner alchemy of the entirety of human experience as taught by the holy Baal Shem Tov.

In Davening, there is usually an aspect of *Keva* / order and routine, perhaps including the time and place of each Tefilah. Yet, as our emotions and mindset frequently change, we need to ensure that we do not get stuck in any specific approach to Davening which may work one day but not the next. We need to be open and responsive to the moment we find ourselves in. We have to work under the assumption that *Lav Davka* / 'not necessarily'; if yesterday singing a Nigun or reciting *Tehilim* helped inspire us to Daven with more intention, commitment, focus and passion, it does not necessarily mean the same method will help us today.

We need to be sensitive to the moment באשר הוא שם / *b'Asher Hu Sham* / 'with whatever and whoever is there'; the moment as it is. There are no

כללים / *K'lalim* / constant principles in Avodas Hashem. We do not need to always Daven with joyful excitement or rapid body movement, or to always Daven quietly or in stillness. We need to be open to how we are experiencing Hashem's presence in this unique moment. It is said in the name of the wise Rebbe, Reb Simchah Bunim of Peshischa, "The one basic rule is that, in Avodas Hashem there are no basic rules, and even this basic rule does not exist." In Yiddish, דער כלל איז, אז לגבי עבודת ה׳ איז נישט דא קיין כללים, און אפי׳ די כלל איז אויך נישט דא.

לא תעשון כן לה׳ אלקיכם / "You shall not do so to Hashem, your G-d" (*Devarim*, 12:4). In this context, to "Do so" means to do everything the Torah described in the verses preceding this one, which speak of idol worship. On the surface, the Torah is telling us that we should not follow those actions (Rashi, *ad loc*). The early Chasidic Rebbes re-read the verse like this: "You shall not do *like this* to Hashem your G-d." We should not think that we always must do things 'like this', in the exact same way. We should not make our Avodas Hashem a particular *Kein* / 'so' this is the way we do it, and never any other way (The Chozeh of Lublin, *Hagadah Shel Pesach, Ma'areh Yechezkel*, p. 25).

In other words, we need to sense what is working in the moment, what is expanding us, or making us feel more connected to the *Ribono Shel Olam* / Master of the Universe — and what is just a fixed routine, even with regards to positive *Hanhagos* / practices. The Chozeh of Lublin (*Zos Zicharon*, p. 4), after writing about the various positive customs he took upon himself, writes, "All the above practices have infinite branches and details. And yet, ולפעמים צריך להתנהג להפך / sometimes a person has to act in exactly the opposite way."

Flexibility is vital in Avodas Hashem. Even within the same day, or within the same Davening, what worked earlier does not necessarily work now. We need to be open to sometimes doing the opposite of our habitual pattern. Before Davening, we need to take a minute to tune into our body, mind, 'heart' and spirit, so that we can sensitively harness them for deeper Davening. Similarly, we need to be attuned during Davening as well, as things shift internally and externally moment to moment. Introspection and self-reflection are fundamental elements in the prayerful encounter. In fact, the Hebrew word for prayer, *Tefilah*, shares its root with *Yefalel* / judgment, and *Palel* / judging. As such, *L'hispalel* / to pray means to assess or judge oneself honestly and lovingly in order to ascertain what is needed in the moment. Tefilah is a simultaneous act of expression and self-reflection.

This great principle of the Baal Shem Tov, that there are no כללים / *K'lalim* / rules, is founded on his *K'lal Gadol* / great principle that Hashem is present in each and every situation and shifting condition. Whenever we choose to see Hashem's Presence, we can and will see His Presence in everyone and everything. This includes our shifting inner conditions, as well; if our moods and states of mind are always at least slightly different, so our ways of 'seeing Hashem' will be different. This also implies that the way we interact with the world around us is directly related to the way that we perceive how we are being treated by the world. If we see the actions of the Compassionate One all around us, we will feel we are being treated with compassion. What we do, say, and even think clearly helps write our stories; therefore, one must choose wisely to create the book which we ourselves want to read.

Understanding the above helps us see why the Baal Shem Tov's path encompassed all different types and modes of Davening. In fact, sometimes he himself Davened with rapture and overt excitement, quaking and jumping about, and sometimes he Davened in total stillness. Sometimes he Davened quickly and sometimes very slowly (as the Medrash says, יש שעה לקצר ויש שעה להאריך / "There is a time to be short and a time to be long": *Sifrei*, 105).

Sometimes he Davened loudly and with outward *Hislahavus* / excitement, and sometimes he would Daven quietly, with inward contemplation, as the holy Arizal himself Davened (*Pri Eitz Chayim*, Sha'ar Olam HaAsiyah, 1. *Sha'ar HaKavanos*, Hakdamah, Birchos HaShachar. The Arizal is connected to the world of *Chochmah* and *Shesika* / silence. Yet, many later Tzadikim write that we should not follow the specific path of the Arizal and we should Daven loudly: Chidah, *Avodas HaKodesh*, Kesher Gudal, 7:18. *Shu't Imrei Aish*, Orach Chayim, Siman 3. Maharam Ash, *Mecholas HaMachanayim*, 7).

Certain students of the Baal Shem and later Rebbes report that the Baal Shem Tov Davened with such great trembling and rapture, even the tiny grains in nearby barrels seem to join him in his trembling (*Divrei Torah*, [Munkatch] Mahadura 2, 60. *Shivchei HaBaal Shem Tov*, 22). One well-known story recounts the time his brother-in- law, Rav Gershon, merely touched the Baal Shem Tov's Talis and was seized with terror, causing him to faint on the spot. Students recalled that his body was so 'charged' during Davening, that even his Tzitzis seemed to be electrified and moving as if they were alive. Yet, other students speak of his Davening in utter stillness and motionlessness, in deep inward ecstasy — not so much in a contemplative state like the Arizal's, rather, in a rapturous yet motionless state of Deveikus.

This approach, characterized by the complementary ideas that 'there are no set rules in the world of spirituality,' that 'sometimes a person has to act exactly the opposite,' and that 'a person needs to tailor their Davening according to what is right for them at that moment,' is a novel, multifaceted *Derech* / path of Tefilah revealed by the Baal Shem Tov. It is a Derech of *Sheleimus* / wholeness, a practice and lifestyle of sensing both Hashem's immanence and transcendence, and including the body and the soul and the worlds of both spirit and of matter. As a *Neshamah K'lalis* / unified, all-encompassing soul, the Baal Shem Tov understood and revealed the all-encompassing unity of the Creator. He revealed that the unity within Creation is an expression of the Unity of the Creator. And correspondingly, he taught that any and all paths lead back to the One.

Now we will explore but a few of many examples of how the teachings of the Baal Shem Tov encompass a variety of Davening modalities. First, we will look at various practices of preparation for Davening through the lens of the Baal Shem Tov's teachings.

To Recite or Not Recite Tehilim before Davening

Before entering Tefilah, says the Baal Shem, one may exert oneself with learning Torah or chanting *Tehilim* / Psalms in order to negate any foreign or negative intruding thoughts, and to expand their consciousness in preparation for Davening. The toil and involvement in Torah and Tehilim before Davening purifies the mind, making one truly ready to Daven. On the other hand, the Baal Shem Tov also teaches that a person should not overextend or tire himself in his preparations for Davening. Sometimes, chanting Tehilim with fervor and devotion before Davening can be detrimental or even counterproductive, as the person may deplete their energy even before starting. If performed too zealously, reciting Tehilim before Davening may consume all one's *Koach* / strength and leave no room for the Davening itself (*Toldos Yaakov Yoseph*, Tazria. *Amud HaTefilah*, 35).

A Nigun to Enter Tefilah, Or a Nigun From Within Tefilah

Singing *Nigunim* / contemplative melodies and songs is another way to help us enter into a deeply prayerful posture before Davening. And during Davening as well, wordless tunes can be used to enhance the impact of the words. Song can assist in concentration and focus, help clear the mind of intruding thoughts, amplify different spiritual emotions, and strengthen one's sense of their soul. Indeed, Rebbe Yehudah HaChasid strongly suggests that we Daven with inspirational songs (*Sefer Chasidim*, 158), and the brilliant sage Rebbe Meir was known to sing various melodies during his Tefilah (*Zohar*, Rayah Mehemnah, Mishpatim, p. 114. *Sha'arei Teshuvah* 2 [Mitteler Rebbe], p. 15).

In general, a Nigun can help calm the mind. The subtle vibrations of a wordless melody can gently direct and focus our attention, and allow us to let go of inner chatter and conceptualizing. When sustained, internally generated rhythms and vibrations can help relax the body and in turn 're-lax' the mind to focus holistically on what is at hand. A Nigun has the capacity, says the Rebbe Rayatz, "to eradicate all extraneous thoughts during Davening" (*Sicha Yud Tes Kislev*, 5708). One of the words for 'song' in Hebrew is *Zimrah*. The etymological root of *Zimrah* is *Zamer*, which means 'to prune' (*Yeshayahu*, 25:5. See Rav Yoseph Gikatalia, *Sha'arei Orah*, Sha'ar 1). When we sing with intention, we are cutting away the weeds that crowd the garden of our consciousness. The Nigun refocuses our attention and removes all distracting thoughts.

Much like how the ebb and flow of the ocean or the rush and flutter of the wind can soothe our splintered psyche, the rhythmic sound of a Nigun soothes our chaotic mind and allows us to go further inward. Through contemplative Nigunim, we enter more subliminal levels of consciousness. They give us a kind of 'behind the scenes' access to parts of ourselves that we are usually denied in a normal state of self-conscious awareness, as our egoic filters are generally set to a utilitarian and defensive mode. When one feels both calm and alert, relaxed and energized, it is then an opportune time to begin Davening.

Besides clearing away the weeds of intruding thoughts, a Nigun can also positively assist us in clarifying and intensifying the *Kavanah* / intention that we seek to actualize. By giving our bodies and hearts something active, expressive and pleasurable to experience, and by investing the intentions of our Davening within it, we occupy more of our faculties in our focus and intentionality. Through singing, which is primarily an act of the heart and soul rather than the intellectual mind, we are able to integrate the conceptual dimension of our Kavanah even deeper into the core of our being. When a person ponders an idea mentally while his heart is soaring in song, the idea literally 'resonates' and penetrates his very being.

Singing opens us up figuratively and literally. It opens our mouths, our lungs, our diaphragms, our minds, our bodies, and our hearts so that *Shefa* / flow and *Brachah* / blessing may stream more freely from, through, and to us. For, as the Zohar teaches, "There are chambers in Heaven which can only be opened through song" (*Tikkunei Zohar*, Tikkun 12). In fact, the words *Shirah* / song, and Tefilah, have the same numerical value: 515.

Sometimes a person may use a Nigun to enter the state of Tefilah, and sometimes it is the other way around: a Nigun emerges from within the Davening itself. Either the Nigun is consciously harnessed to help us Daven, or the Nigun organically arises from the subconscious of the person deep in Tefilah (*Amud HaTefilah*, 21, Note 15). We may be so inspired by the Davening that a Nigun spontaneously flows from our lips (see *Pesachim*, 117 regarding Dovid HaMelech). The Alter Rebbe was once asked why his disciples sang during Davening and he answered that it was an organic and spontaneous overflowing of what their hearts were feeling while in the revealed Presence of Hashem.

It all depends on the situation and mind-heart space of the individual Davening, whether they should recite from *Tehilim* before Davening, or sing a Nigun, or employ another method. A basic understanding of the human psyche will admit that no two days are alike nor are any two moments. We need to Daven from where we are, or from the place we aspire to be, in this specific moment. Sometimes *Tehilim* or a Nigun may be beneficial, while other times they may be superfluous and detrimental. Ultimately, according to the path of the Baal Shem Tov, it is on us to check in and assess our current needs in the moment, and to choose our course of action based on that self-reflective awareness. The same would apply to the tone of voice we use in Davening, whether loud or quiet, in shouts or gentle whispers, in the mode of melodic chanting or conversational tones.

Loud or Gentle Voice

We are generally taught to Daven vocally, out loud and clearly: "Voice arouses intention" (*Shaloh*, Sha'ar HaOsyos, 82b. Taz, *Perisha*, Shulchan Aruch, Orach Chayim, 101:3. *Reishis Chochmah*, Sha'ar HaKedushah, 15). In other words: Our voice helps us concentrate. But what is the appropriate quality of voice to employ during Davening?

On one hand, Davening loudly stimulates our heart and its emotions (*Akeidas Yitzchak*, Parshas Tzav, Sha'ar 58: ואולם כאשר נתפלל אין הכוונה להודיעו צערנו ולהשמיעו לאזניו כי אם להכין לבנו ולהטיב מעשינו לפניו). Often, the more we speak about something and the more our words are loaded with excitement, the more our passions are inflamed and the more enthusiasm we experience. In fact, there were many groups of the early followers of the Baal Shem Tov and his students who Davened quite loudly, with exclamations, shouting, dancing, and revealed ecstatic behavior; some would even involuntarily turn somersaults while Davening. Such behavior creates a loop in which outward expressions of excitement further excite the mind and heart.

On the other hand, the Baal Shem Tov also specifies the need to Daven in a quiet gentle voice, and that any 'shouting' should be done silently: "A person has to accustom himself to pray, even the songs of Tefilah, with a low and gentle voice, and to scream in silence... A cry, a scream that comes from the place of *Deveikus* / the sense of being at one with Hashem, is silent" (*Tzava'as HaRivash*, 33. Amud HaTefilah, 69).

In a state of stillness and genuine Deveikus, our prayers automatically become more inward and quiet. A 'holler' that emanates from a place of Deveikus manifests outwardly with a low whisper, and without a display of emotions or bodily movements. Sometimes, as the Baal Shem teaches, to the outside observer, a person who is Davening can look calm and almost lifeless, yet his soul is inflamed within him, and there is no outward projection. The ecstasy is powerful but silent. The cries of the heart shatter worlds, but are heard only as gentle whispers.

Rebbe Baruch of Medzebuz (1753–1811), the revered grandson of the Baal Shem Tov, once quipped, "A candle wick can be made of cotton or of flax. With one sort of wick, the candle makes a great deal of noise as it burns. While with the other burns in silence. Does the silent candle give less light?"

There is an inward and upward progression encoded into the text of the liturgy. Beginning one's prayers with a raised voice and then gradually receding into quiet whispers represents the progression of the *Seder Tefilah* / the order of the set Davening. In the beginning of Davening, while we still sense ourselves on the 'outside' seeking a sensation of unity with Hashem, we express our desires and yearnings 'externally' with an audible voice and outward physical expressions. From this place, one is still seeking to connect with Divinity outside and beyond oneself. However, once we reach the peak of Davening, and to some extent we enter the inner reality of Unity with the Divine, speech is no longer loudly expressed; we naturally become more inward and quiet. At this point, the quality of our speech moves from ecstasy to intimacy.

The Amidah, the peak of Davening, is said quietly, almost silently. There is a simple reason for this which demonstrates our awareness that Hashem hears our prayers in whatever voice they are proclaimed. Whether loud or quiet, we do not need to scream for Hashem to hear (*Berachos*, 24b). For this reason, a person who Davens loudly is considered *M'Ketanei Emunah /* small in faith (Rashi, *ibid*). Consciously choosing to Daven loudly suggests one does not have faith that Hashem will hear quiet prayers. There is also a more personal reason why the Amidah is said quietly; besides disturbing others (*Berachos*, ibid: אתי למטרד ציבורא), if said aloud, the prayer may come to embarrass one who is confessing transgressions and Davening for forgiveness. Therefore *Chazal /* the sages instituted this Tefilah to be said quietly to allow us the greatest degree of freedom in our expression (*Sotah*, 32b).

Yet, an even deeper reason why the peak of Davening is said quietly is simply that at this stage there is no room for self-expression. If we have Davened the previous stages of the service deeply, we now arrive at an inwardly felt sense of the interconnectedness and unity of the universe. This moment is arrived at quietly and internally, as "A human being is a mini-universe." When we reach this point, we are centered and aligned with the Infinite One, mirroring the perfection Above and below.

This peak of Davening takes place in the super-subtle, higher inner realm of *Atzilus /* nearness or unity (Atzilus and what it represents will be explored later on). In the lower, more external realms of existence and consciousness, we sense a division or even separation from the Source of Life. Hashem is conceived of as being far away, outside ourselves. And so, in order to raise ourselves 'up' into felt connection with our Source, there must first be an outward movement and revealed expression.

When we enter the world of Atzilus (and each person does so relative to their own level), our speech and expression no longer needs to be carried outward, rather it is directed inward (Alter Rebbe, *Torah Ohr*, Parshas Vayechi, 45d). This is represented by the Tefilah of Chanah, the future mother of the prophet *Shmuel* / Samuel, who, when Davening for a child, "Was speaking to her heart, and only her lips moved, but her voice was not heard" (*Shmuel* 1, 1:13). When the Divine is perceived as something outside of self and existence, the natural flow of words is directed outward. Yet the deeper that the reality of unity is felt within, the more refined and subtle the voice becomes.

Eliyahu HaNavi / Elijah the Prophet heard a Heavenly voice telling him, "Go forth and stand on the mountain before Hashem. And behold, Hashem was passing. A great and powerful wind was crushing the mountains and breaking the stones before Him, but Hashem was not in the wind. And after the wind, there came an earthquake, but Hashem was not in the earthquake. And after the earthquake came a fire, but Hashem was not in the fire. And finally, after the fire came a קול דממה דקה / *Kol Demamah Dakah*, a 'still small voice,' or a 'sound of subtle stillness'" (*Melachim* 1, 19. 11:12). This is the state which the prophet, on the most profound and transparent level of consciousness, encounters and communes with HaKadosh Baruch Hu. It is also the place that each one of us, all on our own level, connects with Hashem; the place of the 'still small voice', an inner whisper that speaks volumes.

This idea is echoed in a teaching of the Zohar. The angels on high (higher / deeper vibrations or conduits of Divine frequency), says the Zohar, do not pay attention to any prayers that are *not* whispered below. Indeed, as our words of Davening move into the supernal inner worlds, there is no longer a need for external speech, as they reach a place that transcends all words and outward expressions (*Zohar* 3, p. 210b).

This is because, upon arriving at the apex of Davening, one merges in a timeless moment of intimate Unity with Hashem. At this point, in the language of the holy Zohar, "Everything is silent above and below, with [only] the kisses of desire" (2:128b, *Tikkunei Zohar*, 10). In such a moment, there is utter quiet and stillness; even the one reciting the Amidah, can barely distinguish his own words (*Zohar* 1, p. 210a, *Netzutzei Ohros*, Chida). Rather, what is heard is a gentle humming and whispering sound that evokes intimacy. (As in the quietness of the night and early morning, when spouses speak with each other: *Berachos*, 3a. Perhaps this implies a gentle whisper that will not wake up others.)

This natural progression that we have outlined above, moving from a louder voice to quietness, from a place where it is possible to 'speak' to a deeper place where it is almost impossible to express audibly what we are thinking and feeling,* pertains to the 'linear' view of Davening. Yet, we are

---

* The idea that a person deep in thought or contemplation cannot express themselves audibly is reflected in Halachah as well. Although the Mitzvah of Talmud Torah, as the Alter Rebbe explains, is specifically to learn 'with voice': *Shulchan Aruch*, Orach Chayim, 47:2 as the Mechaber *Paskens* / rules. Orach Chayim, 47:4. See also *Tanya*, 37. Unlike the opinion of the Gra, *ibid.*, 2 and 9. Although see *Shu't Devar Avraham*, 1:16. Yet, the Alter Rebbe also Paskens /rules that וכל אדם צריך ליזהר להוציא בשפתיו ולהשמיע לאזניו כל מה שלומד בין במקרא משנה ותלמוד אלא אם כן בשעת עיון להבין דבר מתוך דבר / "We must ensure that when we learn we speak and hear ourselves learning, whether we are learning Torah, Mishnah or Gemara, *except* in a case when we are delving deeply to understand": *Hilchos Talmud Torah*, 3:12. This is because, as the Rebbe explains, הרהור כדיבור דמי באונס / "In a situation where one is utterly compelled, beyond his volition, *Hirhur* / thinking is then considered like speaking": See *Shulchan Aruch*, Orach Chayim, 62:4, אם מחמת חולי או אונס אחר קרא קריאת שמע בלבו יצא. See also *Pri Megadim, Birkei Yoseph, Be'er Heitiv*, ad loc., and *Igros Moshe*, Orach Chayim 5, 4. This is true specifically with Hirhur, not Mach'shavah. See Rebbe Rashab, *Sefer HaMa'amarim Ayin Beis*, p. 665, where the Rashab brings down from *Likutei Torah* of the Arizal that there are four levels, Mach'shavah, Hirhur, *Dibbur* / speech and *Ma'aseh* / action. Hirhur in this case is *not* Mach'shavah, rather, it is the *P'nimius* / inner essence of Dibbur. It is also possible that the Alter Rebbe is talking about a Hirhur with an open Sefer. See Rav Yaakov Emdin, *Mor VeKetiza*, Siman 47. In other words, when a person is deep in thought and contemplation, certainly deep in inner contemplation and meditation, it is impossible for them to consciously utter words, or for that matter perform any outward act, and thus Hirhur is like Dibbur; they are thus fulfill-

not always so linear; people swing between states, and also move 'horizon-tally' as well as vertically. Therefore, while the teachings about inner silence and stillness generally address individuals who can smoothly transition into the apex of Davening and a sense of Deveikus as they reach the Ami-dah, the Baal Shem Tov also speaks to 'real people' who fluctuate not just from day to day and hour to hour, but sometimes from moment to mo-ment. To them, the Baal Shem Tov teaches that intense body movements and even screaming are valid pathways of devotion, and that through such *Hislahavus* / conflagration, one can attain proper concentration, freedom from negative thoughts, ecstasy, or even rapture.

In fact, we do know, although we are unable to ever truly grasp what was actually occurring in the inner life of a great Tzadik, that the holy Baal Shem Tov himself would sometimes Daven in a state of total stillness and overwhelming sense of awe, and at other times in states of outward ecstasy. During some prayers, he would stand or sit in a "terrifying" mo-tionless condition, sweating profusely and palpably sensing the Presence of the King of the Universe. While at other times, he would clap in great rapture, and run about and shout in tremendous Hislahavus, much like Rebbe Akiva. As we have learned, when Rebbe Akiva would Daven by himself, someone might see him begin Davening in one corner, leave the room, and return to find him in another corner (*Berachos,* 31a. See also *Tanchu-ma,* Chayei Sarah, 5).

The Baal Shem Tov was known to Daven in both modes of outward expression and inward stillness. In other words: he would not necessarily always progress linearly from movement to stillness within the same Te-

---

ing their obligation of learning Torah "with speech" and not just the Mitzvah of *knowing* Torah, in the mind. Note also; וזאת מעלה יתרה גדולה ונפלאה לאין קץ אשר במצות ידיעת התורה והשגתה על כל המצוות מעשיות, ואפילו על מצוות התלויות בדיבור, ואפילו על מצות תלמוד תורה שבדיבור: *Tanya,* 5.

filah. Rather, he would move in and out of these stages many times within a single Davening, depending on what he needed to accomplish on that day or period or even on how he was 'feeling'. Such are the devotions of 'real people,' as mentioned above. In fact, one could even say that the more linear and formulaic one's Davening is, the less 'real' they are actually being.

Rapid Movement or Utter Stillness

Sometimes we need to use our physical voice to anchor our thoughts in the text, or to let go of negative thoughts and maintain Kavanah. And sometimes it is quite the opposite; the 'external' voice is a distraction and breaks our inner focus or sense of Deveikus. The same is true with silence and stillness of the body. Sometimes we might automatically slip into a place of deep stillness and even an absence of inner movement, and sometimes it is only with movement that we can catapult ourselves out of all that is holding us down, vigorously steering clear of any distracting or negative states of mind. With the latter in mind, here is a teaching based on words of the Baal Shem Tov:

"When a person is drowning in water and he moves wildly about to free himself from drowning, certainly onlookers will not laugh at his bodily gestures. Similarly, when a person is Davening and makes wild body movement and contortions, we should not mock him, as he is trying to save himself from the 'sinful waters' that are drowning him, which are the negative and intruding thoughts that are entering his mind to distract him from prayer."(*Ohr HaEmes, Imrei Tzadikim*, p. 83b. *Likutim Yekarim*, p. 15a. See also *Maor Einayim*, Likutei Torah, p. 227).

Tefilah is a time of human-Divine dialogue, progressing toward a point of intimacy. In this way, the linear model of Davening, from movement and noise to stillness and silence, follows the natural course of physical intimacy, as taught by the holy Baal Shem Tov:

"Prayer is similar to being intimate with the *Shechinah*, the "Divine Presence" within Creation. Just as with the first steps of physical intimacy there is back and forth movement of the body and gradually the movement subsides, the same is true with Davening. A person must accompany the beginning of Davening with rhythmic swaying of the body, so that later he can reach the height of union and stay still, with no body motion nor movement, attached to the Shechinah in profound Deveikus." (*Tzava'as HaRivash*, 68. In general, in the *Zohar* (2:128b) as explained at length in the Arizal, Tefilah is a time of Yichud between ZA, the 'Divine Masculine' *Kaviyachol* / so to speak, and Malchus, the 'Divine Feminine'. In the teachings of the holy Baal Shem Tov too, we, Malchus, are in an embrace with Hashem.)

As Davening is likened to *Zivug* / coupling and *Yichud* / intimate unity, the Baal Shem Tov teaches that just as a couple wanting to have a child must conduct their union with passion, joy and desire, the same is true in Davening (*Ben Poras Yoseph*, Noach, p. 19d). To draw down blessings in a revealed manner and to actually bear fruit from our Davening, we must initially enter into prayer with energetic swaying and passionate movement — the first phases of spiritual intimacy — until we reach a point of stillness in which "a cry, a scream that comes from a place of Deveikus, is silent." This is the place of stillness and intimacy toward which all of our prayerful movements and vocalizations strive.

Swaying

Swaying is a classic movement that manifests in the earlier stages of Davening. Besides expressing passion, swaying can ensure that we stay awake and alert (*Nefesh HaChayim*, Eitz HaChayim, p. 432). In fact, one may deliberately sway during Davening to keep focused and spiritually aroused

(*Siddur BeisYaakov*, Hakdamas HaMechaber, p. 12. See also *Tzror HaMaor*, Yisro. *Darchei Moshe*, Orach Chayim, Siman 48).

In general, body motion can keep a person physically and mentally alert. You may notice that it is while taking a walk or doing something active that your best and clearest ideas come to you. The physical dynamic of movement and activity invigorates mental movement and activity as well. The body-mind-soul is a unified, holistic system. A steady rhythmic motion of the body can free up a lethargic or tense mind and allow one to achieve deeper focus.

For our Davening to be wholesome and transformational, we need to get our entire self engaged in the process. "All my bones will declare, 'Hashem, who is like You'" (*Tehilim*, 35:10). All our 'bones' are harnessed in the act of Davening when we sway.* As we enter deeper and deeper states of transcendental consciousness, however, more and more of the physical body is 'dropped' until it is limp or relatively motionless. Yet, until we reach this *Deveikus* / inwardly unified state, we may need to move about and sway in the process of aligning and integrating our whole self in prayer.

Furthermore, swaying is an external expression of the inner states of *Ahavah* / love, and *Yirah* / awe, which are the 'wings' that allow us to 'fly' and reach a place of Deveikus ("*Oraisa* / Torah without awe and love does not ascend on High": *Tikkunei Zohar*, Tikkun 10. In a later text this statement is quoted to include not only Torah, but also Tefilah and Mitzvos). Both love and awe are emotions, and emotions suggest a duality; one is either moving closer, as in love, or stepping back, as in awe. Deveikus is unity beyond such duality. As there is

---

* *Zohar* 3, 218b. R. Dovid Avudaraham. *Sefer HaManhig*, 1:85. *Shibolei HaLeket*, Siman 17. This is brought down in the *Shulchan Aruch*, Orach Chayim, Rama, 48:2. Swaying while learning Torah goes back a thousand or even thousands of years: See *Sefer HaKuzari*, Ma'amar 2:79-80. *Machzor Vitri*, Siman 508. *Kol Bo*, Siman 74. Regarding moving like a leaping flame, see *Zohar*, ibid.

no longer a defined separation, there is no 'love' or 'awe,' hence the stillness at the peak of Davening.

However, before this state of union is achieved, we are encouraged to move. Within the act of swaying there are two general modes: a forward-and-back motion commonly known as *Shukeling* / shaking, and a side -to-side sway or swivel. We will now explore both of these modalities.

Forward & Back

Forward-and-back, or 'in-and-out' shukeling represents a dynamic of coming closer and pulling away, attraction and repulsion, love and awe. This is known as *Ratzu v'Shuv* / 'running and returning'. This movement is symbolic of the paradoxical nature of the process of Tefilah. A person feels himself drawing closer to Hashem as he begins to Daven, and yet, as his spiritual sensitivity expands, he feels further away and the gulf between himself and Divinity seems more acute. But then, precisely from this place of distance and humility, he spontaneously feels close again. Again, as soon as he is aware of himself getting closer, he suddenly feels even more distant. Indeed, the more intimately aware and connected with the Holy One you become, the more you, as a finite being, realize how existentially far away you really are from the Infinite.

In the standard blessing formula, we open by saying, *Baruch Atah* / "Blessed are You," or "You are the Source of Blessing," which is a direct address, born out of a 'first person' encounter. Then, in the next moment, we make a linguistic switch to "Hashem": *Baruch Atah Hashem*, using indirect, third person language. And then we say, *Elokeinu* / 'our' G-d, indicating a very personal experience of Divinity; and then *Melech haOlam* / King of the World, a more distant or impersonal reference. This back and forth language is emblematic of the constant forward and back movements that we experience in Davening.* Mirroring this subtle linguistic pattern, the body as well moves in and out, back and forth, close and far. (For many Tzadikim, the forward and back swaying seems to be the preferred 'method', see *Yesod Shoresh HaAvodah*, Sha'ar HaKorban, Tefilas 18.)

Forward movements are suggestive of bowing down, representing submission and acceptance. The pulling back motion of standing upright again, represents the opposite of submission — resistance, defiance, and non-acceptance. Tefilah is a rich combination of these seemingly contradictory sentiments: both bowing down and humbling ourselves, submitting to and fully 'accepting what is', *and* pulling back in protest and petition, expressing confidence, holy chutzpah and defiant non-acceptance of the status quo.

On the one hand, through the act of Davening we have the opportunity to become aware that everything in our life is Divinely orchestrated and guided by Hashem's 'hand'. Through deeply communing with and entering a Divine space, we come to sense in our gut how, from the highest perspective, the view of absolute unity, Creation is perfect, and we humbly submit to that reality within 'what is'. And yet, the act of Tefilah, which is not only a gift that is granted to us, but also a *Mitzvah* / commandment that we fulfill, suggests on some level a 'non-acceptance' of reality as it is. When we Daven for the healing of someone who is sick, or for wealth instead of

---

* *Noam Elimelech*, Bechukosai: דהנה אנו אומרים "ברוך אתה" הוא נגלה, "אשר קדשנו" הוא נסתר,
מחמת שבהתחלת האדם לעבוד הבורא, נראה ונדמה לו שהוא כבר קרוב לה' מאד, אבל בהתמדתו
בעבודתו ית' בתמידות, אז מבין ורואה שהוא רחוק מאד מהבורא ב"ה, ועדיין לא התחיל בעבודה כלל.
See also *Teshuvas HaRashba*, 5, Siman 52: עוד שאלת: למה נתקן נוסח הברכה, מחצה נמצא,
ומחצה נסתר תשובה: דע, דיש לבעלי החכמה, סוד נשגב, ואין לנו כאן עסק בנסתרות. ואמנם, יש טעם
נגלה, גדול התועלת, במה שתקנו נוסח הברכות כן, ר"ל בנגלה ובנסתר [כלומר: בגוף שני, ובגוף שלישי].
לפי שכבר ידעת, דשני יסודות יש שעליהם נבנה הכל. האחד: לדעת שהוא ית' מחויב המציאות, ושאין ספק
בזה כלל, כמו שנתבאר ונתפרסם המופת עליו, ביאור רב. והב': שאין אמתתו ית' מושגב [מושגת] כי אם
לעצמו ית' לבד, והוא במציאותו נגלה לכל, ובאמתת מהותו נסתר ונעלם מהכל. וכדי לקבוע שתי הפנות
האלה בנפשותינו, קבעו הנוסח בנגלה ונסתר.

poverty, or for peace instead of war, we are Davening for change. We observe what is, and Daven for what we see as better.

These sentiments are paradoxical and contradictory, and yet we strive to maintain both of them as we move through Davening. From our human perspective, we relate to the power of Tefilah as an agent to facilitate change and stand up against what we do not agree or align with. Whereas from HaKadosh Baruch Hu's transcendent perspective, everything is always perfect, and the process of Tefilah allows us to develop a Divine-like consciousness of this intrinsic perfection, or at least a sense of submission and acceptance of the perfection of the Divine will, whatever that may be.

Once, the Baal Shem Tov instructed his students to fervently Daven for a harsh decree to be annulled. An elder student, Reb Ze'ev Kitzes, commented: "But Rebbe, Hashem is certainly compassionate and doing this for our own benefit." "It is fortunate," said the Baal Shem Tov, "that Reb Ze'ev was not among the living during the times of Esther and Haman, for he would have argued the same about the decree of Haman."

We need to entertain both these paradigms. Whatever happens is 'perfect', and that is what Hashem wants us to receive. And yet, Hashem also wants us to Daven for and protest any dire situation or perceived lack in our lives or in the world. On the one hand, we aspire to accept Hashem's will, and on the other hand, Hashem desires for us to be co-creators with Him; in other words: He wants our input. So we Daven with both of these perspectives in mind, as illustrated by our swaying forward and back during Tefilah. 'Bowing', or moving the body forward, is an act of submission. It is a physical way of saying, "Hashem I accept that this current reality is Your will." Pulling the body back up to an erect position, is a movement of non-acceptance and protest, asserting the need for "change" in our life and in the world.

Side-to-Side

Swaying from side-to-side, right to left and left to right, is much like rocking a baby in its cradle, a motion of *Ahavah* / love and nurturing. When we sway from side-to-side, we can feel ourselves cradled and loved by Hashem. Sometimes, in Davening, we do not need to struggle with the issue of submission or protest, we just need to feel safe and protected, that our life is held in the hands of Hashem. Side-to-side swaying represents and evokes this state of mind.

During the Amidah

Whereas swaying, in either direction, throughout the initial course of the Davening is encouraged, during the Amidah swaying is actually strongly discouraged (The Rema miPano, *Asarah Ma'amaros*, Ma'amar Eim Kol Chai, 1:33. *Shu't Rema miPano*, Siman 113. *Avodas HaKodesh*, Kesher Gudal, 12:1. *Shulchan Aruch*, Orach Chayim, 48:9, Magen Avraham, 4). Rashi writes that standing, in general, enhances our ability to have proper Kavanah (Rashi, *Berachos*, 30a. Alter Rebbe, *Shulchan Aruch*, Orach Chayim, 89:9 from the *Magen Avraham*), and perhaps standing in stillness helps even more so. Besides, by the time we reach the Amidah, we are in some level of Deveikus, and in Deveikus there is no room for movement (*Nesivos Olam*, Nesiv HaAvodah, 6). The *Yerushalmi* teaches that when Shlomo HaMelech Davened, כגון הדין נקדים היה עומד / "He stood like a motionless form" (Yerushalmi, *Berachos*, 1:5. *Pnei Moshe*, ad loc. *Aruch*, Erech, נקרים).

וירא העם וינעו ויעמדו מרחק / *Vayar Haam VaYanu'u Vaya'amdu Merachok* / "And the nation saw, they trembled (moved), and they stood from a distance" (*Shemos*, 20:15). Normally the verse is understood to mean that because of what the people saw they trembled and then stood at a distance. However, it could also be understood to mean that they were "moved" (i.e., they trembled) *because* they were still at a distance. They were still observers: they "saw," which demonstrates that they were not in total Deveikus and thus there was still some room for movement.

Not only is there no movement in true Deveikus, but we also need to ensure (however we can do so in a state of Deveikus) that we do not move, as movement may in fact break the Deveikus. In the words of the Baal Shem Tov:

"At times, when you are attached to the Supernal World, to the Creator, blessed be He, you must guard yourself against any type of (inner) movement, even in the body, so that your Deveikus will not cease." (*Tzava'as HaRivash*, 59)

The Baal Shem Tov teaches that there are two general modalities of Davening; loudly, with swaying and conflagration and perhaps even wild body movement, or in total stillness and quietness of body and mind, with amplified inwardness and total surrender.

In the earlier teachings of the Mekubalim there is, as described above, a preference for progressing from movement and swaying to motionlessness and stillness, and from a pre-Deveikus state to full Deveikus, culminating with the Amidah. The Baal Shem Tov offers a subtler, less linear understanding: the issue of which posture to assume and when during Tefilah depends primarily on the state of consciousness, mindset and heart-space of the person Davening. The question is not 'where' you are holding in the Siddur, but rather where 'you' are holding; what state you are in currently. Every person needs to gauge their own internal state of mind and heart, and Daven accordingly.

Moreover, whether one sways or stands still, shouts loudly or cries quietly, should not be so much a conscious, mindful choice, but rather a natural outgrowth of one's state of consciousness. If you are plagued by negative, intruding thoughts, or feel out of sorts, then body movement is not only 'required', but you will probably sway naturally to 'shake off' these thoughts. By contrast, if you are already in the 'zone', motionlessness and quietness may take hold of you organically.

In this way, we simply need to be natural and present while Davening. Whether we are motionless or in motion, standing still or ecstatically shaking, depends on what state we are in (see also *Pri Megadim*, 48. *Mishnah Berurah*, 48:5. *Aruch HaShulchan*, 48:3). We should set the coordinates with our Kavanah, but then also let ourselves cruise on auto-pilot, so to speak, so that we are accessing what is truly authentic to us at that moment, rather than forcing or fabricating some abstract ideal of how we think we should be. Otherwise, if we are Davening the Amidah, for example, and we are willfully forcing ourselves to be still, that in itself is a 'movement'; in fact, it is an aggressive movement of the mind, and it will only cause more distraction and anxiety.

Eyes Open or Closed

How we position and direct our eyes is much like the issue of moving and swaying. In the earlier teachings of the Mekubalim, it seems clear that the earlier states of Davening are to be recited with one's eyes open and with bodily movement, whereas at the peak of Davening, the Amidah, one's eyes should be closed and the body should be still. The Zohar itself speaks of Davening with one's eyes closed (*Zohar* 3, p. 260b), and many of the great sages throughout history would Daven in this way (*Shaloh*, Meseches Tamid 59. *Yesod Shoresh HaAvodah*, Sha'ar 5:2). The Arizal would Daven with his eyes looking deeply into the Siddur, except for the Amidah and listening to the repetition of the Amidah, which he would do with his eyes closed.

A simple reason to close one's eyes during the Amidah is to be free from distractions (*Siddur Beis Yaakov,* p. 12. *Shu't Mor u'Ketziah,* Siman 95). There are also deeper mystical reasons for closing the eyes during the Amidah (*Pri Eitz Chayim,* Sha'ar Kerias Shema, 29), such as not to seem as if gazing upon the *Yichud* / intimate unity between the Divine Masculine transcendence and the Divine Feminine immanence, or embodying the quality of Rochel (within Malchus) who is called "beautiful, but without eyes." (For this reason, on Shabbos, the day of Yichud, the Arizal would Daven the Amidah as well with his eyes open: *Sha'arei Teshuvah,* Siman 267.) Closing one's eyes represents a 'taking leave of the physical', a *Bitul haYesh,* or 'nullification of what is'. This 'endarkening' generates a visceral sense of the integration of our separate 'i' into the Infinite I.

"A person should close his eyes during the Amidah, and if he does so, he will merit to see the Face of the Shechinah at the moment of death" (*Aruch HaShulchan,* Orach Chayim, 95:4). Closing the eyes is a form of 'dying' in relation to this world, and entering a deeper and higher dimension, as in actual death. When we 'close off the world' by shutting out our physical vision, we are moving away from the world and entering into a realm of transcendence and unity, an infinite dimension of pure potential.

Sight is also a sense that re-enforces dichotomy, separation and distance. You can only see something that exists outside of your source of vision; for instance, you cannot see your own eyes. It has to be something that is external to you and your eyes for you to see it. When we close our eyes, we are short-circuiting this sense of separateness. Hearing is the opposite. Physiologically, the act of hearing puts you at the center of what is being heard, thus the concept of 'surround sound'. This is why we cover and close our eyes when we say the *Shema,* a Tefilah that is all about listening and experiencing the all-encompassing Unity of Hashem.

When, in Davening, we close our eyes and transition into an inner world of transcendence and unity, we 'die' from our perception of this world and are birthed into a higher and deeper dimension. This is a metaphorical death, a cessation of perceived separation and individual ego. To merge with the One in such a way is the desire of one whose soul "yearns, to the point of expiration, for the courtyards of Hashem" (*Tehilim*, 84:3). In deep Tefilah, like a moth to a flame, the soul expires in its pining to such an extent that "indeed, it is only the great kindness of Hashem that gives man the strength to complete his prayers and remain alive" (*Tzava'as HaRivash*, 42). With this understanding in mind, there was once a Chasidic Rebbe known as the Seraph of Strelisk, who, every morning before Davening, would sincerely say goodbye to his family, as if for the last time.

While closing one's eyes during Tefilah, especially at the peak of Te-filah, may seem spiritually advantageous, many people find that looking into the *Siddur* / prayer book and seeing the words on the page helps them with their concentration (...אדם שאינו יכול להתפלל בכוונה בלא סידור שכתוב בו התפלה. יקרא בספר: *Sefer Chasidim*, 18). Some people find that with their eyes closed their mind wanders off quickly, and only by seeing the words on the page can they remain focused.

Whether we concentrate better by shutting our eyes to external stim-uli or by looking into the Siddur, depends on our level of consciousness in the moment. When we are in a state of Deveikus and *Mochin d'Gad-lus* / expansive mind, we may almost automatically Daven with our eyes closed. When, however, a person is in a state of *Mochin d'Katnus* / small or restricted mind, a state in which consciousness is not transformed and self-awareness is not transcended, he may need to keep his eyes focused on the letters and words in the Siddur. In the words of the Baal Shem, "When you are on a low level, it is preferable to Daven while looking into a Siddur, as simply seeing the letters will help you have greater intention. When, however, you are attached to the Supernal World, it is better to close your eyes, so that what you see will not distract you from being attached to the Supernal World" (*Tzava'as HaRivash*, 40).

Again, how best to maximize the effectiveness of your current Davening is not a question of where in the Tefilah you are holding, rather, where you are holding in your self. If you are struggling with intruding thoughts or passive mental wandering, you should look into the Siddur and focus on the *Kesav* / written words on the page. The mere act of reading the words on the page will help propel you into a state *Gadlus* / expansion. This is because the letters in themselves are inanimate vessels (also called *Malchus*) in a state of *Katnus* / constriction; it is only when a conscious being, a person with *Binah* / understanding, reads them, that they are 'elevated' into a level of expansion and life. Our Davening is the light that brings the 'dry bones' of the letters to life. Then, through a mirroring effect, this stimulates an expansion and animation within yourself as well — an effect that will be explored more thoroughly later on (see also *Kesones Pasim*, Balak. *Amud HaTefilah*, 46). By contrast, when a person is already Davening with expansiveness, *Mochin* / elevated consciousness and Deveikus, he naturally closes his eyes, and he may not need to use the letters as a visual tool. He himself has become a letter in the Ultimate's Davening.

From the above, it would seem that looking into the words on the page would be the preferred path for those who are struggling with *Mochin d'Katnus* / constricted consciousness, or who are in general less equipped mentally and spiritually to concentrate with Kavanah for an extended time. But this is not quite so. Many great Tzadikim throughout the ages — including the Rebbe, the *Nasi* / preeminent spiritual leader of Klal Yisrael in our generation, and the saintly Chafetz Chayim a generation ago — would Daven slowly, word by word, looking into the Siddur, even during the Amidah (*Toras Menachem*, Tav/ Shin / Mem / Gimel 1, p. 144-145). Perhaps this is because simply looking at the letters themselves is itself a powerful Divine interface; the letters of the Torah are the building blocks of Creation, and thus we are joining with HaKadosh Baruch Hu and co-creating the world when we are reciting these letters, as will be explored in greater detail, further on.

Ultimately, Davening with eyes open looking into the Siddur or with eyes closed "depends upon each person and what he feels will help him in his prayers" (Magen Avraham, *Orach Chayim*, 93:2). Every person must choose the path that they feel is correct for them, and often within the person himself, this changes from day to day or even from one Tefilah to the next; sometimes eyes open looking in the Siddur is helpful and sometimes eyes closed (The Rebbe, *Igros Kodesh* 22, 8,278). Parenthetically, but importantly, if you are keeping your eyes open they should be looking into the Siddur, not wandering about, and not even looking in front of you. This, says the Zohar (3, p. 260b), is because the Shechinah is in front of you and it should not appear as if you are attempting to gaze at the Shechinah.

How to Hold Your Hands while Davening

Our sages provide us teachings and directives regarding the position of one's hands during Davening, especially during the Amidah. In general, the hands are to be positioned in an orderly fashion. Rav Ashi said, "I saw by Rav Kahana that when there was trouble in the world, he would remove his cloak and clasp his hands, 'like a servant before his master'" (*Shabbos*, 10a). Accordingly, the Rama rules, "In times of trouble one should clasp his hands like a servant before his master" (*Shulchan Aruch*, Orach Chayim, 91:6). According to the Rambam, however, Rav Kahana would *always* clasp his hands, both in troubled times and in a time of peace, and he most probably had his right hand over his left, upon his heart (*Hilchos Tefilah*, 5:4. The difference in the various times was with regards to his mode of dress, as *Shabbos* 10a specifies

אמר רב אשי: חזינא ליה לרב כהנא כי איכא צערא בעלמא, שדי גלימיה ופכר ידיה ומצלי. אמר: —
כעבדא קמי מריה". כי איכא שלמא לביש ומתכסי ומתעטף ומצלי" (*Kesef Mishnah*, ibid, 5:4). There
are earlier sources who describe a Middle Eastern custom of placing one's
hands behind their back when speaking to their ruler, and thus one should
do so as well during Davening. This shows that we do not have our own
'hands' so-to-speak, or our own power of agency before HaKadosh Baruch
Hu, and we are Davening with total surrender (*Beis Yoseph*, Orach Chayim, 95.
The Ran brings down this interpretation in the name of Rabbeinu Chananel on *Shabbos*,
10b). This custom is not practiced today, and we should Daven with our
hands in front of the body not behind the back (*Shu't Tzitz Eliezer*, Vol 9, Siman
4).

We know that the Arizal would always Daven the Amidah with his
right hand covering his left (*Pri Etz Chayim*, Sha'ar Kerias Shema, 29); this enacts a dominance of the right hand, which is the attribute of compassion
and kindness, over the left hand, which is the attribute of judgment and
harshness (Rama, *Darchei Moshe*, Orach Chayim, 95:3. *Kaf HaChayim*, 95:13). Later
Mekubalim write, that the custom is to place the thumb of the right hand
in the grasp of the left hand (*Asarah Ma'amaros*, Ma'amar Eim Kol Chai, 1:33. *Magen Avraham*, 95:2. *Shulchan Aruch HaRav*, 95:4. And everyone should practice as is the
custom in their place: *ibid*).

When we place our hands upon our heart, with the right hand over
and perhaps grasping the left hand, we create an image of an archer's bow.
Rav Yehudah Chayit (born in Spain, c.1450), explains that the hands are
the bow and the arrow is the tongue. What pulls the bow back and thus
releases the arrow forward with force is our Kavanah. When we are Davening, we are sending arrows Above to pierce the Heavens and draw down
the flow of Shefa into our lives (*Pirush HaChayit*, *Ma'areches Elokus*, 10. See also:
Nefutzos Yehudah, Derush 24).

We also find that Avraham, who is the first person recorded in the To-rah to Daven, says, "I have lifted my hands to Hashem," which the Targum translates as, "I have lifted my hands in prayer" (See also *Melachim* 1, 8:22. *Divrei HaYamim* 2, 6:13. *Ezra*, 6:5. See also *Shemos,* 17:11. See also *Pirkei D'Rebbe Eliezer*, 44). The lifting of open hands enacts receiving from Above. One stands here below in this world, poised to receive the limitless Divine *Shefa* / abundance and life from the Infinite One, the Most High.

In fact, for many centuries, from the time of Rav Avraham ben Ha-Rambam, in the 13ᵗʰ Century, many Tzadikim would Daven the 'requests' of the Amidah with their hands stretched out above their heads, as the *Sefer Chareidim* brings down (Rav Elazar Azikri, *Sefer Chareidim*, 5:72-73. See also *Zohar* 3, 195b).

Yet, our Sages teach that when a person spreads their hands with the appropriate Kavanah it wields tremendous spiritual potential, and therefore it should be done with the utmost preparation, care and consciousness. The Zohar speaks of the spiritual dangers posed to a person who lifts his hands above his head for no purpose or without proper intention (*Zohar 2*, Yisro, 67a). Even with the proper intentions, there are limitations as to how long a person should stretch out his hands above his head in this manner.* Today, as a conscious and decided practice, we no longer lift our hands above our heads in Davening. This is because it is a way of prayer that has been adopted by the gentiles (*Hagahos Rebbe Akiva Eiger*, Shulchan Aruch, Orach Chayim, 89:1. *Be'er Sheva*, Siman 74), and because it is difficult to attain or maintain the Kavanah that is proper for this powerful posture (*Chavas Ya'ir*, Mekor Chayim, Siman 95:3).

---

* *Sefer HaBahir*, 138: אלא אסור לו לאדם לשהות שלש שעות כפיו פרושות השמים. See also Ramban and Rabbeinu Bachya, *Shemos*, 17:11-12. *Me'iras Einayim*, Beshalach. 17:16. *Pardes Rimonim*, Sha'ar 15:3. *Asarah Ma'amaros*, Ma'amar Chikur Din, 1:22. See also *Shaloh HaKadosh*, Meseches Tamid, 62. *Mekor Chayim*, Siman 95:3.

All of the above hand positions during Davening are premeditated and planned, as one is consciously choosing to place their hands over their heart, for example. Yet in the teachings of the Baal Shem, while the delineated practices of hand placement are certainly encouraged, there is also an understanding of the necessity of spontaneity within Davening, in which perhaps a sense of losing control of the body and the hands may occur, even with wild or unconventional movements happening on their own, so to speak. While the earlier Mekubalim warn us not to Daven with our hands above the head, in the teachings of the Baal Shem Tov there is an understanding that spontaneously and involuntarily lifting our hands is in fact a good omen. As a profound disciple of the Baal Shem teaches, "Know that this (unintentionally raising your hands above your head during Davening) is a sign that your Tefilos have been answered and that in fact you are receiving from On High" (Rebbe Pinchas of Koritz, *Imrei Pinchas*, p. 84).

To Daven with unself-conscious passion, we need to let go and be natural; this 'loosening up' is paradoxically harder than it would seem. We need to enter fully into the words and the experience of Davening, thus allowing the Davening itself to lead our minds, our hearts, and our bodies accordingly. Sometimes your body or hands may be still and limp, sometimes trembling in awe or moving about in ecstasy, and at other times you may even find yourself Davening the Amidah with your hands held high above your head. According to the Baal Shem Tov, all of these are 'right' in the appropriate context and spontaneous flow of your soul in communion with HaKadosh Baruch Hu.

Slowly or Quickly

Sometimes the Baal Shem Tov speaks of Davening very quickly, reciting the words in rapid succession as a person on fire for Hashem, and other times he speaks of saying the words of Davening very slowly, holding onto each precious word like a jewel or a delicacy.

"Sometimes you can Daven very quickly because your heart is on fire with the love for Hashem and the words flow through your mouth, as if on their own." (*Tzava'as HaRivash,* 36)

A student of a student of the Baal Shem Tov, Rebbe Yisrael Hopstein (1737–1814), also known as the Magid of Koznitz, once remarked that if you are still saying the words of Davening through your own volition, still needing to deliberately move your lips, know, that you have not yet reached the deepest level of Deveikus (*Avodas Yisroel,* Metzorah: a teaching by Rebbe Gershon who said this to his brother-in-law, the Baal Shem. See also *Zohar Chai* 1, 5:3. *Notzer Chesed,* p. 75). In other words, when a person truly enters into his Davening, the words come pouring out of his mouth, and usually at a rapid pace. This is considered an advanced method for attaining Kavanah and Deveikus.

In a related manner, for the purpose of shaking off and defending oneself from intruding, negative thoughts taking up space in one's consciousness during Davening, the Baal Shem would advise his followers to Daven rapidly, moving swiftly from one word to the next (*Divrei Moshe,* Bo, in the name of the Baal Shem Tov). It is taught in older sources that reciting an entire *Brachah* / blessing with one exhale will help you rid yourself of any negative or intrusive thoughts (This is taught in the name of the *Reishis Chochmah. Ohr HaGanuz LaTzadikim,* Bechukosai).

On the other hand, the Baal Shem Tov speaks of a profound Deveikus in which one says the words of Davening extremely meticulously and slowly, literally forcing himself to let go of each word and sound as they are emanating from his mouth:

"Deveikus means that when saying a word, you prolong that word extensively. Because of the profound Deveikus, you do not wish to part from the words and you cling to them, holding on to them and drawing them out." (*Tzava'as HaRivash*, 70. See also *Agra D'Pirka*, p. 62)

For the purpose of deepening Deviekus, the Baal Shem Tov advises us to put ourselves fully into the words of the Davening, even into the sound and vibration of each letter. For example, before you are about to say the word *Baruch* / blessed, pause for a moment, think about what the word and concept of blessing means. Then, slowly exhale the first word: *Baaa-Ruuuch*, allowing the sound to resonate in your body.

Many Chasidic Rebbes would in a sense combine both of these modes of slow and fast Davening; they would pace or sit in deep thought for hours, and then, with a single blast of energy, recite large parts of Davening with blinding speed.

In both the path of drawing out each word slowly and the path of Davening very quickly, there is an abstraction of the words from their defined meanings. One distills them to their vibrational essence as conduits or vehicles for transporting Divine consciousness and Light. Through sounding the words in either a protracted or contracted manner, we enter the sonic power of the words and letters themselves, allowing us to connect deeply with the Light and source of the letters, Hashem alone.

As an Adult with Mochin or as a Child with Simplicity

Again, depending on our state of mind and consciousness, we can Daven either with elaborate Kavanah, in a deep contemplative state, or we can express the words of Davening simply and innocently, as a child pleading with his father. We may also weave in and out of different states and thus, when we are consciously in sync with our inner world, our Davening can flow through multiple forms, as discussed. The *Ikar* / main thing to know is that we need to be spontaneous and open, allowing the waves of Davening to carry us along, back to the One.

Sometimes we feel like we need to Daven with *Mochin d'Gadlus* / expansive mindfulness and intricate Kavanah, and sometimes we feel the need to connect on a more visceral level, and reach out to Hashem as a child would call out for a parent; simply, sincerely, unsophisticated and unadorned.

For example: One might at different times pick up the phone to call a loving parent in order to talk about or ask them something specific and important — but sometimes one might call simply to connect. Similarly, sometimes we simply want to speak with Hashem, to reach out and connect. We might need to sing or cry or dance — regardless, whatever comes up can be part of this un-self-conscious interaction, like when a small child reaches out to bond with a parent.

When we Daven like a child there is a strong sense of spontaneity, as we feel like we can and should Daven when we want, and for whatever we want. Nothing is too big or too small, and no time is better than 'now'. As explored earlier, even after Rebbe Nachunya ben Hakana, a famous First Century Rabbi, had mastered all the mystical intentions of Tefilah he would still Daven like a little child. Whether one is Davening in the mindset of a mature adult, with full Mochin and mindful presence, or as a child, with spontaneity and simplicity, the *Ikar* / main thing is to *truly* Daven.

Ensuring That Our Davening Is Not Routine

It should now be clear that whether you sway or stand motionless, whether your eyes are open or closed, whether your hands are swirling with movement or placed neatly on your chest, whether you Daven in a loud or a quiet voice, singing or whispering, quickly or slowly, as an adult with full Mochin or as a child with simple openness — it all depends on being true to who and where you are at while Davening.

Our sages tell us, "He who makes his prayers *Keva* / fixed, his prayers are not *Tachanunim* / supplications" (*Avos*, 2:13. *Berachos*, 29b). Certainly, there is an element of Keva (structure) that is (normally) required to create the proper context of Davening. For example, we need to secure a *Makom Kavuah* / a fixed place in which to Daven, whether that is a fixed place where you Daven every day in Shul or, if for some reason you cannot go to Shul, a special location within your home that is dedicated to Davening (*Berachos*, 6b. *Yerushalmi*, *Berachos* 4:4. Shulchan Aruch, *Orach Chayim*, 90:19). A person concentrates better in a familiar place (*Menoras HaMaor*, Ner 3, Klal 3:10). Yet, the inner essence of the Davening itself should not be fixed. Our most authentic pathways in Davening are revealed to us in the moment, and they are sometimes the 'opposite' of our habitual patterns.

On the *Pasuk* / verse: ובקשתם משם את ה׳ אלקיך ומצאת / "And you shall seek Hashem your G-d from there, and you will find Him" (*Devarim*, 4:29), says the Baal Shem Tov, the emphasis is on the word משם / "from *there*"; we need to seek Hashem from the space that we are in. A person should not say, "Today I really do not have the *Mochin* / mental clarity and open heart to Daven, so let me not *try* to really Daven." This would be a subtle form of idol worship; comparing your living-state to a fixed concept of how you presume Davening *should* feel. Nor should a person say, "Yesterday, singing a Nigun really helped me have Kavanah so let me do the same today." This is another way of relying on Keva, rather than being radically present and open to Elokim Chayim / the Living G-d. HaKadosh Baruch Hu invites us to step into Davening from wherever we are currently standing. We need to honestly and earnestly assess where we are, and from there seek the Omnipresent One.

To Daven with the Whole Self

Part of being aware of 'where we are', the concept of משם / "from there" that we saw in the verse above, and seeking Hashem from that place, is to consciously feel and gauge our bodily state. We need to take a moment (at least) to check in on our current sensations, energy level and general physical experience before we are about to Daven. If one is terribly hungry, for example, it will be impossible for him to concentrate (*Baba Basra*, 12b. *Shulchan Aruch*, Orach Chayim, 89:4). The same would be true if he is exhausted or in great pain, or in a very cold or hot room. There is an intimate interrelationship between the soul, mind and body. For some very self-controlled, strong-minded, or elevated individuals, the movement into Davening always begins with the soul, and the mind and body follow.

In this case, the natural distractions of pain, sleepiness or hunger can be overridden and contained, and he can have Kavanah and *Yishuv Ha-Da'as* / a settled mind in almost any situation. Yet, for most people, the process works in the other direction; most of the time, the body affects the mind and the state of consciousness. We therefore need to be attentive and aware of the state of our body as we are about to Daven, as it will either be the bridge or the abyss between us and Deveikus.

We should not begin to Daven, says the Baal Shem Tov, before we have what he calls הסכמת האיברים / 'the consent of the limbs'. (He discusses this idea as it relates to a collective, i.e., not beginning to Daven until everyone is ready, but it can also refer to the limbs of an individual person.) In other words: Before we Daven we need the consent of our body, to make sure that we are prepared for and attuned to the effort, focus, and opening that Davening requires. For most people, not feeling physically well or comfortable will present significant difficulties in focusing and having Kavanah. We need to tend to the body in whatever manner necessary: perhaps even taking a drink or light food or ensuring that our chair is reasonably comfortable, for example, before beginning to Daven (*HaYom Yom*, 10th of Shevat).

In the words of the Baal Shem Tov:

"When the body ails, the soul, too, is weakened, and one is unable to pray properly, even when he is clean of sin. You must, therefore, guard the health of your body very carefully." (*Tzava'as HaRivash*, 106)

We are a unified system, and each part affects the whole. For the soul to lead the mind and body into Davening may be ideal, but we need to know ourselves; our mind and spirit might be weaker when our body is weakened.

As the Magid of Mezritch, the prime student of the Baal Shem Tov, once put it poignantly "A small hole in the body is a big hole in the soul" (*Magid Devarav LeYaakov*, 191. See also the Rebbe, *B'tzeil HaChochmah*, p. 28). If your body is failing or ailing, lightly injured or irritated, try to the best of your ability to relieve the physical discomfort and mend the 'hole' in the body so that your soul and spirit can be whole and you can truly Daven.

The Baal Shem Tov talks about how sometimes a person wants to Daven with passion and fervor; his mind, heart and spirit are up to it, yet, he cannot get himself to Daven deeply because "his limbs are heavy" (*Amud HaTefilah*, 66. *Ohr Torah*, Ekev). We need to check in and ensure that our limbs are not 'heavy', and acquire the 'consent' of our body, so that we can enter fully — mind, heart and body — into Davening and deeper states of Deveikus.

Beyond making sure the body is not weighing us down, we can actually even do the reverse; we can energize the body and enlist it to ignite the heart, open the mind and stimulate the spirit. In order to jump start our emotions, we can awaken and stir up the body and the heart will follow suit (*Sefer HaChinuch*, Mitzvah 16). This can include clapping our hands or moving our feet, dancing, swaying or singing a Nigun. These external actions can ignite an inner movement and arousal of emotion. If you feel dull and lethargic and your heart feels closed or cut off, some type of intentional movement of the body that gets your heart pumping can kindle the flames of the heart, allowing you to start feeling again.

Sometimes, as a student of the Baal Shem Tov teaches, "A person has to arouse his body with all his strength, in order for his Neshamah to illuminate within" (*Likutim Yekarim*, 33). If the density of the body does not allow you to reveal the light of your Neshamah, you may need to soften and illuminate the body first.

Utilizing Everything

Whatever condition we are in, that is the place from which we need to approach Davening. Yet, to lift off into true Davening, it is not sufficient to merely get the *consent* of our bodies, heart and mind. Rather, we need to enlist all the *capabilities* of our body, heart and mind, to ensure that we experience a real *Hergesh* / feeling and *Geshmak* / 'spiritual-emotional-mindful delight' when we Daven.

To experience an eruption of holy emotions or sensations in the body during Davening, whether overt or subtle, sometimes the subtle stimulation of mere *Hisbonenus* / intellectual contemplation is adequate. Sometimes this kind of contemplative learning, for example of a Chasidic *Ma'amar* / discourse, can ignite the heart and mind and create a conducive internal resonance for Davening. Ideally, the mind controls the heart and our contemplative thought awakens our feelings. Practically, though, since the heart can be dulled with *Timtum HaLev* / closing of the heart, the lights of the intellect and the soul may not penetrate. In such a state, the heart can seem like a large log which cannot catch fire before it is splintered apart.

If Timtum HaLev was a prevalent phenomena in earlier times, how much more so does this spiritual disease prevail today. Today we are living in a world in which apathy and indifference is the norm. When everything is seen as 'relative', nothing really matters any longer. For this reason, sometimes we need to first soften the heart before awakening the mind. Singing a Nigun before or during Davening is one suggestion to arouse and soften the heart. We can also use a creative visualization such as seeing yourself Davening in Gan Eden or in the presence of a great Tzadik from the past. On the other hand, if we ignore the mind completely or circumvent it and operate solely on an emotional level, eventually the mind will resurface and demand our attention. In the end neglecting our mind completely would only allow it to distract us further and shut us down.

Therefore, for the success of our Davening, we need to harness our whole arsenal of capacities. All of ourselves, our body, mind and heart, all need to participate. As such, if we scan our sensations to awaken the body, it should be combined with singing a Nigun to awaken our 'heart space', which should be coupled with *Hisbonenus* / mental contemplation to awaken our 'mind space'. Hisbonenus should then be coupled with visualized imagery, transforming lofty intellectual ideas into vivid four-dimensional mental images. (See *Tanya*, Iggeres HaKodesh, 11).

All the above, from rhythmic motions of the body, to loud outbursts during Davening, from singing to keeping the eyes focused on the Siddur, are external aids to help us get our entire self involved in Davening. When we are entirely involved, then we can lose our sense of self-awareness and slip into a state of Gadlus, and allow the body to become motionless and quiet, and the eyes to close. To consciously involve our entire self in Davening without reservations or holding back is a necessary response to a Katnus stage as we strive toward a point of non-self-awareness. In this space of self-transcendence, we become absorbed in the *Ein Sof* / Infinite No-thing-ness, and finally we enter a full Gadlus and Deveikus state.

Chapter 3

TO PRAY IS TO EXPERIENCE DEVEIKUS/UNITY WITH HASHEM

BEFORE WE GET TO THE ACTUAL *Derech* / PATH OF THE BAAL SHEM TOV IN DAVENING, A FEW GENERAL WORDS ABOUT THE *Tachlis* / OBJECTIVE OF DAVENING ARE IN ORDER.

Our sages teach that if a person has two Shuls in town, one closer to his home and one a little further, he should walk to the further one, as he receives *S'char* / reward for every step taken going to Shul (*Sotah*, 22a). This principle applies only to walking to Shul, but does not apply, for example, if a person has two possible Sukkos to eat in. There is no principle that says if you have two Sukkos, walk to the further one and receive reward; in fact, it could be argued that he should specifically go to the closer Sukkah to go more directly to fulfilling the Mitzvah (ויראה כי אין הדין הזה גבי סוכה שאם יש לו שתי סוכות האחת קרובה והאחת רחוקה שאין לו לילך אל הסוכה הרחוקה בשביל שהוא נוטל שכר פסיעות Maharal, *Nesivos Olam*, Nesiv HaAvodah, 5). Walking to Shul to Daven is unique in that the entire nature of Tefilah is aspiring, longing and yearning to connect, in this way the actual walking to Shul itself is considered to be part of Davening; walking, moving, getting closer, feeling that you are nearing your destination until you have finally 'arrived' and made the connection. This is the essence of Tefilah.

On the heels of this process, upon 'arrival', Davening is all about connectivity, attachment, and a sense of *Deveikus* / unity with Hashem. As in Hebrew, the word for prayer is *Tefilah*, suggesting that prayer is an act of *Tofel* / connecting and joining.* Through the act of Davening, we become, in a revealed and experienced manner, joined with the Creator of all Life.

Our human condition necessitates that we be in a perpetual state of prayer, of hoping, longing, dreaming and yearning. Some dream and yearn for power, while others for money or love, yet the fundamental yearning underlying all of these desires is the yearning for unity — unity with ourselves, with others, with life around us, and ultimately with the Creator.

Deep inside our hearts we are all 'seekers of unity'; we intensely hunger for some sense of connection to 'something' that is beyond all of our brokenness and feelings of being lost or alone. We aspire to make contact and communicate with something larger than ourselves, something more whole and complete.

---

* *Targum Onkelus*, Bereishis, 30:8. Rashi, Rashbam and Seforno, *ad loc*. Rav Mattisyahu Delecreta on *Sha'arei Orah*, Sha'ar 2, p. 63. *Pri HaAretz*, Vayigash. *Torah Ohr*, Terumah, p. 79d.

While all of our individual yearnings are real, sadly we may set our sights on empty goals such as fame, money, or trivial and transient sensations, in hopes that their attainment will generate a lasting sense of wholeness, beauty, self-worth or simple satisfaction. But all this 'down-grading' of our true Divine desire really does is make us feel less satisfied and whole. Sensing such a devastating emptiness, some people try to fill the hole with materialism, obsessively sacrificing their lives for their career. Others try to fill the void with food, compulsively attempting to escape the feeling of spiritual hunger. And still, the emptiness prevails. Not only does the hunger, discontentedness or feeling of lack not disappear, it becomes increasingly exacerbated. The more we attempt to fill ourselves with 'things', the emptier we feel. This is because the fulfillment of desire only expands one's vessel of desire. As the vessel expands, so too does the feeling of need or yearning, along with the sense that one's appetite is never quite quenched or pacified. Only by uncovering and revealing our own wholeness, our soul, the part of us that is One with the One, with Hashem, can we feel truly and lastingly whole, full, complete and satisfied.

A human being is driven to seek out, uncover and openly reveal perfection within this imperfect world, a place of wholeness within all of the brokenness, joy in the place of sadness, transcendence within tediousness, light in the place of darkness, and holiness hidden within foolishness. That is our nature, as we are created in the image of the Infinite One.

We all deeply yearn and fervently hope for change, either inside of us or in the outer world, and we want more out of life. This inner hunger is the root of prayer. When we become aware of this inner hunger and turn it toward our Creator, rather than toward transient phenomena, prayer emerges naturally, catalyzing radical shifts in our life and perception. From this raw and vulnerable place deep within, Tefilah is born.

Davening is like peeling an onion. As you peel away layers of yearning, going deeper and deeper into what your yearning really is, tears begin to form. You may start to weep because as you are going deeper into the core of your humanity, more of the real you is being revealed, and along with this, the wholeness and beauty that you always so passionately sought. All of the hidden layers of your psyche and soul — the sense of emptiness, the traumas, and fears that you harbor, both willingly and unconsciously — are being shed. As your body and mind open up, you make contact with your deeper self. You reach out and reveal a sense of *Tofel* / 'joining' with the Creator of the Universe. Through this process of yearning and opening and reaching out, you are effectively establishing the lines and rhythms of open communication fundamental to any sustainable, committed relationship. Tefilah is the technology that allows this connection to occur.

To establish a revealed, felt connection with the Source of Being, you must peel away the layers of *Kelipos* / husks, the coverings that conceal your deepest self, your Neshamah. In the process of moving inward, you also reach deeply 'outward', toward self-transcendence. In this way, you experience a visceral and profound sense of Deveikus with HaKadosh Baruch Hu. All the techniques of Davening, including the intricate Kavanos on the various names of Hashem, are meant "only to cleave and connect oneself with Hashem" (*Toldos Yaakov Yoseph*, Parshas Vaera).

To paraphrase the words of the holy *Zohar* (*Zohar* 2, 250a), "Praiseworthy are the righteous who know how to set their prayers correctly, because as their prayers ascend on high, they too ascend with their prayers and are elevated until the door of the innermost, highest chamber is opened and they are in the Presence of the King."

Deveikus, Beyond Love and Awe

As will be explored in greater detail, *Ahavah* / love and *Yirah* / fear or awe are the dominant sensations experienced and expressed in Davening. Love and awe are the wings upon which our spirit takes flight. One without the other — love without awe or awe without love — no matter how profound or powerful, does not allow our soul and prayer to soar upwards.

Ahavah is the sense of feeling closeness with Hashem, whereas Yirah is the trepidation we sense when we are approaching the Infinite Mystery. There is a repulsion and sense of terror and dread in nearing the inconceivable magnitude of The Infinite One. Ahavah without Yirah is inspiration without 'vessels' to contain it and put it to use in the world of action. Yirah is the prime vessel that contains inspiration. Ahavah without Yirah can be an inspiration or desire that becomes 'wasted seed', so-to-speak (*Imrei Tzadikim*, p. 3). Without Yirah there is no 'receiver', no vessel to collect and contain the *Shefa* / flow that the inspiration and desire generate, and so the flow dissipates, and the yearning for wholeness is unfulfilled and even exacerbated.

Generally, growth into psycho-spiritual maturity travels along the trajectory from Yirah to Ahavah. But in a healthy process, it will also move from Ahavah into a higher form of Yirah, and then from that Yirah into a deeper Ahavah, ad infinitum. This is the spiral staircase of prayer, upon which our spirit ascends and blessings descend.

Deeper dimensions of Ahavah and Yirah will be explored later on, but relevant to the discussion at hand, it is important to understand that both love and awe are 'feelings'. Any kind of feeling suggests separation, whether it is one that draws us closer — as in love — or repels us from something, as in fear. Even awe and wonder, at least the way they are normally experienced, are still 'emotions'. *Yichud* / unity and Deveikus are beyond all emotions. Love and awe are the wings that lift us and move our life upwards, but in the moment that a person touches a state of Yichud and Deveikus with Hashem, there is no more movement. This can manifest when the person is including higher love and higher awe simultaneously, or when they have transcended the sensations of feelings all together. In either case, once you are 'one' in Yichud, there are no longer 'movements' or 'feelings' as we normally experience them.

After Adam and Chavah / Eve ate from the 'Tree of Knowledge of Good and Evil', they entered the world of duality and were banished from the Garden of Eden; Eden being the inner space of Yichud. Once they were outside of Eden, "Hashem stationed the *Keruvim* / angels of 'nearness' with their fiery spinning swords to the east of the Garden of Eden, to guard the way to the Tree of Life" (*Bereishis* 3:22-24). Accordingly, the function of the Keruvim is to guard the Tree of Life, representing the world of unity. The *Ma'areches HaElokus* (A *Sefer* / text attributed to Rav Todros Abulafia, 1225 to c.1285) interprets the Keruvim as wielding two swirling swords which represent Ahavah and Yirah. Love and awe carry us to the gates of Eden, but to pass through those gates and attain Yichud, the Tree of Life, even these emotions need to be transcended.

Ultimately, Edenic consciousness is beyond all duality. Emotions such as love, fear, and even awe imply two separate entities coming near to each other but always remaining on some level apart and alone. *Deveikus* means not only 'cleaving', but on the deepest level implies a full Yichud 'beyond' emotions, when our personal 'i' becomes subsumed within the embrace of the Infinite 'I' of the Creator.

When we achieve, even momentarily, this state of utter *Bitul* / nullification of the sense of 'i', we transcend our limited, finite and defined ego-self and slip into the limitless, nondual space of Infinity. This is much like physical intimacy, when approached with intentionality and integrity, in which one is able to transcend their boundaries of separateness and achieve a total melding of two into one, as the Pasuk says, ודבק באשתו והיו לבשר אחד / "...and [by] cleaving to his wife, they shall become *one* flesh" (*Bereishis*, 2:24).

Such experiential awareness and identification with the infinite unity of Hashem is the point of all Tefilah.

Chapter 4
THE SIX STAGES OF TEFILAH

W HILE THE BAAL SHEM TOV HIMSELF DID NOT TRAN-
SCRIBE HIS TEACHINGS, NOR DID HE LEAVE US ANY
BOOKS, HE DID LEAVE US WITH A TREASURE TROVE OF
DEDICATED STUDENTS, WHO BECAME VERITABLE 'LIVING BOOKS' AND
FULL EMBODIMENTS OF HIS TEACHINGS. THESE DISCIPLES EVENTU-
ALLY WROTE DOWN SOME OF THEIR REBBE'S TEACHINGS, AND IT IS
FROM THEM THAT WE GET A GLIMPSE OF THIS REVOLUTIONARY, PRO-
FOUND YET 'SIMPLE', SPIRITUAL GIANT.

Parenthetically, it is important to keep in mind, as his spiritual 'grandson', the Alter Rebbe, points out (*Igeres HaKodesh*, 25), that the Baal Shem
Tov spoke Yiddish, while his disciples recorded his teachings in Hebrew.

Therefore, we need to have a fine-tuned ear to discern when perhaps a nuance may be hidden in translation, and whether we can uncover deeper meaning by closely paying attention to the text, meaning, not only to *what* is written, but to *how* it is written and in what context.

The Baal Shem Tov's Path of Prayer, in Brief

One foundational principle of the Baal Shem Tov's worldview to understand, before we move any deeper into his teachings on prayer, is the idea that the world is filled and formed with the *letters* of the Aleph-Beis. Our sages reveal to us that the world was created with *Asara Ma'amaros* / Ten Utterances, which literally means Ten Divine Sounds or Vibrations (*Pirkei Avos*, 5:1). The Torah describes the process of creation as a series of Ten Divine Utterances which give rise to the world as we know it. It is through these primordial 'words' that Creation emerges and becomes physically manifest. For example, "G-d said, 'Let there be light', and there was light" (*Bereishis*, 1:3). Each time there was a Divine utterance, a new dimension of Creation came into being. From this deceptively simple statement describing Hashem's creative process, we learn that speech, and by extension sound, are creative mediums in and of themselves.

Bereishis Bara Elokim Eis / In the beginning G-d created [the Heavens]..., can also be translated as, "In the beginning G-d created *Eis*...." The word *Eis* / את, which is a preposition that serves as a definite direct object marker, can alternatively be understood as an acronym made up of the first and last letters of the Hebrew alphabet, meaning 'In the beginning G-d created the 22 letters from Aleph to Tav'. According to this interpretation, the first creation, even before the formation of the Heavens and the Earth, was that of the 22 letters of the Aleph-Beis. These primary building blocks and vibrations of communication and creativity preceded all other phenomena.

Bara is the second word of the Torah, a word that is normally translated as 'created', yet it comes from the word *Bar* / outside or external. Therefore, we can read the first verse as, 'In the beginning, G-d *externalized...*' This Self-externalization process begins with a swelling of sound and spiritual vibration, which gives rise to the initial formation of the letters, and then to the words that give birth to all energy, matter, form, movement, and consciousness that appear as seemingly 'outside' of the Creator. The fruit of Creation manifests 'out' of its root in Divine Speech.

Speech is rooted in the breath and thought within the speaker. Creation thus emerges from deep within the Creator, and manifests outwardly through the Divine 'Mouth' by means of the letters, which then combine to form words, which generate inhabitable realities.

If we can understand the spiritual mechanics of the letters — their power, structure and depth — we can attain enhanced creative powers. It is for this reason that the main architect of the *Mishkan* / Sanctuary in the Desert was Betzalel, whose name literally means, 'in the shadow of G-d'. Betzalel was chosen for this most cosmic of creative projects specifically because "Betzalel knew the combinations of letters that the Creator used to create the world" (*Berachos*, 55a). This knowledge gave Betzalel the wisdom and insight necessary to construct a finite container that could paradoxically conceal and reveal the Infinite Presence of Hashem.

Every 'letter' of creation is a distinct building block, a conduit of Divine life-force, which combines with other such letters to vibrate and animate a specific life form or phenomenon. In other words: The letters are the means through which Divine Creativity expresses, sustains and regenerates Creation.

The sound 'Ah' of Aleph, for example, creates an energetic or vibratory opening. When this sound is joined to the sound 'Oh' of the letter Vav, and then to the 'R' of Reish, the word *Ohr* / light is formed, and actual light is brought into being. The spiritual sound wave created by the combination of these three letters is the metaphysical source of light. When Hashem said "Let there be light," and revealed the word *Ohr*, light was immediately present.

To create a physical entity, a spiritual vibration, a metaphysical sound is uttered, giving rise to a defined physical vibration and flow of energy, which gradually condenses and is solidified as actual matter. Hashem said, "Let the earth sprout vegetation…," and it was so.

While the Torah recounts only ten Divine Utterances creating the entire world (lights, spheres, vegetation, fish and birds, etc.), there is an almost infinite variety of 'Utterances' vibrating throughout manifest reality. Even two raindrops are distinct from one another, requiring unique articulations to bring them into being. The Ten Utterances of *Bereishis* are therefore best understood as the root expressions of Divine creativity, and through the creative act of *Tzirufim* / letter permutation, all of the unique, creative 'words' are spoken to form, enliven and sustain all life.

This complex of ideas is summarized in the *Tanya* when considering the creation of a stone, which is not mentioned specifically in the Ten Divine Utterances: "Now, although the word אבן / *Ehven* / stone is not mentioned in the Ten Utterances recorded in the Torah (how, then, can we say that the letters of the Ten Utterances are the life-force present within a stone), nevertheless, the stone is animated through the Ten Utterances by means of letter permutations and substitutions…so that ultimately the specific combination of letters [that forms] the word אבן descends from the Ten Utterances… And so it is with all created things in the world" (*Sha'ar haYichud ve-haEmunah*, 1).

Everything in this world has a distinct vibration and frequency; all phenomena that we can observe in the world are manifestations of their corresponding 'letters'. The Hebrew word *Devar* means 'thing', as well as 'word' or utterance. Everything is thus essentially a physical manifestation of a unique Divine word. 'Things' are *Devarim* / 'words' that are based on *Tzirufim* / combinations of letters and sounds.

All the world is filled with the 'letters', vowels and vibrations of the Aleph-Beis (R. Avraham Abulafia, *Otzer HaGanuz* 3. p. 367. שכל העולם מלא אותיות הקדש. *Meor Einayim*, Likutim, p. 477. כי האדם כולו מראשו עד רגלו מלא אותיות) And for that reason, everything in this world, no matter how lofty or lowly, is merely another expression of Divine Speech. Yet, these Divine vibrations are concealed within reality, so what we see and experience are mere physical manifestations of spiritual vibrations. This apparent dichotomy between Divine vibration and physical matter occurs because there was a *Sheviras HaKeilim* / shattering of the vessels and thus a scattering of the Divine sparks of energy, in which their presence is concealed within the world. These fallen sparks, descending from the Sheviras HaKeilim, are in fact the letters of creation, themselves, hidden within the 'things' of this world.

Having fallen, the Divine letters are now capable of creating 'negative' as well as 'neutral' *Tzirufim* / combinations. Our task is to 'elevate' them to their Source. In the context of Davening, we activate this elevation by gathering all the far-flung sounds of the universe into our Tefilah, and speaking them in the Presence of the Creator, thereby integrating them back into their Source. By doing so, we participate in revealing the inherent wholeness, goodness and holiness of Creation, as will be further explored in Chapter 9.

This is a unique *Chidush* / novel understanding from the Baal Shem on the essential necessity to verbally express our desires and yearnings, to 'speak' our Davening in words. In general, regarding all other positive Mitzvos, there is a debate among the sages whether they need Kavanah or not to be considered accomplished/complete (*Berachos*, 13a. *Eiruvin*, 95a. *Pesachim*, 114b. *Rosh Hashanah*, 28a. In Halacha there are Poskim who draw a difference in this matter between the Mitzvos of the Torah and the Mitzvos of our sages: *Magen Avraham*, Orach Chayim, 60:3, Alter Rebbe, ibid. *Derech Pikudecha*, Hakdamah. *S'dei Chemed*, *Klalim*, Mem. Klal 61). Yet, all opinions agree that with regards to Tefilah, Kavanah is essential, and without a general Kavanah there is no Tefilah at all (*Chidushei Rabbeinu Chayim Halevi* [Brisker] on the Rambam, *Hilchos Tefilah*, 4:1. See also, Alter Rebbe, *Shulchan Aruch*, Orach Chayim, 98:1, regarding a person who cannot have Kavanah of the *Pirush HaMilos* / literal meaning of the words of Davening. Although see *Chazon Ish*, *Gilyonos* regarding this Reb Chayim (1974. Page 4), and his simple reading of these (*ibid*, and 10:1), seemingly contradicts the Rambam's. Principally, at first the Rambam offers the general idea, and then later on he elaborates — this is the general method of the Rambam. See also Radbaz, *Hilchos Shavuos*, 1:4).

The Rashba, Rebbe Shlomo ben Aderet (13th Century, Spain) makes a distinction between כוונה לצאת / the Kavanah to fulfill the obligation and the Kavanah of doing what you are doing. Regarding the Mitzvah of Davening, certainly regarding the first passage of the Amidah which is the "opening of Tefilah" (Rashi, *Berachos*, 34b: שהוא תחלת התפלה) and posits the address to which we are about to send our prayers, there is no Mitzvah without Kavanah on what you are doing.* This is the case also in the reading of the Shema, where we accept upon ourselves the yoke of Heaven, as well

---

* As the Rashba, *Berachos*, 13b, writes, ואפשר לי לומר עוד דפסוק ראשון צריך כוונה ואפילו בדיעבד. ואין דבר זה תלוי באידך דמצות צריכות כוונה דהתם בכוונה לצאת הדברים אמורים, אבל כאן צריך כוונת הענין כלומר שלא יהרהר בדברים אחרים כדי שיקבל עליו מלכות שמים בהסכמת הלב. וכענין שאמרו גם כן בברכה ראשונה של תפלה בשלהי פרק אין עומדין. והטעם שבשאר המצות שהן מצות עשה כל שעשה מצותו אף על פי שלא נתכוין לה הרי קיים מצות עשייה אלא שאין זה מן המובחר, וכל שכן שיצא אם כיון לצאת אף על פי שהרהר באמצע המצוה, אבל אלו שהן קבלת מלכות שמים או סדור שבחים אינו בדין שיהא לבבו פונה לדברים אחרים. It should be noted that there is also Machshava / thought and Kavanah / intention. Machshava means you are thinking of doing this action, Kavanah means you are having intention, knowing what and why you are doing it. *Tzafnas Pone'ach,* Rambam, Hilchos Ma'achalos Asuros, 4:22.

as in speaking Hashem's praises. Just as the 'mail' will not arrive without a correct address, so too without Kavanah at the beginning of the Amidah, the prayer will not arrive at its destination, and therefore, by definition, no 'prayer' will have been offered. But with the correct address, even if some of the words are not legible, perhaps some 'Kavanah' can be assembled from what *is* clearly written.

Indeed, Kavanah of the mind and heart are essential in prayer. This reinforces the fundamental question, "Why, if the *Ikar* / the main aspect of Tefilah is the intention of our mind and heart, do we need to *speak* the words out loud?"

It appears from various sources that the purpose of speaking our Davening, rather than just 'thinking' our prayers, is that we tangibly 'give voice' to our desires (*Chovos HaLevavos*, Cheshbon HaNefesh, 3). Without externalizing our thoughts, longings and desires, they remain in the inner recesses of the heart and do not surface into our waking consciousness. Giving voice to our yearnings, dreams and aspirations makes them real and concrete, from there we can actualize and elevate them.

From a similar perspective, since "voice arouses intention," we need to Daven with voice in order to arouse our hearts and actions (*Akeidas Yitzchak*, Parshas Tzav, Sha'ar 58). Yet, there is a poignant Chidush in the teachings of the Baal Shem Tov. For him, the purpose of speaking is not merely to help arouse Kavanah, nor to make our needs conscious by articulating them out loud (as the Mabit writes, *Beis Elokim*, Sha'ar 3), rather, verbalizing the Davening has its own unique purpose.* In this way, the literal vocalization of our

---

* Although, since voice helps with intention, many Chasidic Rebbes would Daven in private, so they could Daven loudly. This is based on the words of the *Perishah*, דר' יונה כד / הוי צליל דעתיה היה מתפלל בב״ה וכד לא הוה צליל דעתיה הוי מתפלל בביתו בקול לעורר הכוונה "Rav Yonah (the *Yerushalmi* tells us) when his mind was settled, he would Daven in Shul, and when it was not, he would Daven in his home, loudly, to arouse intention": *Perishah*, Orach Chayim, 101.

yearnings and praises is the essence of our Davening. But how? Simply: It is the most direct way to elevate all of our personal experience along with all of Creation. The question of how our Tefilos are actually answered, and when they are answered, will be further explored in Chapter 9.

All of the above is but an introduction to the role of the letters in creation, as well as within our consciousness. These ideas will continue to be developed and will become more comprehensible as this text progresses. Now we will begin to unpack the actual steps of how to Daven.

Presence, Awe and Love

The most fundamental obstacle that stands in the way of a deep, fulfilling and transformative prayer experience is lacking a sense of the Divine Presence. It is therefore essential to recognize, when shifting into the posture of prayer, that you are standing before the Infinite One. In fact, beyond the circumscribed experience of Davening, one should seek to orient their entire life around the recognition that they are constantly in the presence of the Omnipresent.

To cultivate such a tangible awareness and experience of Divine Presence, it helps to ponder the sheer magnitude of Creation and then to associatively infer the infinite greatness of the Creator. When we consider the myriad ways that the macrocosm mirrors and synchronizes with the microcosm of Creation, we cannot help but marvel at the limitless power and unfathomable brilliance of its Creator. This contemplative cue is designed to inspire a sense of *Yirah* / awe within the consciousness of one who internalizes its essential implications. The quality of Yirah is often translated as 'fear', but it should not be confused with being scared or panicked, which are actually *Kelipos* / negative traits rooted in the *Sitra Achra* / other side. Yirah, properly understood, is an experience of sensing the numinous mystery of being in the presence of the Ineffable. It is being existentially overwhelmed by the unfathomable immensity of and luminosity of the Creator.

If you were walking along an unfamiliar forest path and suddenly the trees parted, revealing the nearby presence of a sheer thousand meter sea cliff and a vast, panoramic view, your hair might stand on end or your knees might begin to buckle from the beauty, and you might step back in awe. Only once you had found a stable, safe place to sit and settle your nerves, might you then begin to delight in the subtlety of the scene, and feel embraced by it. Similarly, the *Yirah* / awe and wonder that result from an experience of the vast panorama of the Divine Presence eventually opens us up to the experience of *Ahavah* / love, the Divine embrace. The experience of Ahavah is a gift, not a state that we can achieve or occupy on our own. However, Yirah is a key that opens our heart to receive this gift.

In this way, Yirah precedes Ahavah. This is another important part of Davening according to the path of the Baal Shem Tov; we open ourselves through Yirah, and then Ahavah settles in. If we were to bypass the state of Yirah and seek to begin our devotions with an arousal of Ahavah, there would be a possibility that whatever feelings of closeness we stirred up would be mere fantasy and empty imagination. Thus, it is advisable to begin Davening, or at least a segment of one's Davening, with the arousal of a visceral sense of standing in the Divine presence, this leads naturally to feelings of awe, which then allow deep emotions of love to emerge and flow throughout one's being and expression.

Thought, Speech and Surrender

Once both the emotions of Yirah and Ahavah have been revealed, one should then contemplate and form a *Kavanah* / intention, a thought-anchor, for the words of Davening. An occupied mind is a focused mind; at least it is more anchored and not as easily distracted. Therefore, having an intellectual, mindful Kavanah throughout Davening ensures that little or no intruding thoughts enter the mind and distract you from truly Davening.

However, according to the path of the Baal Shem Tov, once one begins to intone, speak or sing the words of Davening, one should then let go of all thought and enter fully into the letters and sonic vibrations of the words themselves. Such an immersion in sound allows one to 'ride' the sound waves, as it were, higher upward and deeper inward. To 'enter' into the letters and sounds of 'speech' means to divest yourself from left-brain intellectualizing, and to invest yourself into the actual embodiment of your prayers; this is achieved by shifting your focus from the semantic meanings of the words to the sonic quality of their sounds. This in turn shifts your consciousness from the cognitive capacity of the intellect to the affective realm of visceral sensation.*

The last step is surrender, otherwise known as Deveikus.

In summary, there are six general stages in the Baal Shem Tov's path of Tefilah, in sequence: 1) Presence, 2) Awe, 3) Love, 4) Thought, 5) Speech, and 6) Surrender. We will now explore these stages one by one.

---

* In the Baal Shem Tov's sonic-oriented practice of 'entering the words', if there is no mindful intentionality, there is more risk that intruding or even negative thoughts will enter the mind during Tefilah. For this reason, the Baal Shem Tov and his students developed a system of handling negative thoughts during Davening. For example, in the Arizal's system one is always 'thinking' while Davening, and it is thus a 'mind heavy' practice, and leaves little room for intruding thoughts. However, in the system of the holy Baal Shem Tov, one alternates between 'thinking' and letting go of all thought in order to 'enter the words', as described above, making it a more 'heart heavy' practice, thus the issue of intruding thoughts needs to be specifically addressed. See the Appendix for a more detailed discussion on this very important issue of what to do with one's thoughts during Davening.

Chapter 5
STEP ONE: PRESENCE

Entering Presence

RESENCE IS A PRIMARY ISSUE IN DAVENING, AND ITS LACK OBSTRUCTS MOST PEOPLE'S ACCESS TO A DEEP, FULFILLING AND TRANSFORMATIVE EXPERIENCE. TRULY ENTERING A POSTURE OF PRAYERFULNESS DEMANDS AN INTERNAL SHIFT OF CONSCIOUSNESS; ONE CANNOT JUST SIMPLY START DAVENING AS ONE WOULD FLIP ON A LIGHT SWITCH. THEREFORE, WHETHER IT IS IN REGARD TO OUR OWN AWARENESS AND FOCUS, OR IN RELATION TO THE ONE IN WHOSE PRESENCE WE ARE STANDING DURING THE DAVENING, THE IMPORTANCE OF PRESENCE IS PARAMOUNT.

The (Lubavitcher) Rebbe once used the phrase זיך-שטעלט איד א / דאוונען "A Jew *stands up* to Daven" (heard from Reb Yoel Kahn). In Yiddish, צו זיך-שטעלט actually means more than just 'standing up'; it means to ready oneself, to gather oneself, like a soldier who straightens himself as the general enters. It is a type of readiness, of total presence and focus. One must fully 'arrive' and transparently be 'present' and present themselves in order to begin Davening.

"No one shall ascend with you," (*Shemos*, 34:3) Hashem tells Moshe, as he is about to ascend the Mountain to receive the Torah. Says a student of the Baal Shem Tov, "As you stand in a posture of Tefilah, you should feel that you are standing alone in the world, and that only you and Hashem exist" (*Ben Poras Yoseph*, 88d). This is the thought we need to contemplate as we are about to Daven: 'There is nothing else going on, and there is nowhere else to be; in fact, there is nothing else, just me and Hashem.'

Cultivating Presence

"*Shevisi Hashem l'Negdi Tamid* / I have placed Hashem before myself at all times" (*Tehilim*, 16:8). What does it mean to place Hashem before ourselves at all times? In response to this verse the Rama writes (*Shulchan Aruch*, 1:1. See Rambam, *Moreh Nevuchim*, 3:51-52. Rashi, Radak, *ad loc. Reishis Chochmah*, Sha'ar haYirah, 1): "This is a great principle of the Torah and is a paramount attribute of the Tzadikim who walk in the ways of Hashem. For the manner in which a person sits, moves around, and carries out his daily activities while he is alone in his house is not the same way he would engage in these activities while standing before a great king (or a person he deeply respects). In addition, the way one speaks while among those in his home and the conversations he partakes of with his relatives is not the same manner in which he would speak while in the presence of a mortal king. Surely when one considers in his mind that the mighty King — The Holy One, blessed be His Name...stands always before him and constantly sees his deeds... then everything he does will be done with more caution."

By sensing that we are always in the presence of the Omnipresent, our whole manner of being and doing, thinking and speaking will be transformed, refined and elevated. Our life becomes that much more infused with urgency, meaning, and ultimate purpose when we cultivate an awareness of living perpetually within the all-pervasive Presence of HaKadosh Baruch Hu. This reality can be considered conceptually in the mind or it can be experienced viscerally in the heart and body.

Additionally, the idea of *Shevisi* has also been interpreted to suggest that one should literally envision the Four Letters of Hashem's Name in their mind's eye (*Be'er Heitev*, Ibid). Rav Yitzchak of Acco, a student of the Ramban when the Ramban lived in Acco, writes that the placing of Hashem in front of you means placing the four letters of the Name of Hashem, the Yud-Hei-Vav-Hei / י-ה-ו-ה in front of your mind's eye constantly. These four letters, he writes, should be visualized written out in the script of the Torah (as if written in black ink on parchment: *Maggid Mesharim*, Parshas Miketz. Parshas Vayikra. *Sha'ar Ruach HaKodesh*, Derush 1. *Sha'arei Kedushah* 3, Sha'ar 4). Each of these four letters should be infinitely large, filling your entire inner screen of vision. While your inner eye is gazing at these letters your mind and heart should be directed towards the Infinite One, the 'Light' that is beyond the 'vessels', which in this case are the letters. The *Habata* / seeing (of the letters) and the *Mach'shavah* / thought and intention directed towards the Reality beyond the letters should be simultaneous (*Me'iras Einayim*, Ekev, 11 – 22. Rav Chayim Vital, *Sha'arei Kedushah*, 4:5).

Corresponding to this concept of *Shevisi* is the practice of being נכח / facing Hashem, so to speak. In fact, the holy Arizal teaches that a person should visualize in his mind's eye, the Four Letter Name of Hashem in each direction you face. Regarding the Pasuk עיניך לנכח יביטו / "let your eyes look forward" (*Mishlei*, 4:25), the Arizal comments, the word נכח in numerical value is 78, the same as the Name of Hashem three times (26+26+26=78). Thus, to be נכח means to place the Name of Hashem literally in front of you 'three times'; one to your right, one forward, one to the left. In other words, in the directions that your eyes naturally see (*Sha'ar Ruach HaKodesh*, 8a. *Likutei Torah*, Parshas Toldos, on the Pasuk *L'Nochach Ishto*).

In the path of the Baal Shem Tov, the concept of being נכח means to live consciously in the immediate Presence of HaKadosh Baruch Hu, no matter what 'direction' you are facing. When you live your life in the presence of the King, the נוכחות / *Nochechus* / immediate presence of Hashem is experienced viscerally, not just conceptually or in the mind's eye. These teachings, while containing great force, gently invite each of us to sense Hashem's tangible presence surrounding us as we become increasingly aware of being embraced within the radiance of Hashem's light. To quote:

"There is great value when a person continuously considers in his heart that he is near the Creator, and that Hashem is surrounding him at all times. One should be so experientially connected to this concept that he does not need to be constantly reminded of its truth. For he 'sees' Hashem's Presence with his inner eye and understands that Hashem is the *Mekomo Shel Olam* / Space of the World. Since Hashem was present before the Creation of the world, the entire world is founded upon and exists *within* the Creator, may He be blessed. Most people see the world first, and through (the lens of) nature they may see Hashem. But when one places Hashem before himself always, he is able to see Hashem first, and through the Creator to see Creation." (*Likutim Yekarim*, p. 3. *Baal Shem Tov Al HaTorah*, Ekev, 42)

A sense of seeing begets a sense of being seen. When your life is lived consciously in the perpetual Presence of Hashem, and you are constantly *seeing* the guiding Hand of the Creator in every detail of your life, you are also aware of being *seen* by the Creator of the world. In the words of a student of the Baal Shem:

"This is a deep level (of living): to always see the Creator, blessed be He, with your mental eye, as if you are looking at another person. And one should think to himself that the Creator too is looking at him, in the same way that another person can look at him. This should be your continuous pure and clear thought." (*Tzava'as HaRivash*, 134. *Baal Shem Tov al HaTorah*, Ekev, 37)

Here is a similar teaching by another student of the Baal Shem Tov:

"A person should always be in a joyous state and think and believe (sense) with complete faith (clarity) that the Shechinah (Divine Immanence) is at his side and is watching over him. You are looking at the Creator, blessed be He, and the Creator, blessed be He, is looking at you." (*Tzava'as HaRivash*, 137. *Baal Shem Tov Al HaTorah*, Ekev, 38)

Joyful Judgement

In the above teachings, 'Seeing' is not meant as literal physical seeing, rather a sense of seeing with higher or inner vision. The same would apply to hearing; we can and should aspire to 'hear' Hashem's Presence in this world and gain a sense of being heard by Hashem. Essentially, the above teachings are describing the cultivation of an overwhelming sense of being cared for, empowered and understood. This awareness then generates the reassuring sensation that all of your life is of great value. Your life is being recorded for eternity, not for judgmental reasons, Heaven forbid, but because every moment is infinitely precious and meaningful.

'Living in the presence of the Ultimate Observer and Listener' and sensing this truth moment to moment is another way to describe the concept of קבלת עול מלכות שמים / *Kabbalas Ol Malchus Shamayim* / accepting upon yourself the yoke of Heaven. In such a state of awareness, you realize that your life is serious, and that your thoughts, feelings, words and actions really do matter to Hashem. In the powerful words of the *Tanya*, which would be a good passage to meditate upon before Davening (see the Rebbe, *Igros Kodesh*, 17, 6,259): "And indeed, Hashem is standing over him, and the whole earth is full of His glory, and He searches his mind and heart, to determine if he is serving Him as is fitting" (*Tanya*, 41). Who is not gripped by trembling at the very thought that the Great and Awesome King is keeping watch over him? Yet this awesome awareness is not stifling or repressive in any way — it is quite the opposite — it is tremendously empowering and emboldening. It charges the person with a sense of heightened purpose, alacrity and alertness.

As mentioned earlier, to stand in front of the Creator of the Universe is to be rooted in purpose, direction, and intentionality. You cannot honestly say, 'I am standing in front of my Creator and the Creator of All Life, but I don't care about my life or the world.' That would be a contradiction in terms. To stand in front of Hashem is to align yourself with Hashem's 'vision' of you, *Kaviyachol* / as it were.

Securing this consciousness of literally standing in the Presence of Hashem is the ultimate key and motivator to live a deeper, higher, holier, more meaningful life. If we can truly believe, feel and 'see' this, not just conceptually, but experientially, then we almost have no choice but to live in an exemplary manner. We feel alert and ready. How can we 'sleep' away our lives if our lives are so meaningful and important? This is ultimately the orientation of one who has accepted the Ol Malchus Shamayim. They are charged with purpose and ready to act with consciousness, creativity and compassion.

What does HaKadosh Baruch Hu see as my greatest potential in this life? What does He want from my life and from human life in general? Where is my life heading? What should I dream and pray for? Where is the world heading, what should I pray for the world?

This awareness awakens us. The overwhelming sense of being seen, heard and valued arouses a sense of urgency, empowering you to embrace the fact that every detail of your life has tremendous import and meaning. We each have a mission and are imbued with a deep purpose. We are soldiers of peace with vitally important marching orders. Every one of us is entrusted to be a channel of the Master of the Universe and a co-creator tasked with making this world a kinder, holier, more just place for all. This is an almost overwhelming sense of the majesty of the human spirit and the magnitude of our abilities. Living consciously in Hashem's Presence produces within us an awesome and awe-inspiring sense of being alive.

Our sages teach a fundamental prerequisite to Davening: "One should not begin to pray before attaining Koved Rosh" (*Berachos* 30b). *Koved Rosh* means humility (Rashi, *ibid*), although the literal meaning is "heaviness of the head," which also conveys a sense of serious-mindedness. Life is serious, but not sad. It is seriously alive, awake, inspiring; there is thus a deep sense of 'heaviness', weight or awe in the simple fact of just being alive. Every moment is unimaginably precious and potentially profound.

If you ponder this idea well, that life is immeasurably valuable, you will be awe-struck. Indeed, this is the sensation that is awakened in us on Rosh Hashanah, the Day of Judgment and our collective birthday. This is quite literally the 'awe' referred to in the Days of Awe. It is not the shallow fear of being judged and punished that makes these days so awesome. Rather, it is the existential urgency and the awesome responsibility of being alive and in the Presence of Hashem that inspires us. We can truly impact and alter reality with our thoughts, speech and actions. Every single thought, word and deed therefore has tremendous value in the eyes of Hashem, so how can we waste even a single moment? How can we live with this awareness and not be overwhelmed by the immensity of it all?

In truth, we are being judged every day and even every moment (*Rosh Hashanah*, 16a). However, a 'judgmental' judgment would make you feel small, but this sense of being judged is *Mamash* / literally and completely the opposite: it is a Heavenly acknowledgment and empowering affirmation of your inestimable worth.

Similarly, we are being born and reborn every day and with every passing moment — entrusted anew with the awesome mission of our unique life. On our every birthday, Hashem tells us, as it were, "I'm glad you're alive; you are important to Me." And the truth is, every day that we wake up is our 'birthday'; every moment that we are alive is a cause for celebration. Each and every moment we are alive Hashem is saying to us (*Kaviyachol* / as if there is a 'need' Above), "I need you." The whole world is saying, "You are a necessary part of existence." All of Creation is saying, "Without you, all of life would be different." This is a joyful recognition, reverberating throughout the chorus of creation. On the other hand, it can also feel overwhelming when you recognize that every single moment of history has led up this very instant in time, and that the future is waiting for you to make the right choices and further Hashem's Presence in the world now and forever. Such a sense of urgency and responsibility can either carry or cripple a person, pushing them to persevere with faith or paralyzing them with self-doubt.

Thinking about how Hashem believes in us and gives us life every moment, causes us to stop in amazement and ponder: 'How can a person ever sin?' How can there not be a *Pachad Norah* / tremendous sense of terror in the act of doing, *Chas v'Shalom* / Heaven forbid, an Aveirah? What would motivate me to put my hand in a blazing fire even for a moment? How could I ever willingly let myself waste even a single second of this incredible life?' This is true Yirah.

Beware of False Humility

Merely reading the above words and considering this perspective can arouse you to accept upon yourself the *Ol Malchus Shamayim* / yoke of Heaven; to sense your responsibility and to be aware of the Koved, the 'weightiness', of your life at every moment, and recognize that you are empowered, even commanded, to impact this world. Related to this, here is another important teaching by the Baal Shem Tov:

"Too much (false) humility causes one to distance himself from the path of serving Hashem (which, by extension, is serving humanity and benefiting one's soul as well). On account of his humility, he does not believe that his actions, whether Torah (study), prayer or acts of loving kindness, cause a *Shefa* / flow to all the worlds. But the truth is that even angels receive nourishment from his actions. And if he would truly believe in this (the power and magnitude of his actions), he would serve Hashem with joy and awe. How careful and scrupulous he would be with every word and every slight movement, if he would really ponder this and put his heart to the matter. Certainly, who would not be gripped by trembling and sweating when considering how the Great and Awesome King is keeping watch over his lowly lips (observing what will come out of his mouth).... The same person should open his heart and say, 'I am a ladder that is firmly planted on the ground, but the upper part of the ladder reaches Heaven. All my movements, words and actions create an imprint in the upper worlds.' As a result of this awareness, he will be scrupulous that everything he does and says will be for the purpose of Heaven (to further the revelation of Hashem's Presence in this world). However, if he thinks, 'Who am I? How can I possibly affect any change or make any difference above or below?' This will cause him to be lax in his behavior and do as his (ego) pleases with no sense of consequence...." (*Toldos Yaakov Yoseph*, Ekev. *Baal Shem Tov Al HaTorah*, Amud HaTefilah, 137. See also *Zohar Chai*, Yisro, p. 80b)

Every one of us matters; we each make a difference to all of life. And we can make an even greater difference if we understand that every moment, the Creator of All Life is telling us, 'I believe in you and I need you to believe in yourself and your mission.' This is part of accepting upon ourselves 'the yoke of Heaven'. 'The yoke' means the awesome weightiness of our lives, as well as the gift and privilege of having responsibility for Hashem's Creation, and having the G-d given power to Daven and affect changes that benefit the whole.

The foundational experience of *Nochechus Pnei Hashem* / 'standing in the immediate Presence of Hashem' is the awareness that we are in a face-to-face relationship with the Creator, and that Hashem wants us to be a co-partner in Creation. This awareness is overwhelming and tremendously empowering. In the context of Tefilah this means that we need to believe that our Davening actually has an effect on our lives and in the world, and not lower ourselves in false humility. We need to know clearly and feel deeply that HaKadosh Baruch Hu wants our Davening, and that our Davening is powerful.

Before the Great Flood, Noach was told to build an Ark and that a catastrophic flood would sweep over the land — and yet it never occurred to him to Daven for his generation to be saved. Unlike Avraham and Moshe, says the *Zohar*, who did Daven for the people of their generation, Noach did not. Why not? Noach was מקטני אמנה היה / a small believer (*Medrash Rabbah*, Bereishis, 32:6. *Bereishis*, Rashi, 7:7). Perhaps it was not only that he was a small believer in Hashem and in the prophecy that the flood would really occur, but also that he was a small believer in himself. He had little faith in his potential and in the power of his Tefilos to make a difference, and as a result, he did not Daven. To truly Daven, we need to both believe in Hashem and believe in ourselves; we need to believe that our Tefilah has a truly transformative effect. We need to believe in the possibility that things can be different, and that *we* can make that difference through our actions and through our Davening.

General Kavanah

Tefilah needs *Kavanah* / intention, beginning with the general Kavanah of being in the *Nochechus* / direct presence of Hashem. The Kavanah of Nochechus is more than mere *Mach'shavah* / thought; it is not just 'thinking about' being in the immediate presence of the Master of the Universe, rather it means to direct your entire will and desire, your entire inner life and orientation, towards Hashem (כוונתו ומחשבתו, says Rashi, בקשתו ומחשבתו / "His Kavanah and his thought are his *desire* and his thought": *Kerisus*, 19b. See also *Tzafnas Pane'ach*, Hilchos Ma'achalos Asuros, 4:22).

When Davening, we should imagine ourselves standing in front of the Shechinah, the Immanent Presence of the Most High (Rambam, *Hilchos Tefilah*, 4:16); "standing in front of the King" (Rashi, *Berachos*, 25a). Without this Kavanah of Nochechus, there is no Tefilah whatsoever; not only has the גברא / *Gavrah* / person not fulfilled his own obligation to Daven, but there has been no חפצא / *Cheftzah* / 'object' or act of Davening at all (*Likkutei Sichos* 22, p. 117). In order to properly Daven, we need to be in a prayerful mode of mind and heart, and this occurs when we have a *Hergesh Penimi* / inner 'feeling' of literally being in the presence of the Shechinah, ready to enter, see and be seen.

Therefore, our Kavanah of Nochechus has to be made with our entire being, not merely in our mind. Years after growing up and not seeing his childhood friend Rebbe DovBer, the great Magid of Mezritch, for such a long time, his old friend asked, "Why does it take you so long to Daven? I too Daven with all the Kabbalistic *Kavanos* / intentions, and yet it takes me a much shorter time to get through the Davening." The Magid answered him, "Since you are now a merchant, let me ask you a question, 'Why do you need to travel to the market place to buy your goods? Why can't you just meditate and be there in your mind, without having to actually schlep there?'" "Well," he answered, "I need to literally buy and sell my goods, not just in my mind." "Ah," said the Magid, "me too; I need to actually *be there*...."

One should not be satisfied with a mere intellectual understanding of the Kavanos or a conceptual comprehension that Hashem is immediately present, rather, one needs to fully "be there" in the Davening.

In addition to comprehending the simple *Pirush HaMilos* / meaning of the words which transform the written letters on the page into the living words of one's own heart, we need to sense where we are standing, and in front of Whom. Tefilah is a time for genuine communication and nurturing a living relationship with the living Presence of Hashem. Davening is not a mere monologue, rather it is a space for open and profound dialogue. While our Tefilos are always heard, it is through Davening that we open ourselves up to 'hear' the Divine Presence as well. We must initiate and maintain an immediate awareness of the Presence of Hashem in order for the real dialogue of Davening to transpire. In reality, Hashem is always present and always listening; we can consciously recognize this when we are prayerfully receptive and open to HaKadosh Baruch Hu's Presence in our Davening.

In addition to Nochechus, attaining a deep understanding of the *Pirush HaMilos* / the meaning of the words of the Siddur is also extremely important, and the best approach is to hold both of these 'intentions' simultaneously (Mitteler Rebbe, *Sha'ar HaEmunah,* Hakdamah) In fact, being cognizant of the Pirush HaMilos can help us enter deeper into the dialogue and thus arouse a deeper awareness of standing in the Presence of Hashem. In this way, the Pirush Hamilos are not a distraction, rather an enhancement of our awareness of Whose Presence we are standing in.

And once we have established a strong sense of Nochechus Pnei Hashem, we are automatically induced into a state of *Yirah* / awe, which is the next step in the Baal Shem Tov's path of Tefilah.

Chapter 6
STEP TWO:
YIRAH/FEAR AND AWE

Fear and Awe

OFTEN *Yirah* IS TRANSLATED AS FEAR, AND BECAUSE OF THIS, IT IS AN EASILY MISUNDERSTOOD CONCEPT. FEAR IS NOT SOMETHING THAT MOST PEOPLE HAVE A POSITIVE RELATIONSHIP WITH, AND RIGHTFULLY SO. THEY ARE ALL TOO FAMILIAR WITH EGO-BASED FEARS, SUCH AS THE FEAR OF DEATH OR BEING HURT. WHEN SUCH *instinctual* FEAR IS PROJECTED ONTO THE SPIRITUAL IDEA OF YIRAH OF HASHEM, IT SOUNDS CONSTRICTIVE, OPPRESSIVE, OR EVEN PETTY, AS IF OUR RELATIONSHIP TO HAKADOSH BARUCH HU IS SOLELY BASED ON WHAT WE RECEIVE.

Yet, instinctual fear is a Divine gift in many situations in life, serving to protect us from serious threats and negative patterns of behavior. That being said, it constitutes the very lowest level of Yirah. The higher levels of holy Yirah are more akin to reverence or awe. Such Yirah is similar to a sense of holy terror or dread, which arises when one realizes they are in the presence of the mysterium tremendum of the All-Powerful Omnipresence. Higher Yirah is a product of recognizing our paradoxical importance and insignificance within the world and in the Light of the Infinite One.

Yirah is the gateway to all Divine service, personal transformation and rectification (*Shabbos*, 31b). Let us therefore seek to better understand what exactly Yirah is and how this emotion can be a positive force in our spiritual development.

There are people who Daven and even walk around in life with a certain feeling of smallness, self-limitation, meekness and mild melancholy, mistakenly assuming this to be an expression of Yirah of Hashem, and a deep way of Davening and living. Says the Baal Shem Tov, this sensation is nothing more than *Far-kvetsh-keit,* a form of spiritual depression and constriction. Certainly, it is not a commendable or desirable emotion, and it is definitely not Yirah (*Likutim Yekarim*, p. 3. *Baal Shem Tov Al HaTorah*, Amud HaTefilah, 59).

Other people think that Yirah, the 'fear of Heaven', means living their lives in a hypervigilant state, as if they are constantly being punitively surveilled and judged. They are perpetually afraid of being caught doing something 'bad'. Such fear, even if it has some limited behavioral benefits for themselves and others, is simply ego-based. The ego is that which is afraid of rebuke or punishment. Any threat to the ego's authority is unacceptable and thus it triggers anxiety. This Yirah is actually referred to as יראת העונש / *Yiras HaOnesh* / fear of punishment, and it "is only for the lowly (immature, unintelligent, or unsophisticated). This is not the Yirah of the wise and the mindful" (*Mesilas Yesharim*, 24).

Yiras HaOnesh / fear of Divine punishment is an inferior state, similar to natural, instinctual ego-rooted fears, whether they are well-founded or illusionary. One such example of a well-founded fear is fearing a drunk driver on the road. An example of an illusionary fear is the fear of darkness or of public speaking. Either way, the root of all these fears is the ego's instinctual avoidance of pain and insecurity.

Ultimately, the ego fears its termination. From the greatest to the slightest fears, all are based on an avoidance of experiencing any level of physical or psychological annihilation. Ranging from the fear of being physically hurt or losing a large amount of money, to being emotionally crushed by rejection or punishment, all fears are manifestations of the core fear of losing the ego. When thus triggered, the ego has many cunning schemes available to secure its survival and self-perpetuation, from methods of fleeing and avoiding, to fighting and outsmarting. Anything or anyone that threatens the ego's survival is ascertained as worthy of fear and defense.

If Yirah is not Far-kvetsh-keit, and higher Yirah is not Yiras HaOnesh, what then is the type of Yirah we seek? It is a dynamic awareness in which embracing our fears elevates us to a place of awe, wonderment and astonishment. This is called יראת הרוממות / *Yiras HaRomemus* / the awe of the exaltedness of Hashem.

Earthly Fear and Heavenly Fear

There is יראת שמים / *Yiras Shamayim* / 'fear' of Heaven, and there is יראת הארץ / *Yiras HaAretz* / fear of the earth. Yiras HaAretz is lowly fear, egoic fear of being punished or threatened in relation to matters of the earth.

Yiras Shamayim is awe of Heaven, of Hashem's Presence (*Aderes Eliyahu,* Bereishis, 1:1,4). The lower Yirah, as Rabbeinu Yonah explains (on *Mishlei,* 2:5), is based on reward and punishment, whereas the higher Yirah is based on the soul sensing the awesomeness of Hashem and His limitless power and presence.

Unresolved or subconscious fears can cause a person to grasp at objects and at the earthly ego itself. When these self-preservation instincts are enfolded within a relationship to Hashem, they are called *Yiras HaAretz.* For example, someone installs Mezuzos because they are afraid of robbers, or someone starts wearing Tefilin because they are afraid of losing their income. There is obviously nothing wrong with these reactions; indeed, performing Mitzvos does protect us, and Hashem's will was done in the Mitzvah, no matter the motivation. However, *Yiras Shamayim* means letting go of the ego-self and earthly anxieties within the Heavenly majesty of Creation and the Creator. This is the experience of losing yourself in the vast, overwhelming Presence of HaKadosh Baruch Hu. In Yiras Shamayim, one might install Mezuzos or wear Tefilin without any personal pay-offs whatsoever, but simply out of the urgent responsibility and awesome opportunity to fulfil the will of the Infinite One.

We can move from Yiras HaAretz to Yiras Shamayim by recognizing that the root of all our fears is the fear of letting go of control. We can ask ourselves, 'Do I really have full control over the circumstances of my life anyway?' Our *responses* to what life throws at us are certainly in the domain of our control. But we cannot control what life throws at us. We cannot control the weather or other people, whether we make money or keep it, or whether we have children or not. None of these basic turns in life are fully up to us or what we do. Certainly, doing Mitzvos and *Ma'asim Tovim* / good deeds, and asking Hashem for what we need, all predispose us to receiving blessings and abundance, but this is not 'control', per se.

The illusory thought that somehow one can control every situation they encounter is in fact the root of all fear. The very thought that one can control life at all is the fruit of the ego's twisted root, a threatening sense of separation from life itself, as well as the Source of Life. All control belongs to Hashem, the Master and Guide of the Universe. The deeper we see our fear for what it is, the more it dissolves into awe, surrender, and loss of self within the Divine Guidance. This is *Yirah Ila'ah* / higher Yirah. In the words of the Maharal (*Nesivos Olam*, Nesiv Yiras Hashem, 1), "Yirah means to make oneself as if he did not exist." Higher Yirah is the sensation of the collapse of the I, the ego.

Awe descends at the moment that we surrender the self in an *aha* (or 'awe-ha') moment. At the moment of awe, there is very little self and self-awareness. There is just Hashem.

We can access a form of this higher Yirah even in an encounter with the unfathomable beauty of nature or majesty of human heroism, especially in the moment we feel astonished, bewildered or overwhelmed. We just need to firmly acknowledge that this beauty or majesty belongs to Hashem alone. Yet, sometimes the only way to access *Yirah Ila'ah* / higher awe is through *Yirah Tata'ah* / lower fear, the fear of losing control of the self.

In order to open lower Yirah into a passageway to higher Yirah, one needs to meet it head on and penetrate to its root: the desire to control life. When one releases their sense of personal control into the Hands of Hashem, one is more able to access the higher Yirah, the total dissolving of selfhood in the Presence of Hashem. Ultimately, this higher Yirah is a gift bestowed upon you from Above. In the words of the Baal Shem Tov:

"There are those who pray with sadness because they are depressed, and (yet) they think they are praying with great Yirah…. True Yirah is a Yirah that is bestowed upon one (i.e., it falls upon him spontaneously), not the Yirah that he himself awakens. The latter Yirah is considered 'feminine waters' (inspiration that comes from below, from oneself). True Yirah falls upon one from Above, causing him to tremble and quiver. And because of this great fright, he has no idea where he is. As a result, his mind (thoughts) become clear and tears begin to flow involuntarily from his eyes." (*Likutim Yekarim*, p.3. *Baal Shem Tov Al HaTorah*, Amud HaTefilah, 59)

In summation, the steps to receiving higher Yirah are as follows: Perhaps you begin from a fear of punishment or of losing control over your experience. By sitting with this fear and following it to its root, you are able to release it and begin to tap into a higher Yirah. You realize that there is an Ultimate Controller of the world beyond you, and you let go and let G-d into your life. Your fear then transforms into awe. Finally, the highest Yirah descends upon you from Above, completely washing away your sense of separate self-consciousness and agency in the Infinite Omnipresence of the Creator.

Here is how the Baal Shem Tov speaks about the movement from lower fear to higher and deeper awe:

"Commenting on the verse (*Koheles*, 3:14), 'Hashem has made it that men shall (be in) fear before Him,' the Sages say (*Berachos*, 59a), 'Thunder was created only to straighten out the crookedness of the heart.' Hashem desired that all of Israel have true Yirah of Hashem. One who is smart will achieve Yirah by thinking (to himself), 'Hashem is the Master of the World and the Source of All Reality, and if the Divine animating force would leave Creation for one moment, all of Creation would disappear.' Because of this focused thought (about the majesty and absoluteness of the Creator) he will attain awe of Hashem until all the limbs of his body tremble.... It is not like the ignorant people who say that Yirah is depression....

"This (thought process) works only for people who have *Seichel* / clear intellect. Only they can contemplate Creation and initiate an internal state of Yirah for themselves. For one who does not possess Seichel, and yet Hashem also desires that he too should have Yirah, Hashem gives him reason to be in fear according to his small intelligence — for instance, through the sound of thunder, as explained above. In such a case, the Divine intention is for him to move from this lower form of Yirah to the higher Yirah. He should think to himself, 'This thunder is merely one expression of the Mighty Creator, and if I am scared of it, then certainly I should have Yirah of the Creator, who created the thunder.'

(Here is the main point that is relevant to our discussion:)

"And the same is true for all externally generated fears, such as the fear of the government, or the fear of (G-d forbid) losing a child. The reason Hashem created these types of fear is so that we can move from this lower Yirah to the higher Yirah." (*Meor Einayim*, Yisro. *Baal Shem Tov Al HaTorah*, Ekev, 26)

When we do not have the proper Seichel to initiate our own sense of holy Yirah, we should contemplate all of our lower fears in life, and inquire into their roots, and this may in the end inspire us and lift us out of these fears, and into a life of wonderment and awe. In other words, we can move deep into the experience of any given lower fear, and then ask ourselves what the primary fear is that is at the basis of that fear.

If we look closely at a fear of losing a specific job, for example, there may be a deeper fear within it, such as losing money, honor or property. Within that deeper fear, there may be a fear of lacking basic control over our lives, such as the ability to procure food to eat and a place to live. However, as we contemplate this level of fear, we will be able to recognize that we have survived many potentially fearsome situations, and that Hashem has cared for us and guided our lives until now. We can then see that although we do have very little control over our lives, there is a Controller, and that is Hashem, the Compassionate, the Omnipresent.

This realization both alleviates and elevates our fears, transforming them into awe and wonderment. For example, if Hashem had not intimately orchestrated our nourishment and development as an embryo, we would not even be here. In fact, Hashem's awe-inspiring orchestration of life and care for us have been constant, and He clearly wants us to exist and be nourished.

For this process to be effective, we really need to consider our own minuteness and seeming insignificance in the face of the majesty and magnitude of the cosmos. Once we realize how small we really are and how little control we actually have over the unfathomable details of life, we are able to release our egoic grip on reality and let ourselves slip into the Divine embrace. This feeling of relinquishment and release is a pathway into 'awe'. When we are able to let go of our fears, anxieties and worries, tears of joy and wonderment, radical amazement and awe, begin to flow from our eyes, and praise from our mouths.

Clearly, true, healthy Yirah has nothing to do with anxiety, fear and worry, nor depression, melancholy or despondency. On the contrary, a sense of joy, elation, ecstasy, desire, bliss and *Deveikus* become quite palpable in the higher levels of Yirah. A person feels more whole, more 'infinite' and powerful, by being at one with the Ultimate Omnipotent Power of the Universe. And furthermore, true Yirah begets *Ahavah* / love, a tremendous desire to intimately connect with that Source of Power.

Yirah and Joy

For this reason, the Baal Shem Tov taught that Yirah and joy are meant to be simultaneously expressed and felt in Davening. To quote:

"Tefilah that is uttered with joy is more readily accepted on High, much more than a Tefilah that is said with sadness and weeping. This is similar to a pauper who comes in front of a king (or a wealthy person) and beseeches the king with great weeping. In such a case, the king only gives him a small amount (just to get rid of the annoyance). However, when the king's minister speaks lovingly and with joy to the king, joyfully recounting the king's praises before him, and in that context also submits his request, the king will give him a very large gift as befits the minister's status." (*Tzava'as HaRivash*, 107. *Amud HaTefilah*, 60)

Our sages tell us that it is essential that we Daven with joy (*Medrash Shocher Tov*, Tehilim, 100). We therefore need to try to Daven from a place of elation and positivity (*Berachos*, 31a. *Mishnah Berurah*, 1:10. This is the reason why we "juxtapose *Geulah* / redemption and *Tefilah* / prayer": *Shulchan Aruch*, Orach Chayim, 93:2. Indeed, "The root of Tefilah is the heart's rejoicing in Hashem": *Sefer Chasidim*, 18). On the other hand, "All the heavenly Gates are closed, except the gate of tears" (*Baba Metziya*, 59a); as a student of the Baal Shem Tov teaches that when one *involuntarily* cries during Davening, this is a sign that his Tefilah has been accepted on high (Rebbe Pinchas of Koretz, *Imrei Pinchas*, p. 84). Based on this, we need to understand that just as one can have bitter tears of sorrow, pain, hardship and suffering, which are certainly powerful agents of prayer, one could also have tears of yearning, of hoping, and even of joy, and these are just as, or even more, powerful.

"Joy breaks down all barriers" (Rebbe Rashab, *Sefer HaMa'amarim*, Ranat). This certainly includes the opening of any negative blockages within the person

Davening, but it also refers to the blockages on a cosmic level. Joy, love, vulnerability, desire, yearning, passion are what allow for real intimacy to occur, and thus the possibility of new life to be born. Similarly, says the Baal Shem Tov, for our Tefilos to manifest and produce fruit, our Davening must be evocative expressions of these same positive emotions. In fact, the words of our Davening are more readily accepted on High and more speedily answered below, when they are uttered or sung in joy. As the Baal Shem Tov teaches, if you feel joyful, elated, and unburdened at the conclusion of your Davening, this is the biggest proof that your Tefilos have been received on High and answered (whereas if you feel down, depressed, dispirited, this shows that your Davening was not effective: *Toldos Yaakov Yoseph*, Ekev. *Amud HaTefilah*, 168). Simply, joy is essential to Davening.

If one Davens from a place of depression, besides the possible spiritual harm that may occur (and beside the fact that joyful prayer is more effective), says the Arizal, he will not be able to receive any of the *Ohr* / light and *Shefa* / flow that comes down to him during the Davening (*Shulchan Aruch Arizal*, Orach Chayim, 1:1. *Pri Eitz Chayim*, Sha'ar Olam HaAsiyah, 1. *Sha'ar HaK'lalim*, Hakdamah. See also *Kaf Hachayim*, Orach Chayim, 90:32).

Simply being in a state of sadness or *Far-kvetsh-keit* while Davening shuts a person off from experiencing any revelation of whatever Ohr they were able to circulate and tap into during their prayers. A person stuck in their sadness, wallowing in their melancholy, is marred in darkness and no light can possibility penetrate. In such a condition, there is no way to feel the Light of Hashem, or to feel connected, answered and whole.

By attaining the higher form of Yirah, our ego has been broken open, and thus we can vividly feel elation and real pleasure. This Yirah is literally the opposite of ego-driven 'fear'; it is the surrender of the egoic self within the Infinite expanse of HaKadosh Baruch Hu.

Here is a short mental practice that may help a person achieve some form of Yirah.

Quiet your mind and gently think:

Have I ever felt like I was losing control? Think of a situation in your past where life seemed beyond your control.

How did it make you feel? Small? Powerless? Afraid? Feel the fear. Sit with it; acknowledge it in your body.

Recognize that most of life is simply beyond your control — both the seeming detriments and the benefits. Recognize that there is a Controller and that is Hashem, the All Powerful King and Guide of All.

Relinquish your egoic need to control and simply let go.

How does it feel to let go? If tears well up, allow them to flow.

Sit and rest for a few minutes.

Chapter 7

STEP THREE: AHAVAH/LOVE

Ahavah / Love

THE PROFOUND AND WONDERFUL TEXT OF THE REBBE RASH-AB, *Kuntres HaAvodah*, WHICH IS DEDICATED SOLELY TO THE *Avodah* / INNER WORK OF DAVENING, BEGINS WITH THESE WORDS: "THE ENTIRE AVODAH AND HARD INNER WORK OF THOSE WHO TRULY SERVE HASHEM DURING TEFILAH IS TO COME TO THE ATTRIBUTE OF LOVE." FOR DAVENING TO OCCUR, WE NEED BOTH YIRAH AND AHAVAH, BUT AHAVAH IS THE HIGHER OBJECTIVE.

Yirah and Ahavah are the wings of our Davening, which allow us and our *Tefilos* / prayers to 'fly upwards' as it were. One without the other, is like a bird trying to fly with only one wing (*Tanya*, 41. *Tikunei Zohar*, Tikun 10), and like a bird, we need both wings to fly (See regarding birds *Chulin*, 52a: כיון דבהאי לא מצי פרח בהאי נמי לא מצי פרח). In other words, we need both awe and love, working in unison, for our soul to fly upwards and inwards in Tefilah and Deveikus.

Yirah is a תנועה / *Tenuah* / movement of contraction, stepping back, and being humbled in the presence of the Omnipresent. Ahavah is a *Tenuah* / movement forward, an expansion, a drawing near. The two are expressed in attraction and repulsion, closeness and distance, familiarity and reverence, intimacy and transcendence, Hashem as 'Father' and Hashem as 'King'. A healthy relationship demands both movements.

Speaking of the Mitzvos of Ahavah and Yirah, the Rambam does something very unusual from the way he generally codifies the Mitzvos. He writes about both of these Mitzvos as one idea: הא-ל הנכבד והנורא הזה מצוה לאהבו וליראה אותו / "To this glorified and awe-inspiring G-d, there is a Mitzvah to love (seemingly corresponding to glorified) and fear (corresponding to awe-inspiring)" (*Hilchos Yesodei HaTorah*, 2:1).

The ancients postulated that there were two forces in the universe: one that gave life, vitality and sustenance, and thus that would have been the one to whom they would express love, glory and gratitude — and a force of darkness, that caused death, destruction, drought, and thus that would the one to whom they would express fear, appeasement and humble reverence. In the Rambam's teaching, above, he seems to point out a fundamental and foundational precept of Torah: there is Only One force in the universe, for HaKadosh Baruch Hu is the Source of All reality, and there is no bifurcation nor dichotomy in Him. Hashem is glorified, intimate and loved, and simultaneously awe-inspiring, transcendent and feared. HaKadosh Baruch Hu is both our loving Parent, and our demanding King. Hashem is both the Immanent and the Transcendent; both 'beyond all' and 'including all'.

Ahavah is about moving closer or expanding 'outward', while Yirah is more about retreating away or contracting 'inward'. Regarding Yirah, for an 'inward' movement to occur, the person needs to establish an element of aloneness or even some type of existential isolation. As Rashi writes, speaking of the *Kohen Gadol* / High Priest (*Yumah*, 4b): "He would separate himself from other people so that *awe* could rest upon him." Being alone allows you to enter a state of awe. Ahavah, on the other hand, is a movement outward, toward the 'other'; it is a shared experience that opens us up to others, and to deeper aspects of ourselves. In Yirah, we contract and eventually cease all movement, both outwardly and inwardly. In love we open up and move freely outwards and upwards.

In the path of the Baal Shem Tov, awe brings one to love. The love of Hashem flows naturally out of the state of being overcome with awe of Hashem and His Creation. The state of awe is initially stimulated when we open ourselves up to connect to some grandeur that is outside and beyond us, whether a painting, a piece of music, or a natural landscape, etc. As the awe of Hashem propels us inward, we expire into the infinite expanse of HaKadosh Baruch Hu. Then, when the state of awe becomes somewhat tempered, tremendous longing and Ahavah for Hashem is aroused.

As we ponder the awesomeness and the Infinite greatness of the Creator of life, we can enter a state of Yirah. When this state is slightly mitigated, it automatically transforms into longing, yearning and love (*Tzava'as HaRivash*, p. 7b. *Amud HaTefilah*, 58), as "Yirah is the gate to Ahavah" (*Likutim Yekarim*, p.3. *Ibid*, 59). First there is Yirah, and only then real Ahavah.[*]

---

[*] Yirah is the gateway that leads to Ahavah: *Akeidas Yitzchak*, Ekev. *Avodas HaKodesh*, 1:25. The Rambam writes, on the other hand, that Ahavah comes before Yirah. *Hilchos Yesodei haTorah*, 2:1. Yet, it is clear that the Baal Shem Tov is speaking about a higher Yirah. With this all in mind, the progression is from a lower Ahavah to a lower Yirah (Rambam) and then from a higher Yirah to a higher Ahavah (Baal Shem Tov). Ahavah is the higher level. *Tana D'vei Eliyahu Rabah*, 28. See also *Sotah*, 31a. *Sifri*, VaEschanan, 7. See also *Tanya*, Chap, 43. Thus עשה דוחה לא תעשה / a positive Mitzvah — which is rooted in Ahavah —

Following the sensation of feeling completely overwhelmed and over-awed, we then slip, almost effortlessly, into love. In this way we must actively work on developing our Yirah, while Ahavah comes on its own (*Keser Shem Tov*, 2, 17d. *Bnei Yissaschar*, Tishrei 4:14. *Derech Pikudecha*, Hakdamah 7. The idea that Yirah slips automatically into a joyous state is also expressed in the *Zohar*, בקדמיתא בעי יראה, לדחלא מניה, ובגין דחלא דמאריה, ישתכח לבתר דיעביד בחדוותא פקודי אורייתא :*Zohar* 3; p. 56a).

We cannot force love. It is a gift from Above that flows organically from true Yirah. In the state of deep Yirah there are no feelings, and hence no love either, yet, once the intensity of that holy awe begins to fade, we slip into the sweetest Ahavah.

What is Love?

What is love? It is actually a very difficult emotion to describe, define or quantify (*Keser Shem Tov* 2, 24:1. *Baal Shem Tov Al HaTorah*, Vaeschanan, 51). Suffice it to say that when we are talking about 'love of Hashem' we are not talking about the kind of love one feels when they say they love ice cream, or pizza, for example. To love ice cream just means you enjoy the taste and texture on your palate. You do not really love the ice cream itself. You just like what the ice cream does for your palate or stomach. At best, you can say you 'love' how ice cream tastes.

---

pushes aside a negative Mitzvah that is rooted in Yirah: Ramban, *Shemos*, 20:8. Also, keep in mind that to the Rambam, Ahavah is not an 'emotion' as in a feeling in the heart, a *Hergesh*, rather a desire to *know* Hashem. In the words of the Rambam (*ibid*, 2:2), "What is the path [to attain] love and fear of Him? When a person contemplates His wondrous and great deeds and creations and appreciates His infinite wisdom that surpasses all comparison, he will immediately love, praise, and glorify [Him], ומתאוה תאוה גדולה לידע השם הגדול / "yearning with tremendous desire to *know* the Great Name." Whereas to the Baal Shem Tov, Ahavah is an emotional yearning for closeness, for Yichud. Note, Rambam, *ibid*, 4:12.

A more subtle, refined form of love, such as love between people, is a 'contingent' or 'dependent' form of love (the Rebbe Rashab, *Sefer haMa'amarim 5666* ("Samach Vav"), Ki Na'ar Yisrael). It is dependent on who the other person is, and the conditions of your relationship. Love between humans is, in this way, often self-serving. You love what the other person does for you, or how the other person makes you feel. This is actually a more-subtle kind of self-love. Most relationships are founded on what each participant can obtain from the other; one gives to the other in order to get something from them. This is a conditional love — if it can even be called 'love'. Such a relationship will last only as long as both parties are getting what they want from the other. For example, an employer may appreciate or even 'love' an employee for what he does for the company. The moment, however, the employee ceases to produce the desired results, the employer will cease to experience those warm feelings for the employee.

There are other forms of human relationship which are rooted in a higher reality. For example, many spousal couples that stay connected across many seasons and through many ups and downs are not limited to this give-and-take modality. Their interactions express a higher measure of unconditional love. They may never even consider the question, 'What has s/he done for me lately,' as both partners might be focused only on fulfilling the other person's desire or will. Yet most spousal relationships, even long lasting ones, begin with a conditional love — initially contingent on physical, emotional, social or intellectual attractions. In the end, these loves, as powerful and magnetic as they may be, are also conditional.

Perhaps the closest thing to the love for Hashem (and experiencing Hashem's love for us) that we can experience in our daily life is love for our children. Parental love is intuitive and instinctual, because a child is in a very real way a part of the parent. A parent's love is intrinsic and unconditional and is not founded in a dynamic of give-and-take, nor in any physical sensations, emotions or intellectual constructs.

Pause for a moment and imagine you are a parent instructing your child to clean his or her room. The instruction is for the child's own benefit — to teach responsibility — but for whatever reason, the child does not listen. The room remains uncleaned, and your will has been disobeyed. Your initial reaction is frustration. You delineate a consequence for the child, again intended for the child's own benefit, to realize that his or her actions or non-actions are significant and consequential. Although tearful and hurt, the child instinctually turns to you and reaches out for a comforting embrace. Suddenly, you are in touch with a place deep within yourself where your love for your child is more powerful than your desire to be obeyed, or even to teach the child a lesson. This natural, instinctive, and yet unconditional love is the true essence of the relationship between children and parents.

As discussed, Yirah is aroused and then eventually bestowed upon us when we meditate on the awesomeness and greatness of the Creator, which then brings into sharp focus our own relative emptiness and no-thing-ness. We lose a sense of selfhood when faced with the Infinite power of the Ein Sof. Ahavah, by contrast, is unconditional connectivity. Having contemplated the awesomeness and infinite power of the Creator of this vast and magnificent universe, we are then infused with a profound love for Hashem. This occurs because we recognize that, despite such inconceivable disparity, we are intimately and essentially bound to Hashem, and Hashem to us.

Parenthetically, it is important to note here that in general, in our world of duality, there are different dynamics in our relationship with HaKadosh Baruch Hu. Perhaps when we are doing a Mitzvah, a Divine command, we feel ourselves as servants serving their master. Learning Torah, we feel like students sitting before our teacher. And when we Daven, we are like children in front of their father (*HaYom Yom*, 26th Tamuz).

Infinite Love

For a moment, let us truly consider the vastness of the universe and by equivalence the minuteness of man. We know that light travels at a constant, finite speed of 186,000 miles per second. If you were traveling at the speed of light, you would circumnavigate the equator of the earth approximately 7.5 times in just a single second. Now try to imagine 60 times this distance; this is only one 'light minute'. Now imagine 60 times that distance; it might seem infinitely vast, but it would amount to just one light-hour. Try to imagine 24 times that distance — one light-day, and 365 times that distance — one light year. It is simply too inconceivable to imagine how vast a space would then be traversed in 365 light years. Now, consider 100,000 years of travel at the speed of light. This practically immeasurable span of space is the approximate diameter of our galaxy alone. Now imagine that there are not just two, three, 100, 1,000, or even 1,000,000 other galaxies, but that there are billions, in fact over 200 billion known galaxies.

This contemplation alone can arouse a deep sense of awe, yet, now try to assimilate the truth that despite this incomprehensibly massive universe, and despite the fact that our entire planet is but a tiny speck in the orbit of our galaxy, and despite the fact that we are just one tiny living organism among billions upon billions of life-forms on this planet alone, still, Hashem makes room for you, cares about you, knows everything about you and loves you unconditionally, as if you are His only child. Hashem trusts and entrusts each of us with a vital mission to accomplish. Hashem chose you out of this immense universe with the mission of revealing and manifesting the entire purpose of Creation. This paradoxical and miraculous realization arouses a deep feeling of love — both of being loved and of loving in return.

Once this innate love and connection is awakened within us, all we then want and desire is to be closer to our Beloved. A person who is truly in love wants only to please their beloved one. Shlomo HaMelech / King Solomon says of himself, **חולת אהבה אני** / "I am lovesick" for Hashem (*Shir HaShirim*, 2:5). A person who is lovesick cannot think of anything else besides his beloved, as all his thoughts are focused upon them. One who is **חולת אהבה** / lovesick for Hashem, in the words of the Rambam (*Hilchos Teshuvah*, 10:3), is "someone who loves Hashem with **אהבה גדולה יתירה עזה עד מאוד** / 'a great, exceeding and very powerful love', until his soul is totally bound up in the love of Hashem. As such, he will always be obsessed with this love as if he is lovesick. [For a lovesick person's] thoughts are never diverted from the woman whom they love. They are always obsessed with her; when they sit down, when they get up, when they eat and drink. How much greater then is the love for Hashem which is [implanted] in the hearts of those who love and are obsessed with Hashem at all times."

Love is not about the pleasure of consuming something, as in eating the ice cream, nor is it about self-centered gratification, such as how the beloved makes you feel. Rather, true love is focused entirely on the one who is loved.

When our love for Hashem is aroused, all we can think about is Hashem. We are lovesick, infatuated with our Beloved. All our thoughts, feelings, and our whole life, are directed towards 'pleasing' and making our Beloved 'happy'. All we truly desire is to live a life of *Kidush Hashem* / 'sanctification of Hashem's Name' by revealing the light of our Beloved One in this world. In the words of the Baal Shem Tov:

"There are those who pray and think they are Davening with love when in truth they are just in a good mood (i.e., they are feeling good about themselves and their life, so they think this is what it means to love Hashem). The truth is that when a person is really in love with Hashem a great humility falls upon him. All he wants to do is beautify the Name of Hashem (to live his life as a Kiddush Hashem), and all he desires is to overcome his negative (ego-based) inclinations. When he experiences this, then he knows that he is experiencing true love." (*Likutim Yekarim*, p.3. *Baal Shem Tov Al HaTorah*, Amud HaTefilah, 59)

From Awe to Love and Back Again

As discussed, the general pattern of psycho-spiritual development that leads to Ahavah begins first with a practice of contemplation that stimulates a state of awe, until one is open to receive a higher level of Yiras Hashem, and then finally one is granted Ahavas Hashem. In a more quantum view, as we progress on the path of Davening, Yirah and Ahavah vacillate continuously. This is a form of what is known as *Ratzu v'Shuv* / running and returning, as well as expansion and contraction. Even across the span of a single Tefilah, we may alternatingly experience love and intimacy with Hashem's Presence, as well as awe and trepidation in the awareness of our distance from the Utterly Transcendent One.

When love morphs into Yirah it ensures that our love does not become subtly selfish and ensnared by our own sense of *Yesh Mi she-Ohev* / 'there is someone (the *Yesh* / ego) who feels love.' In fact, some sources in Chasidus even speak about intentionally pausing, if possible, one's rapture and Deveikus during Davening to guarantee that their love does not, perhaps later, spill out into emotional or physical lust or other negative Kelipos.

For it is quite possible that when the heart is aroused and expanded in holy love, if unchecked and allowed to flow without any *Havdalah* / separation, or mindfulness, that such love will spill out into unwarranted spaces. For example, after an ecstatic or emotional Davening, some people can collapse into compulsive overeating, mindless humor — or even anger, one of the Kelipos of imbalanced *Chesed* / expansiveness. Spiritual love can overflow its intended vessels when it is not tethered to mindfulness and Yirah. The Holy Viledniker writes of practicing *Tzimtzum* / contraction and *Havdalah* / separation during Davening for precisely this reason (*Sh'eiris Yisrael*, p. 111-112). This is the movement of *Shuv* / returning — and specifically returning to the touchstone of Yirah, which purifies and renews the state of Ahavah.

At the beginning of Davening, we may feel dramatically overwhelmed in what we must undertake and experience — standing with humility and awareness in the Presence of the Infinite Omnipresence. This humbling sensation inspires a person to feel their own lowliness, smallness and observable existential 'distance' from Hashem. It can even create a resistance in some people to begin the process of Davening altogether. But as we move into Davening, begin to ascend the ladder of prayer, and travel into deeper and higher states of consciousness, we begin to feel closer and closer. This generates, circulates and reciprocates more love and feelings of connection and belonging. This is the standard telos of moving from Yirah to Ahavah, as explored.

However, although the general trajectory in a life of psycho-spiritual maturation is from Yirah to Ahavah, in a healthy spiritual process it will also vacillate from Ahavah back to Yirah, and then again from Yirah back to Ahavah, and so on. The spiritual path is not purely linear or progressing ever-forward. Nor is the path only cyclical, as in coming back to the same place in the same way, day after day or minute after minute. Rather, Creation seems to be organized in a series of spiral dynamics. We continue to come back to the same root of reality and identity, but from a different, deeper level and perspective.

An illustration of this process of vacillation is revealed to us in the standard six-word blessing formula. The structure of a blessing begins with *Baruch Atah*, "Blessed (or 'Source of blessing') are You," which is phrased in the *Nochach* / second person. This is a very direct personal address — "You." But then, we continue and refer to HaKadosh Baruch Hu in the *Nistar* / third person, "Hashem." This is a more formal and less intimate address. According to this linguistic formula, we start by feeling close and intimate, as if being cradled by Hashem. When we say "You," we mean literally *You*, as if we were speaking directly to a loved one or a dear friend. Hashem, the Creator, in our prayers becomes a 'You', a subject we can address. From this perspective, Hashem is no longer an abstract object or idea, but a living presence in our life — a real 'You', with whom we feel close and intimate.

And then an even deeper, higher awareness sets in and we begin to feel distant again, because every level that we attain through love, opens up to a more expansive conception of Divinity and to a more pronounced awareness of our own smallness within that immensity. An overwhelming sense of the Holy Transcendent Other sets in and we feel small, alienated and distant. With what little strength we have left, we say, "*Hashem...*" And from this state of awe, suddenly a breakthrough occurs and once again we feel close, embraced, cradled and loved. From this place of love, we are able to say the next word of the Brachah, *Elokeinu* / "our G-d..." Immediately, a deeper realization sets in and we once again feel distant as we address HaKadosh Baruch Hu as *Melech HaOlam* / "King of the World..." We experience this back and forth, running and returning, expanding and contracting, moving deeper into and out of love and closeness and awe and distance throughout these six words, as well as throughout the Davening in general, and our spiritual path as a whole. In fact, we need both of these modes of awareness so that our relationship with Hashem does not become one of callousness or carelessness (*Yalkut Shimoni*, Iyov, 1:891).

This vacillation from Yirah to Ahavah and back again continues throughout the process of our Davening until we reach the Throne of Unity, the highest level, where both feelings of closeness and distance, love and reverence, exist simultaneously as one.

Through this dynamic of feeling first close and then distant, first loving and then reverent, we are able to sense the transcendence of the Holy Other and become overwhelmed by the mystery and majesty of the Creator of All. And we are able to sense as well the immanence, closeness and familiarity of Hashem, as if we were being held in a Divine embrace. We are perpetually moving in and out of these perceptions. They are in fact two poles of a greater emotional spectrum, and each one strengthens and sensitizes us to its opposite. Yirah and Ahavah can thus be understood as complementary and even collaborative for the greater project of spiritual flight — Deveikus.

Our body too, when attuned to our inner consciousness during Davening, moves in sync with these oscillating states. At times during Davening, we Shuckel from right to left, and at times, almost involuntarily, we Shuckel from front to back. Moving from front to back is a movement of Yirah — as we bow the head forward in reverence and then move backward in awe. Moving from right to left, side-to-side, is a movement of affection and love as we feel ourselves 'cradled' by Hashem.

While these states appear to be two separate movements, on a deeper level, they are aroused and awakened simultaneously within the context of Davening. It is taught in the name of the Ramban: "Although it is impossible for these two attributes (Ahavah and Yirah) to coexist in general, it is possible for these two emotions to exist simultaneously in the context of Divine service" (Baal Shem Tov in the name of the Ramban, *Ben Poras Yoseph*, 45:3. See also *Toldos Yaakov Yoseph*, Mishpatim).

There can even be a 'simultaneity' of Yirah and Ahavah when our Ahavah brings us to a fear of letting go of the Ahavah, or the fear of 'harming' the presence of Ahavah. Think about the first time you picked up a newborn baby. While there is tremendous love and pleasure in picking up this tender infant, yet, extremely delicate hands are needed. One is nervous, perhaps even scared, of holding him gently enough, not too tight, while making sure to cradle the head to support the fragile neck. It is a great love that is felt throughout, but it comes with a deep 'fear' of not taking the correct precautions and necessary care. So too, our love for HaKadosh Baruch Hu is so overwhelming that it makes us concerned about the loss of even a single moment of serving Him. The responsibility that we bear on our shoulders is so great that we appropriately fear 'dropping the ball' that Hashem has passed us. This type of Yirah is not a Yirah of 'awe', rather a Yirah of 'distance', of Transcendence. However, in Avodas Hashem these apparently conflicting emotions, feeling close and feeling distant, can simultaneously exist.

Only in serving Hashem can we concurrently experience two seemingly conflicting and opposite states, for outside of contact with the Divine, this is not possible: "There is no Ahavah in the same place as Yirah, or Yirah in the same place as Ahavah; this only occurs with Divine attributes" (*Sifri*, Parshas Ekev. *Reishis Chochmah*, Sha'ar Ahavah, 1. Also quoted in the name of the Ramban. *Ben Poras Yoseph*, p. 54d). On a deeper level of unity within, one feels love and closeness with Hashem, while concurrently feeling awe and perhaps even a fear and trepidation of approaching the Mystery. In this case, the experience of Yirah instills within us an awareness of our smallness and inadequacy before something infinitely greater than ourselves. Paradoxically, however, such Yirah does not create a sense of terror and a desire to flee, but rather a sense of gravity and a corresponding desire to connect. The recognition of the superiority of the Holy Other, in fact, establishes a connection and a feeling of being lifted, enlarged, magnified and elated. In the words of the Medrash, יראתי מתוך שמחתי ושמחתי מתוך יראתי / *Yareisi MiToch Simchasi, V'Simachsi MiToch Yirasi* / "Within my joy I fear (am in awe), and my joy is within my fear" (*Tana D'vei Eliyahu Rabbah*, 3).

Yirah is the *Bereishis* / the 'in the beginning', the foundation of *Avodah* / Divine service. For this reason, the word בראשית / *Bereishis*, as the *Tikunei Zohar* writes, contains the letters that spell the word ירא / Yirah. Yet, in small numerical value the word *Bereishis* is 13 (Beis/2, Reish/2, Aleph/1, Shin/3, Yud/1, Tav/4 = 13), which is the same value as the word Ahavah. In other words, when you boil Yirah down to its essence, you find Ahavah. Bereishis, the hidden utterance of Creation, is thus an interinclusion of Yirah and Ahavah as one.

How can Ahavah and Yirah exist together? When you are in awe (and certainly if you are fearful), there is no room for love and being drawn closer. And conversely, when you are reaching out in love and feeling close there is no room for the contracted emotion of awe and feeling vast distance. They are antithetical. And yet in Davening these conflicting emotions can be maintained simultaneously.

The reason for this is that when a person is in a true state of Deveikus and *Ayin* / nothingness, or emptiness of self and self-conscious awareness, all opposites are reconciled (*Magid Devarav leYaakov*, 7. Ohr Torah, Vayera 27-28). This is because there is something paradoxical in the way the world was created and within the relationship between the Creator and Creation. Let us use the body and soul as an example. On one hand, the body is part of Creation; it was created and formed at a particular time and will return back to the elements by the age of 120 years. On the other hand, we possess a spark of the Creator, which makes us infinite and eternal and therefore connected to a world beyond Creation, beyond space and time. And so, by maintaining both of these perspectives at once, as a physical body and as a spark of the Divine, we relate to Hashem both as our 'external' Creator, and paradoxically also as the deepest Essence of *who we are*.

HaKadosh Baruch Hu is both the 'distant' Creator as well as the 'intimate' Emanator of Creation. In relationship to our Creator we are both 'close' and 'far', 'small' and 'big'.

In the world of interpersonal relationships, when we are feeling the pull of love and connection, our egoic boundaries are eliminated and we are able to experience a genuine sense of intimacy. We have the capacity to fully enter into the other person's 'space' and they in turn are able to fully enter into ours. Yet, when we are feeling this type of intense love, there is no room for Yirah, trepidation, withdrawal or reservation. By contrast, when we are feeling intimidated by another person's presence or we sense their grandeur, we feel hesitant to move any closer out of a sense of humility and smallness. When Ahavah wells up in response to this distance and we do move closer, then there is less Yirah.

In the context of human 'romantic' love, we are experiencing a 'created' love; it is not innate and it has a beginning and potentially an end. Additionally, it is a love that is trying to bridge a gap, implying that there is a 'distance' between us and our beloved. In this sense, the sense of love is needed in order to draw us closer to that which is separate from us. This is in contrast to a parent-child love, in which there is a sense of inseparability.

Love of Hashem is often likened to the love of a child for a Parent. Yet, to an even greater degree than parent-child love, love for Hashem is a) innate, and b) not trying to fill a gap. Rather, love for Hashem is more an experience of revelation or realization of what has always been present. Our love for Hashem is revealed when we begin to feel the innate connection we have with our own Source and Sustainer. It is actually a connection that is deeper than that of Creation-to-Creator or child to parent: we are actually an inseparable 'part' of Hashem.

Despite this essential inseparability, it is equally true that Hashem 'created' us, and the Creator is unique, apart and infinitely beyond us. In this way, the experience of Yirah awakens and reveals the potential for 'relationship' with Hashem, the relationship of a finite creature approaching his Infinite Creator. Sensing such an existential gap between Creator and Creation is necessary in order to cultivate the reverence and yearning for connection that will ultimately pull us closer than ever, closer than if we were to have never felt any distance in the first place.-

In Summary: Yirah represents our experience of Hashem's Transcendence and grandeur, while Ahavah represents the experience of Hashem's Immanence and accessibility. On one hand, we sense Hashem as completely beyond us and the world, and yet we sense that Hashem is also immeasurably close and deep within us. Hashem is Infinite and incomprehensible, and also immediate and more real than any observable reality. In fact, both Immanence and Transcendence are definitions and manifestations, whereas 'Hashem Himself' is beyond all manifestations and expressed through all manifestations, no matter how seemingly contradictory to our binary logic. Every-thing and no-thing are all present and included within Hashem. In this way, the opposite emotions of Yirah and Ahavah can be experienced simultaneously.

Nochechus / presence, Ahavah and Yirah, all reflect the general mindset and emotions required to put us in a conscious state of connection with the Source of All Life so that we can Daven with openness and authenticity. The next step in the Baal Shem Tov's path of Davening is establishing a particular meditative Kavanah in relation to the words we are going to utter in Davening.

Chapter 8
STEP FOUR: KAVANAH /
THOUGHT-INTENTION-DESIRE

Thought-Intention-Desire

AVING ESTABLISHED A STRONG SENSE OF *Nochechus* / BEING PRESENT WITH AND WITHIN THE DIVINE, AND HAVING IN-SPIRED AND AROUSED EMOTIONS OF *Yirah* / REVERENCE OR AWE AND *Ahavah* / LOVE AND YEARNING, WE ARE ALMOST READY TO BEGIN DAVENING.

For Tefilah to commence, there also needs to be some sort of *Kavanah* / intellectual intention. And all opinions agree that Tefilah without inten-tion is "like a body without a soul" (*Chovos HaLevavos,* Sha'ar Cheshbon haNefesh,

3:9. *Sefer HaYashar,* Sha'ar 13, p. 124. The *Nefesh* / soul is missing without Kavanah, thus such Tefilah is unlike a Korban with a Nefesh, although it is still considered as an offering of Minchah, wheat offering, that lacks Nefesh anyway: *Keser Rosh,* 22. Thus, there is still a *Cheftzah* even without the Kavanah: Brisker Rav, *Reshimos Talmidim,* Yesodos HaTefilah, p. 237).

'Mindless' Tefilah, or Tefilah without Kavanah, has also been described as "bringing a fork and knife to the table without serving the food" (Chidah, *Chomas Anach. Yeshayahu,* Chap. 29), or like going through the mechanical motions of chopping wood (see Rambam, *Moreh Nevuchim,* 3:51*). In fact, without a general Kavanah in what you are doing there is no real *Metziyus* / existence of prayer at all. To ensure that one maintains their Kavanah throughout Davening, the Arizal taught a detailed practice of *Kavanos* / formulaic intentions and *Yichudim* / formulas of unification. It was strongly suggested by the Holy Arizal that one should establish and maintain these formulas of intention within his mind during the recitation of one's prayers. In this way, the Kavanah and the *Dibbur* / speaking of the words of Davening occur simultaneously.

The *Chidush* / novelty of the Baal Shem's teaching, which contrasts slightly but significantly with the prescription of the Arizal, is that he strongly encourages us to focus on our Kavanah just *before* we recite the words of Davening, and then, when we are vocalizing the words, we should drop any intellectual formula and just be present in the resonance of the words themselves. In the Baal Shem's approach to Kavanah, the intention should illuminate what is about to be said, and then the words should be pronounced without any 'thought' whatsoever (*Toldos Yitzchak,* Noach. *Amud*

---

* In the words of the Rambam, אבל אם תתפלל בהנעת שפתיך ופניך אל הכותל - ואתה חושב במקחך וממכרך...כמו שיחפור חפירה בקרקע או יחטוב עצים מן היער מבלי בחינת ענין המעשה ההוא לא מי שציוהו לעשותו ולא מה תכלית כונתו - לא תחשוב שהגעת לתכלית.

HaTefilah, 20). This allows us to fuse our mental and emotional energy with the themes and ideas of the Davening right before we speak them. But once we begin reciting the words, we need to just be present in their sounds and vibrations and not be distracted by any mental gymnastics or even any thoughts beyond the words themselves. Just be present with the words as you recite them in Davening. This may sound simple, however, when one considers the fact that our minds are constantly grasping at thoughts to hold onto, this practice of radical presence is not as easy as it may sound.

'Think before you speak' is a principle that is appropriate always, even in casual conversation. Prior to opening your mouth to saying something, it is a common sign of compassion, consideration and mindfulness to think about what you want to say, and whether or not you should even say it. How much more so with Davening.

Speaking without *Mach'shavah* / thought, says the Baal Shem, is like someone 'spilling seed', wasting bodily energy (*Likutim Yekarim*, p. 4b. *Amud HaTefilah*, 44. Similarly, speaking without thought is like *Sheviras HaKeilim* / the Breaking of the Vessels, as without thought there is no 'life' in the vessels, the words that are spoken: *Keser Shem Tov*, 2, 2b. *Amud HaTefilah*, 77).

In such a case, one is taking their vital energy and most Divine-like quality — the ability to communicate and create — and wasting it with empty, meaningless, mindless words. As a result of thoughtless speech, he squanders his *Chayus* / life energy on triviality and empties himself and his energy into a vacuum, with no purpose or direction.

There are two basic elements to the unique Davening practice of the Baal Shem Tov: a) think before you speak the words of Tefilah and when saying the words 'stop' thinking, and b) do not just think of what you are about to verbalize, rather scan the words themselves as you contemplate their meanings, before saying them. Mach'shavah and Kavanah before Dibbur means to literally contemplate the actual words — not only their ideas — before saying them. Only after you have thought about the actual words of a segment of prayer do you say them with full presence.

This practice entails more than just a general thought or quick review of the words and ideas you are about to say, rather it implies a detailed contemplation and even expanded visualization of the actual words before saying them. For example, if you are about to say the four letter-word *Baruch* (Beis, Reish, Vav, Chaf), before vocalizing the word, you might scan the word itself, then imagine its separate constituent letters drawing together, then internalize what the word *Baruch* / bless really means to you, and finally say the word (Rebbe Ze'ev Wolf of Zhitomir, *Ohr haMeir*, Shoftim).

This practice is similar if you are saying one or three words at a time, as is suggested by numerous teachers. For example, *Baruch Atah Hashem* / 'You are the Source of all blessings, Hashem….' First, take a moment to collect all the letters from these three words, read them in your mind's eye or in the Siddur, and think about what they mean. Then stop thinking and say them with all the clarity and strength of your being. Around a century after the Baal Shem Tov, the Chafetz Chayim writes (*Hashmatos l'Sefer Shemiros HaLashon*) that HaKadosh Baruch Hu planted a good piece of advice on how to have Kavanah while Davening: before each blessing of the Amidah, pause a few moments and consider what you are about to say, and then actually vocalize it.

An earlier source that perhaps suggests this practice can be found in the writings of the Ramban, Rabbeinu Moshe ben Nachman (1194–c.1270). There is a well-known letter that he sent to his son, Nachman. At that point in time, the Ramban was living in Israel, in the city of Aco (Acre), as he needed to escape his birth-land of Spain following a series of contentious theological debates. His son was living in Catalonia, Spain. The letter was meant to strengthen and inspire the character trait of humility within his son. He instructed his son to read the letter at least once a week. In fact, he assured his son that every day that he would read this letter, Heaven would answer his heart's desires. This letter became publicly known after being printed in Mantua, Italy in 1623, and over time it has become quite famous. It is a letter that is recited and studied regularly by many people throughout the world on a daily or weekly basis.

"Think about your words before you let them out of your mouth," the Ramban urges his son. If we read this carefully, we can see that he is referring to more than just 'thinking before you speak', which everyone understands to be a considerate way to live in general. The letter is saying something more specific — you should think clearly about the *actual words* that you are about to say in Davening, and only then should you say them.

In the teachings of the Baal Shem Tov, the quality of thought that you should apply to your words of Davening before you speak them goes beyond merely formulating them in your head, as in simple 'Mach'shavah before Dibbur' (as many Mekubalim teach us. See *Rabbeinu Bachya*, Vayikra, 24:10. *Shaloh*, Meseches Tamid, Mer Mitzvah, 9). Rather, he suggests that you put all your attention and intention into what you are about to say, before you say it. See the words with your mind's eye, let them sink into your psyche, fill them up with light. Then, when you finally recite the words of Davening, do so free of contrived thinking, and enter completely into the sounds and vibrations of the sacred words.

Speech without Kavanah

When we recite the letters, words and sounds of Tefilah, our minds should not be occupied with their intricate meanings and interpretations, no matter how lofty these Kavanos are. Rather, we should be simply and fully present with their actual sounds, and the raw, unfiltered sensations of their vibrations.

In other words: We should enter into and relate to the words of Davening as "letters without any interpretation" (האותות בלי פירוש. *Degel Machaneh Ephrayim*, Eikev. *Amud HaTefilah*, 23). Just be present in the sound of the words, and while reciting them, do not get caught up in any intellectual grasping for meaning; simply be *in* the idea itself and express yourself from there. When you first secure the Kavanah and meaning of the words before saying them, you can then let go of Kavanah and 'enter' the words and be present 'within them'.

In a one-on-one encounter with another person, if I am immediately 'analyzing' the words they are telling me, rather than allowing them to first sink in and then to contemplate them, then I am not being present with the person nor their words. If I am engaged in intellectually dissecting the information even while they are talking, my *Da'as* / awareness and presence is caught up in an egoic pursuit. In fact, if one is caught up in the meaning of their own words as they are speaking them, they will not be present in them either, and perhaps even become too self-conscious to speak.

As an exercise: If you are ever in a conversation and your mind drifts into dissecting the meaning of the other person's words, observe what happens. Do you cease to listen to them as a whole person, ignoring their tone and body language? Do you seem to be surrounded by a buffer of your own thoughts, and perhaps even thoughts about your thoughts? How does the other person respond to your lack of presence? Now drop your inner 'thinking self', be quiet and present and absorb the other person's words directly, without that analytic filter. Allow yourself to fully hear the other, to receive their words and digest them fully, to pause, and only then to respond.

Tefilah is our time to have a 'conversation' with HaKadosh Baruch Hu, a time of Divine encounter. And so, as all encounters, we need to ensure that we are present within the words we are speaking, without becoming trapped in our head. When saying the sacred words of Tefilah we need to ensure that we are present with the Light of Hashem within the words, to *hear* them, digest them and let them vibrate within our body and soul. We need to avoid getting caught in the beautiful cage of our intellect in order to fly into the wide-open expanse of our heart. This is the difference between Torah and Tefilah, learning sharpens the mind while prayer softens the heart.

'Thinking' the sacred words of Davening while verbalizing them not only decreases your presence with them, it actually limits the spiritual power of their holy, *Ohr* / light. Whatever meaning you construct in your limited understanding pales in comparison to what truly lies within the sacred, holy and light-filled words of Tefilah. If you are thinking about a particular Kavanah while reciting them, you are limiting their true capacity, because then the words only mean what you *think* they mean, from your limited perspective, and not what they really mean on their own. If, however, you are simply saying the words of Davening without any personal, subjective, and limiting understanding of what they mean, then the words retain their maximum and Infinite potential. In the words of the Baal Shem Tov:

"One who holds a particular intention (that is known to him) while Davening or performing a Mitzvah, only has access to what is currently known to him. However, if one says the words (of prayer) with deep connection to their *sounds*, then all the Kavanos are automatically included within them. Every letter is an entire world. Thus, when a person recites the words of prayer with deep connection, the corresponding upper (inner) worlds are aroused and activated to create shifts and impacts in the world below." (*Tzava'as HaRivash*, p. 14b. *Amud HaTefilah*, 26)

Sweetening Din / Judgment through Vocalizing the Words

Words create realities, as will shortly be explored; such is the power of the sonic vibrations of the words of Tefilah and Torah study. Yet, this is only so once the words are spoken, when the letters are combined and verbalized (thus, a mere visual reading is not enough: *Shulchan Aruch*, Orach Chayim, 47:4. The Gra holds a different opinion: *Biur haGra,* ad loc. Alter Rebbe, *ibid*, 47:2). Until that moment, the letters on the page are considered 'dead'. Without a sentient consciousness to vocalize them, the letters on the page amount to nothing more than ink on paper. They need to be 'listened to', absorbed and felt, and then animated, enlivened and sounded. By means of our emotional arousal and mindful Kavanah, these letters and words become charged with *Chayus* / life force, and then through their verbal articulation they become fully 'living words'. In this way our prayers can make waves in the world.

Accordingly, when a scribe writes a *Sefer Torah* / Torah Scroll, it is more scrupulous of him to actually vocalize every word he is about to write, before he writes it, even if he is looking into another Torah intermittently while writing (*Menachos*, 30, Tosefos. Mordechai, 957. Tur, *Orach Chayim*, 32). The reason for the stringency of vocalizing while writing, in the profound language of the *Bach* (Rav Yoel Sirkis, 1561–1640), is that the *Kedushah* / sanctity that emanates from the breath or 'vapor' of his mouth when he recites each word will be drawn down into the letters of the word that he then writes on the parchment, infusing it with vitality (צריך שיקרא כל תיבה ותיבה קודם שיקראנה נראה דס"ל דלאו משום שלא יטעה הוא אלא דכך היא מצות כתיבת ס"ת תפילין ומזוזות שיהא קורא כל תיבה ותיבה ואח"כ כותב כדי שתהא קדושת הבל קריאת כל תיבה ותיבה היוצא מפי הקורא נמשכה על האותיות כשכותב אותן בקלף).

Letters on a page of the Siddur are inanimate and lifeless, existing in a form of concealment, although their actual purpose is to reveal. This is the case in both written and spoken language; before we speak them, conceptual words have no life. Yet, a distinction must be made between written and spoken words, as they function differently. With speech there is a higher degree of *instantaneous* revelation. As the word is spoken, it is also heard. However, there does still remain some element of concealment in the spoken word as one can never fully express what he truly feels and experiences. As such, spoken words are simultaneously a revelation of experience and a concealment of understanding.

With regards to written words, the situation is a bit different. Whereas in speaking there is one revelation, with writing there are two revelations. The first is when the writer puts down his ideas to the paper. At this moment, insight is revealed to him, even though it is still concealed from the world. The second revelation occurs when a reader comes and reads these words, perhaps even hundreds of years later; their light and meaning are thus revealed even more in the world. In other words, from the perspective of the book itself, the words on the page are still concealed or 'dead' until a reader reads them.

When the author commits the ideas to paper, it is 'book one', as it were. Later, when someone reads these words, the reader creates 'book two' (See the Pirush of the Gra, *Sifrei de Tzniusa*, Chap. 1). There is thus no instantaneous revelation in writing, as with speech; a book is defined by its process of delayed revelation. In this way, writing suggests a 'double' concealment: one prior to 'book one', an expression of the writer's inspiration, and one prior to 'book two', the reader's activation and understanding of the words.

This explains how the words on the page are lacking vitality, and are as if 'dead'. It is only through the act of reading, chanting, singing, and understanding their meaning that these letters of *Din* / concealment become 'sweetened' and assume their full meaning, purpose, and life. Certainly, words do become 'alive' and animated by the mere act of reading them, but they become truly infused with meaning and intention only when understood. This is illustrated in Halachah: a printed word of Torah (not handwritten with intent), is not yet considered 'holy' until a human being reads it. Until then, the writing can actually be burnt or perhaps even discarded.* Only once a human being has read from a *Sefer* / text do the printed words become holy and the book needs to be treated with the respect of a sacred item. Only through the reading and vocalizing of the words do the letters become alive and thus 'sweetened' of their inherent quality of Din.

One of the fascinating features of Chasidic thought as expressed in the teachings of the holy Baal Shem Tov is that previously abstract and metaphysical concepts of Kabbalah and spiritual cosmology became practical 'psychology'. The mystical structures that were previously used to map out and understand the nature of the universe were transformed into frames through which we can understand the inner workings of the human psyche and soul. Hence making these previously, perhaps, obscure teachings more personal and practical.

For instance: Malchus, the final Sefirah of the Tree of Life, is classically understood as a Sefirah that has "no (substance) life of its own." Malchus is the ultimate 'receiver' of the Ten Sefiros; the 'vessel' par excellence. Malchus represents the Feminine aspect of the Divine referred to as 'Daughter'. Binah, the upper Feminine Sefirah, is considered the 'Mother', the one that births the lower eight Sefiros. Inwardly, says the Baal Shem, Malchus

---

* Printed books, before being learned, are considered תשמישי קדושה, not Kedushah itself: *Mas'as Binyamim*, Siman 100. Furthermore, the Avnei Nezer writes that printed Sefarim (not a Tanach) until they are learned, since *Hazmana Lav Milsa* / "An object *prepared* for a Mitzvah is not yet considered as an object of a Mitzvah," they do not yet have Kedushah. Perhaps as printing machines are completely automated and books are printed with no human intent or involvement, this is even more true.

represents the areas in our lives, whether within us or around us, that 'have no life of their own', remaining lifeless without any influx from Above to activate them. They have potential for purpose and impact, but without the right 'fuel', they will not give off any light. Binah represents our mindful consciousness; the aspect of awareness that has the power to animate and energize dormant potential, if channeled properly. When we join our Binah with our Malchus, we inject vitality and life into the areas in our life that seem lifeless and full of concealment. When Binah transmits its light to Malchus, Malchus can reveal its potential.

"The root of Tefilah is to sweeten the *Din* / judgment of Malchus by connecting it to its source, which is Binah," says the Baal Shem (*Ben Poras Yoseph*, p. 116b. *Amud HaTefilah*, 77). "If a person understands (has Binah) what the words mean…he thus connects Malchus (which is speech and the letters) with Binah, which is thought" (*Toldos Yaakov Yoseph*, Vaeschanan. *Amud HaTefilah*, 76).

What this means is as follows. When a person is sick, G-d forbid, or for that matter whenever there is anything amiss in a person's life, it is considered an expression of *Din* / concealment, an aspect of Malchus. When we Daven for healing or for whatever is lacking in our lives with intention and mindfulness, it is an aspect of Binah. By reciting and giving life to 'dead' letters on the page, we are *Mamtik haDin* / sweetening the Din by infusing Malchus with Binah.* The act of Tefilah itself is an act of sweetening the

* There is a principle of המתקת הדינים בשורשם / "sweetening the judgments (concealments) in their source" — see, for example, *Sha'ar HaKavanos*, Shofar; and there are many levels of this dynamic. The deepest source of *Dinim* / concealments is the *Tzimtzum* / constriction of the *Ohr Ein Sof* / Infinite Light to create and reveal the *Koach HaGevul* / the power within Hashem to conceal and reveal finitude. The Tzimtzum comes about because there is a Divine desire to express the Koach HaGevul from within the Ein Sof. This level of Gevul within the Ein Sof is called בוצינא דקרדינותא / "the lamp of darkness." See, for example, *Zohar*, Bereishis, in the beginning: 'The Koach HaGevul is the בוצינא דקרדינותא.' See also *Shemen Sason*, on *Eitz Chayim*, Igulim V'Yosher. And the בוצינא דקרדינותא is also called the *Kav HaMidah* / the measuring stick, as it were, that defines and delineates

the *Gevul* / boundaries for each Sefirah: *Zohar*, Vaeschanan. These are the first levels of what can be called *Dinim*, constrictions and limitations, as it were. Following the *Sheviras HaKelim* / breaking of the vessels, which occurs because the intense Lights are too overwhelming for the vessels, the Ten Sefiros, begins the process of Tikun, measured Light, the perfect amount of Light in the appropriate vessels that can contain that Light.

The 'first' of these worlds of Tikun is the world of Adam Kadmon, abbreviated as *AK*. Then comes the spiritual world of Atzilus. Then begins the more manifest, physical worlds of Beriah, Yetzirah and finally Asiyah. Each of these worlds contain Ten Sefiros, which are: Keser (and within Keser the level of *Atik* / removed and *Arich* / long, flowing downwards), Chochmah and Binah. These three are called the ג' ראשונות / first three, known as the acronym ג"ר. Then come Chesed, Gevurah, Tiferes, Netzach, Hod, Yesod and Malchus. These seven are called the "seven lower ones." All these Ten Sefiros are present within all worlds. Yet, in the world of AK, the level of *Atik* / removed or detached, Keser is most dominant.

In the world of Atzilus, the level of *Arich* / elongated Keser (and Chochmah) is most dominant. In the world of Beriah, the Sefirah of Binah is most dominant. In the world of Yetzirah, the 'six' emotional Sefiros are most dominant. In the world of Asiyah, the Sefirah of Malchus is most dominant. The *Partzuf* / persona and world of AK contains all Ten Sefiros (albeit with Atik being most dominant) and thus there is the level of Gevurah within AK. The Gevurah within AK is another place where Dinim show up. Following the world of AK is the world of Atzilus. The higher *Partzuf* / persona, world, always becomes enclothed within the lower Partzuf, yet, just like within the body, the head, and upper part of the body are literally less clothed, the same is true with the Partzufim, the ג"ר / 'Higher Three' do not become enclothed within the lower Partzuf. The ג"ר remain detached and are not enclothed in the lower world; only the seven lower Sefiros, from Chesed to Malchus become enclothed. In this way, the Atik of the Above world always remains detached from the lower world, and the lower seven are vested within the lower Ten Sefiros.

In the world of Atzilus (where Arich is dominant), which can also be seen as an intermediary between the Infinite Worlds Above and the Lower finite worlds below, this process of the enclothment of the lower seven of the higher world (AK, Atik) into the Ten Sefiros of Atzilus is as follows (*Eitz Chayim*, Sha'ar HaArich, 1-3): Keser of Arich receives and becomes enclothed within the Chesed of Atik, Chochmah of Arich becomes enclothed within the Gevurah of Atik, Binah of Arich within the Tiferes of Atik, Chesed of Arich within the "upper third" of Netzach of Atik, Gevurah of Arich within the "upper third" of the Hod of Atik, Tiferes of Arich within the Yesod of Atik, Netzach of Arich within "middle third" of Netzach of Atik, Hod of Arich within the "middle third" of the Hod of Atik, Yesod of Arich within the end of the Yesod of Atik (and the two "lower thirds" of Netzach and Hod of Atik remain 'open' and penetrate, giving sustenance to the lower worlds of Beriah). Malchus connects with the highest level.

Din. By giving Binah to the letters of Malchus, we are, in turn, stimulating a sweetening of any Din in our lives.

For our purposes, we see that Chochmah of Arich (Atzilus, as Atzilus is the *Keser HaK'lali* / general Keser), which is also called *Chochmah Stima'ah* / hidden Chochmah, contains and is enwrapped by the Gevurah of Atik. So Chochmah contains and is enmeshed with Gevurah, manifesting the idea of Dinim. And thus, בחכמה אתבריר / through Chochmah there is a *Birur*, an elevation of Din and all concealments, since Chochmah (of Atzilus) has traces of Din (from the Higher World), and can mitigate Din. This is another place where Din shows up. Yet, since Chochmah and Binah are always in unison "like two friends that never part," there is an implanting of the Gevurah within Chochmah in the 'womb' of Binah and thus Binah is also דינין מתערין מינה. Thus, there is Din in Binah.

Now for the המתקת הדינים on all these levels. The greatest המתקת הדינים is the sweetening of all Din, and of the Tzimtzum itself. This will only occur in the time of Moshiach, when paradoxically "the Tzimtzum itself will become illuminated," when concealment itself will be experienced as revelatory. This type of המתקת הדינים is beyond our level of doing or even rationally thinking about. For our purposes, there are three levels of המתקת הדינים: on the level of Atik, on the level of Chochmah and on the level of Binah. The המתקת הדינים on the level of Atik, the Gevurah of Atik, is that since לית שמאלא בהאי עתיקא / there is no left side (concealment) in Keser to experience the sweetening of Din on this level means to look at your life and experience only goodness and blessings in life. This is not simply to see that "this too is for the good" although it seems 'bad', rather there is *only* good.

When a student of the Maggid of Mezeritch asked him how he could achieve the state of "Just as one recites a blessing for his good fortune, so too must he recite a blessing for misfortune," the Maggid told him to go visit Reb Zusha. When he came to Reb Zusha's dilapidated home, and sat down to a meager meal of some crumbs of bread and water, he told Reb Zusha that the Magid sent him to learn from him how a person can recite a blessing for his misfortune, for the bad as well as for his fortune. Reb Zusha looked at the man puzzled and said, "Me? Why is the Maggid sending you to me? I don't have any bad or misfortune in my life."

The המתקת הדינים on the level of Chochmah is where the negative, the Din, the bad, becomes like *Ayin* / nothing. You live in a state of Bitul, in nullification of the egoic I. So while there still may be hardship and Din, you can detach yourself from the suffering, and remain in a joyous state. On the level of Chochmah it is as if the Din, that is very real, disappears and dissipates.

The המתקת הדינים on the level of Binah is the comprehension and understanding that although it is not yet lived and experienced, we know and understand that everything Hashem does is for our best. Everything originates from Hashem's kindness and compassion, even though a person does not yet see and experience this in his personal life.

Through our Kavanah and consciousness, we flood the 'dead' letters on the page of the Siddur or Sefer with life and energy. We awaken the letters and give them *Chayus* / vitality, and the letters thereby become activated and animated. The letters themselves are the *Olamos* / worlds, the tangible vessels. Our consciousness and intention are the *Neshamos* / souls, and through our intention we reawaken and reconnect the *Elokus* / the Divinity, the Life Force, to 'resurrect' the letters and flow through them into the world and into our lives.

Sometimes the opposite process occurs. If the Davener lacks the clarity of complete and full *Mochin* / intelligence and the energizing strength of *Chayus* / vitality, they can still inject a very simple Kavanah into the recitation of the letters themselves. There can thus be a *Hamtakas Din* / sweetening of the 'concealment' of the dead letters, which then causes an opening and expanding of *Mochin* / clarity and transparency of mind, within the person himself. Rather than the Davener arousing the letters, they in turn awaken him, allowing for the individual to attain Deveikus and Mochin through the letters themselves.

This is the amazing, transformative power of linking our Binah with our Malchus — our deeper understanding and intentionality with our words and actions. Indeed, this theme of connecting *Mochin* / mind with speech and action is a critical and fundamental principle in the Baal Shem Tov's teachings (*Keser Shem Tov,* p. 4). Mindfulness – being mindfully aware that we are living in the Presence of Hashem and thus perpetually conscious of our every thought, word and action – is integral to living a holy, wholesome and meaningful life.

This is because everything we experience in the outside world, according to the Baal Shem and many other sources, is merely a projection filtered through our internal, subjective prisms. Our *Mach'shavah* / thought creates our reality. Prior to the interplay between observed objects and the observing subject, the objects themselves do not really 'exist', per se; at least not in the form in which they exist in relation to us when observed. Not only does observation create a transformation of *context*, but it can even create a transformation of *content*. An example of this was given above: the act of reading a printed word renders the page sacred. On a 'quantum level', a particle's behavior will change depending on whether or not there is an observer. Observation is a creative act. Reality does not exist until it is measured, at least on the atomic scale. Spiritually, this means that our Mach'shavah is the most integral part of our existence, and in fact it creates our existence. We therefore need to ensure that we cultivate the most beneficial form of attention, intention and interpretation. Everything that we experience is dependent on our thoughts. If we have good, healthy and holy thoughts, our life will be experienced, felt and enacted in a good, healthy, holy way. This is the *Ikar* / main point of connecting our words and actions (Malchus) with our conscious understanding (Binah).

Mach'shavah / Thoughts and Da'as / Awareness

From another perspective, Mach'shavah is a *Levush* / garment imposed on top of a preexisting form or 'content'. Prior to the manifestation of Mach'shavah is a process of Chochmah, Binah and Da'as. Our Da'as is linked to our *Keser* / Crown which is our inner world of Atzilus. Even beyond these exceedingly subtle levels of consciousness is our access to the higher emptiness of all forms of existence: our inner *Ayin* / No-thingness.

Let us explore, for a moment, our higher Da'as. There is a tradition that a great ambition of the holy Baal Shem Tov was to teach people how to untangle themselves from their emotions and even their bodily sensations so that they could be fully present and mindful. Only through such psycho-physical untangling are people able to experience a real *Yishuv ha-*

Da'as / settling of the mind. How is this practically cultivated? How do we go beyond merely attempting to force the mind to be present, and actually step into full presence?

Da'as is the part of you that is observing your experience right now. The word *Da'as* contains the letters *Eyd* / witness. It is the part of the self that is always observing and witnessing life. Wherever there is a duality, such as 'being present' versus 'not being present', there is a third option that reconciles the two opposites by transcending and including them both. Da'as is a good general term for the experience of 'the third path, which reconciles the two'. Da'as experientially transcends the objects that are known, yet also includes and unifies them within the experience of the knower. By including both the state of presence and the state of distraction, Da'as is the impartial and unaffected common ground for both. Yet it is of a totally different order as well. It is off the map, so to speak, as it is not part of the spiritual struggle or game; rather it is the very field upon which the 'game' is played.

True presence is attained through higher Da'as. The effort exerted in trying to avoid or banish distraction, and any attempt to directly strengthen presence, both merely intensify the manic swing between the opposite states. In other words, every time you powerfully assert presence, distraction comes swinging back with equal power. The only way off this perspectival pendulum is to reject the binary and simply settle into Da'as, the knowing witness. Only from this place can one access the higher context of consciousness that allows both presence and distraction, to emerge and exist. The end result of this expansive embrace is an authentic, lasting presence.

Whenever you feel that you are not being present, or lacking Kavanah, stop and take notice. Ask yourself: Who is the 'you' that is looking at the distraction itself, as well as the distracted 'you'? The answer is *Da'as*, your knowingness, your intrinsic ability to notice. Consciously knowing your non-presence is the only real way to become truly present. Be the *Eyd*, the witness beyond the opposite manifestations of distraction and focus. This 'practice' is not something you need to believe in. You can experience it and verify it for yourself. Our consciousness is structured like a series of nesting dolls, which level upon level contained within; Da'as is the empty space that surrounds all of the Tchochkes of the mind.

Kavanah and Mach'shavah are essential and pertinent in all areas of life and in Tefilah. Yet, on the path of the Baal Shem Tov, it is important to remember that our attention to Kavanah needs to be secured prior to reciting the words of Davening. When we then recite the words, without our mind occupied with its own thoughts, we can then enter into and become absorbed by the sounds and vibrations of the sacred words themselves. When you chant the holy words of Tefilah do not *think about* their meaning, do this beforehand, rather, allow yourself to experience their sounds and inner vibrations viscerally through your senses.

Chapter 9
STEP FIVE: DIBBUR / SPEECH

A S WE HAVE SEEN, WHEN WE ARE ABOUT TO SPEAK THE WORDS OF DAVENING, WE SHOULD LET GO OF THE MIND, WITH ALL OF ITS DEFINING AND THUS LIMITING PERCEPTIONS OF MEANING, AND SIMPLY BE PRESENT IN THE WORDS THEMSELVES. IN THE STORY OF THE GREAT FLOOD, *Noach* / NOAH IS TOLD TO CONSTRUCT AND THEN "ENTER INTO" THE *Teivah* / ARK.

Commenting on this passage, the Baal Shem Tov teaches that the word *Teivah* also means 'word'. In this way, Noach is being told — and as the Torah is eternal, we too are being told every day — that in order to protect ourselves from the floods and turbulent waters of the world, what King Shlomo / Solomon called the *Mayim Rabim* / the raging great waters, we need to fully enter into the words of Torah and Tefilah. These 'revealed' words are designed to create a sanctuary of meaning and purpose amid the raging flood-waters of life. And וכל מה שמדבר בכח גדול יותר / "The more forcefully one speaks words of Torah or Tefilah, the more of the animal soul's energy he introduces and clothes within these words (thereby, converting more Kelipah to holiness)" (*Tanya*, 37). Yet, to allow these holy words to have the maximum effect as a sanctuary and means of transformation, we need to "enter into" them with great force. What does this mean and how can we put it into practice?

Connecting to the Ohr / Light within the Letters

The essence of the *Koach Eloki* / the Divine creative force is *Ein Sof* / Infinite. As the Creator is Infinite, so too is the power, the force that emanates from Him. This G-dly Infinite power is *Mufshat* / transcendent of all definitions or contextualization. However, for this Infinite force to create finite existence, it needs to be 'tamed', named, and defined. The primary medium for such 'taming' of Infinity is the *Osyos* / letters of the Aleph-Beis. Every letter of the Aleph-Beis is another *Hagbalah* / definition. In the letter Aleph, the Infinite *Ohr* / Light shines through the prism and context of an Aleph, and in the Beis the Infinite Light shines through the form and vibration of a Beis, and so forth.

You can think of this process as an infinite ocean of water which spreads into and circulates through many different streams. In each stream, the water takes on a new shape and flow; each stream looks and moves differently than the others, but it's all one body of water. The Ohr within the letters is always the same Ohr, just contained and expressed within a different package or vessel.

צהר תעשה לתבה / "Make illumination for the ark" (*Bereishis*, 6:16). Noach is instructed to create a window (or, place a precious stone) to provide light for the ark. As noted, תבה, in addition to 'ark', also means 'word'. We are thus bidden to create an opening for the Infinite Light to shine through our words of Davening. The Light of HaKadosh Baruch Hu is always present, everywhere and at all times. Our task is to carve out a space within ourselves so that we can connect via our consciousness (Neshamos) to the Infinite Light (Elokus) contained within the letters/words/vessels of Tefilah (Olamos).

The sacred letters of the Aleph-Beis are the conduits that transmit Divine flow from a purely infinite, undefined, non-contextualized statelessness into a particular object or idea. Every letter itself is a distinct building block or channel transmitting Divine Light and Life-Force. Every word is a combination of blocks or packets of defined light, which combine with each other to vibrate and animate a specific reality or life form. The letters are therefore the means through which Divine Creativity animates, sustains and evolves Creation. As such, every word has both a defined, specific meaning, as well as containing the Divine Light that is pulsating through it. This is the *Ohr* / Light of every word.

When we are focused only on the meanings of the words and their limited definitions, we relate to them as something to be grasped, outside of ourselves. Yet, when we enter *into* the words and experience them in Deveikus, we go beyond their semantic meaning and connect with the Ohr that lies *beyond* the letters. In the words of an early Chasidic teacher, "The main *Avodah* / service of Hashem is to speak the words of Torah and Tefilah with all your strength… when a person puts himself fully into the letters his body becomes refined.

This is due to the fact that within the letters the *Ein Sof* / the Infinite Light of Hashem rests, the letters, [when fully entered into], thus have the power to burn away the coarseness of the body, thereby revealing its spiritual essence. And this is indeed the "divestment from the body" and through this a person can come to actual *Ruach HaKodesh* / prophetic consciousness, and access a deeper, transcendental wisdom (*Toldos Aharon*, Vayigash).

Perhaps this is what the Baal Shem Tov meant when he taught, "When Davening, have in mind that Hashem is vested in the letters…Utter the words with all your *Koach* / strength because that will connect you fully with [Hashem], blessed be He, since your strength is in invested within the letter, and the Holy One blessed be He dwells in the letter as well" (*Tzava'as HaRivash*, 108. *Amud HaTefilah*, 84). In other words, when we put all our *Chayus* / vitality and *Koach* / strength into the words we are saying, we are connecting *our* inner Ohr with the *Ohr of Hashem* / the Infinite Light of HaKadosh Baruch Hu that resides within the letters.

In this way, putting all our Koach and Chayus into our Davening as we say the words is not about Kavanah or even 'understanding', as the Kavanah needs to be established before the recitation of the words. Rather, it is about being fully present *in* the words. This requires us to Daven with our whole self — body, mind, heart and soul. In fact, even if we are not reciting the words exactly and precisely, and do not fully understand what we are saying, we can still connect to the light of the Osyos. "If One reads the Torah (or Davens) with great devotion and 'sees' the lights within the letters, even though he does not intone the words correctly, Hashem is not scrupulous with him, since he is reciting these words with such great love and passion. This is similar to a father who loves his young child very dearly. When the child begins to ask something from the father, although the child speaks very unclearly (as he has hardly learned to speak), the father takes pleasure in just listening to his words" (*Likutim Yekarim*, 3'). With

---

* As the Medrash says, אמר ר' אחא: עם הארץ שקורא לאהבה איבה, כגון: ואהבת, ואייבת. אמר הקדוש *Shir HaShirim Rabbah*, 2:1. Or as the Sefer Chasidim writes; אם ברוך הוא: ודילוגו עלי אהבה יפלא בעיניך על אותן המגמגמין בלשון וקורין לחי״ת ה״א ולשי״ן סמ״ך ולקו״ף טי״ת ולרי״ש דלי״ת איך מתפללים או איך קוראים בתורה ואומרים דבר שבקדושה כשמגיעים לנפשנו חכתה לא נמצאו מחרפים

the love and devotion of a child speaking to their Heavenly parent, we can connect with the Ohr of the Osyos, no matter our level of understanding.

Every letter contains three dimensions: *Ohr* / light, *Chayus* / vitality, and *Koach* / power (*Tanya*, Sha'ar HaYichud v'haEmuna, 12, note. These three correspond to *Ohr* / light, *Mayim* / water, and *Rakiah* / the firmament that the *Zohar* speaks of: *Zohar* 2, 167a. *Eitz Chayim*, Sha'ar 39, Derush 5-5. *Siddur Im Dach*, p.1-2. *Likutei Levi Yitzchak*, Igros Kodesh, p. 327). We too, and all of Creation, having been created by these letters, as it were, are also composed of Ohr, Chayus and Koach. When we connect to and place our entire Ohr, Koach and Chayus into the words of Davening we connect it to the Divine Ohr, Koach and Chayus within the letters. The act of putting ourselves and all our light, strength, and vitality into the Osyos we are saying, attaches us to the Ohr within the Osyos that radiates from the Creator.

This profound connection with the light within the letters is of the utmost importance to truly effect change in our lives and in the world, as will be explored.

In Greater Detail

Every word we utter in Davening should be invested with the full involvement of our body and spirit. "Know that every word is an entire *Partzuf* / structure. A person needs to put his entire strength into each word, otherwise it will be missing a limb" (*Tzava'as HaRivash*, p. 4b. *Baal Shem Tov al HaTorah*, Amud HaTefilah, 25). If we are not fully present in every single letter

---

ומגדפים אל תתמה על החפין כי בוראינו אשר הוא בוחן לבות אינו שואל כי אם לב האדם אשר יהיה תמים עמו ואחרי שאינו יודע לדבר בענין מעלה עליו כאלו אומר יפה: *Sefer Chasidim*, 18. In the words of the Chasam Sofer, ישראל לפנים ממלאכי השרת ואינם צריכים מליץ לפני אוהבם ית״ש והוא מקבל בסבר פנים יפות אפילו בלשון עלגים וגמגום: *Shu't Chasam Sofer*, Orach Chayim, 166.

and word that we utter, we will be missing a part of the whole. Our mind needs to be involved in holding the preparatory Kavanah before we say the words. Our body needs to be involved in the physical vibrations and movements of energy generated by the sounds of the words themselves, which pulsate throughout our body. And our spirit needs to be involved in the breathing and articulation of the actual sounds, as they initiate and carry the words of our Davening into the world.

In other words: We need to enlist our Koach, Chayus and Ohr to participate when we "enter into the word." We can say the words of Davening slowly if it comes naturally, or say them quickly, if this is more effortless and flowing. Either way, we should aspire to feel their vibrations penetrating and permeating our entire being, and to ride the sound waves as they rise and fall, swell and recede, run and return. Entering into the words allows the words to enter into us.

Allow yourself to simply be present with every sound, movement, and vibration. Let the emanating Ohr and pulsating *Koach* / power of the letters fill and infuse your entire body. Perhaps you can not only sense the Ohr of the letters, but maybe even 'see' it with your deeper vision, as the Baal Shem Tov teaches, "Focus all your attention and thought on the power of the words, until you may begin to 'see' the sparks of light that shine from within them, and how they sparkle and ignite one another, and from these sparks more and more *Oros* / Lights are born" (*Keser Shem Tov*, 2, p. 4b. *Magid Devarav L'Yaakov*, 47. *Amud Ha Tefilah*, 88). Feel the rhythm and light of the letters, and even 'see' them, making sure to let go of trying to think about the meaning of the words, and allow yourself to be totally present with every sonic vibration and movement. We can thus experience the entirety of the sounds of the letters with the entirety of our senses. In this way, Davening becomes a whole-system experience that integrates all parts of our being in a unified purpose.

One way to practice this profound yet simple method of Davening is to utilize the natural rhythm of breath. Before you are about to recite a word or short phrase, inhale and reflect on the meaning of the words you are about to say. Gently hold and retain your breath. Then, as you are exhaling, recite the words with your full presence, Koach, Chayus and Ohr. Invest all of yourself into your Davening, say the words with your entire body.

It may even be possible that you do this with each letter and sound you recite. For example, before you say the word *Baruch*, as you are inhaling, pause a moment and think about the word and concept of blessing. Then, slowly exhale the first syllable: *Baaa....* Take another inhale, pause and exhale the rest of the word: *Ruuuch....* Again, any contemplation of the word's meaning transpires before the actual speaking; in the speaking itself, there is no thinking, just the intimate experience of sound, vibration, light, vitality and Divine power.

Most people find this practice too difficult or too time-consuming, so instead of pausing for each letter or word, pause before reciting every two or three words. In fact, there are many Tzadikim who suggest we should never utter more than three words in one breath during Davening (*Yesod Shoresh HaAvodah*, Sha'ar 5:1). Between every two to three words, pause for a brief moment, inhale and reflect on the meaning of the next two to three words, and then recite them. Pause, inhale, reflect, and then recite another two-three words. What is unique about this path is that when you recite the two or three words, free from any mental activity and meaning-making, the words truly speak for themselves — not merely to your mind, but to the deeper strata of your being.

This is especially important before reciting a blessing. And so, prior to reciting *Baruch Atah Hashem* / 'You, Hashem, are the Source of Blessings', pause, inhale, and think deeply about what these words mean. Hold that meaning in your mind and inhale it, as it were, deep into your body. Then with one powerful exhale, say the words *Baruch Atah Hashem*, entering their sounds fully and riding their vibrations out into the world. Then, pause, inhale, and reflect on the meaning of the next two or three words in the blessing; when you are ready, exhale and articulate them with your whole body. Repeat this sequence until the Brachah is complete.

Another approach would be to say the entire blessing in one powerful and extended exhale — especially if you are struggling with extraneous thoughts that are distracting your focus (A suggestion by many Tzadikim from the last 500 years: *Totzaos Chayim*, 36. *Ohr Tzadikim*, 5:15. *Ohr HaGanuz*, Bechukosai. *Siddur R. Shabtai*, Seder HaLimud).

Whether you say one letter, one word, or many words in one exhale depends on your level of concentration and focus, as well as what comes more naturally and effortlessly. In fact, this can change from day to day, from Tefilah to Tefilah, and even within a single prayer session, page, paragraph or sentence. Sometimes you may feel that taking a pause before every syllable is appropriate and natural, while at other times you may feel like you can hold your concentration on a longer passage, and then let the whole passage come tumbling out of your mouth in a waterfall of sound (See *Tzava'as HaRivash*, 36). The point is to always check in with yourself beforehand to know what is appropriate. Do you currently have an expansive or constricted state of mind? Do you feel like moving quickly or slowly? What do you feel and need in this moment?

Whereas it is much easier to place our full self into the sounds and words of Davening when we are Davening out loud, such as in the earlier stages of *Shacharis* / the Morning Service, it becomes more challenging to enter the sounds and vibrations during the *Amidah* / silent Standing Prayer. Although, the recitation of the Amidah is not actually completely silent, rather it is recited in a very soft voice, just loud enough to be heard by the person uttering the words (*Berachos* 20b. *Berachos,* 31b. Rambam, *Hilchos Tefilah,* 5:9. *Shulchan Aruch,* Orach Chayim, 101:2, *Magen Avraham,* ad loc). As such, riding the vibrations of this Tefilah requires one to either imagine the sounds or to sensitize themselves to hear ever-subtler sounds, like a tuning fork capable of picking up the slightest frequencies.

Elevating the Entire World through the Words of Prayer

When we vocalize our Tefilah out loud, besides clarifying what we want and clearing the mind of all other thoughts, we elevate the entire world. The Osyos of Davening are the mediums through which we are able to not only perform the Avodah of *Ha'ala'as HaNitzutzos* / elevating the sparks of holiness in the world, but to elevate the actual world itself. In other words, the path of the Baal Shem empowers us to elevate the entirety of Creation; not merely to sift out the latent Divine, sparks of Infinity that exist within it. Such full-scale transformation and elevation occurs not merely through an intellectual process, rather entails the engagement of the actual physical world itself. In terms of Davening, this requires the activation of the 'physical' words themselves. To quote the Baal Shem Tov:

"A person should have in mind that through his prayer he is arousing the Osyos and sounds that created the entire world, including both the upper and lower worlds. As such, when he recites his prayers and sings Hashem's praises, he is doing so together with all the worlds and all the creatures. Since he aroused the Osyos, and the Osyos are the life force of all of Creation, everyone and everything is praying with him and helping to elevate his prayer. Additionally, he is elevating all of Creation with his prayers and intentions." (*Darchei Tzedek,* 39. *Amud HaTefilah,* 80)

On one level, we are connecting with the entire world and the entire world is Davening with us. All of Creation is seeking completion. All of Creation yearns for perfection and to be connected to its Source. When we are asking for healing, it is not merely we who are asking, but the whole world is praying with us — all people, all animals, plants, microbes and even minerals that need healing or rectification. When we are asking for rain, so is the earth. Every parched piece of land is yearning for rain, and when we Daven for rain (see *Chulin*, 60b), we become the mouthpiece for the earth, and for everything that needs rain. We are Davening for everything and everything is Davening through us, as there is an intrinsic synergy and interconnectivity between all of life. Thus, our mouths, invested and enlivened with Kavanah, love and awe, become the mouthpiece of all Creation, reaching out and reaching up in collective yearning and redemption.

When we Daven this way, connected to and on behalf of everything, we ourselves are elevated as well, along with everything else.

To review: Divine Osyos form and fill the world. The letters and sounds of Divine speech that say, "Let there be light," for example, are the metaphysical vibrations that trigger corresponding physical vibrations that manifest as energy and eventually matter. In other words, the existence of light is a physical manifestation of the Divine word *Ohr*, spoken into being. In this way, everything in our universe has a unique structure, sound, vibration and rhythm. The countless objects that we observe with our senses are but physical manifestations of their respective spiritual frequencies. As discussed, the Hebrew word for 'thing' is *Devar*, which also literally means 'word' or 'utterance'. Every 'thing' is essentially a product and physical manifestation of a unique Divine 'word' or vibration.

As a result, when we say the words of Davening or a *Brachah* / blessing, we are simultaneously gathering together all the sounds and letters that make up the universe as well. When we then speak them with presence, love and awe, the 'wings' of Tefilah, we too fly up with our prayers, as it were, and elevate the world in the process. Everything in Creation is reflected within everything else. "A human being is an *Olam Katan* / small world, and the entire world is called *Adam Gadol* / a big human being." What happens in a microcosm affects the entire macrocosm, and vice versa.

All the expressions of Divine *Dibbur* / speech that fill the world, carrying their inner spiritual quality into all of Creation — all yearn to reconnect, in a revealed manner, to their Source Above. Through Davening we elevate everything in the world to its Source, and reconnect all of Creation to its Creator. In the words of Rebbe Avraham *HaMalach* / the Angel (the son of the Maggid of Mezritch, who, in turn, was the most important student of the Baal Shem Tov):

"This is why the verse says, 'I long, I yearn for the court of Hashem' (*Tehilim*, 84:3). Speech desires to rise upwards to its Root. What is the root of speech? Speech is rooted in the *Maskilim* / the primal cause of 'awareness', the Divine level of *Chochmah* / wisdom and *Binah* / understanding…. This is what it says regarding Noach: 'Make yourself a *Teivah* / ark (or word)…with lower, middle and upper decks.' Meaning, with regards to speech there are three levels. The lower level is foul and negative speech. In the Ark the lower level was for animal dung. The middle level of speech is ordinary everyday conversation. This corresponds to the Ark's dwelling for the animals themselves. The third level of speech is holy speech, such as Tefilah and Torah spoken with love and awe of Hashem. Through this level of speech all of Creation is elevated back to its Source. This level corresponds to the third deck in the Ark, which was for the dwelling of the humans…." (*Chesed leAvraham*, Noach)

Every *Alul* / effect yearns for its *Ilah* / cause. The whole world, and every creature in it, yearns to be elevated. The letters, sounds and vibrations within each being long to return to their Source in holiness, and this longing is the song of the Unity of Hashem. When we speak or sing holy words in Davening, we are gathering and elevating all of Creation to resonate with the sound of HaKadosh Baruch Hu's Presence.

A Chasidic story tells of a villager who was not able to read the words of Davening, and instead would say, "Master of the Universe You know that I am an ignoramus and I cannot even read the words of Davening. All I know is the Aleph-Beis. But You surely know all the words. So I will recite and give You the letters of the Aleph-Beis and You form them into words."

This is not merely a touching tale, rather it is a profound teaching that reveals the essence of what Davening is really all about: the creative power of the letters of Davening. And in Davening, both the simpleton and the Tzadik are returning the letters of Creation to their Source Above so that new vibrations can be formulated and drawn down, carrying new blessings into this world.

Here are the words of the Magid of Mezritch, the most prominent student of the Baal Shem Tov:

"The deeper purpose of Davening is to elevate and uplift the letters and words (and by extension, the entire world) to their Source Above. The world was created by the downward flow of Divine letters, and our task is to create words from these letters and return them back to Hashem. When we know this process, our Tefilah may be joined to the constant flow of creation: (from) word to word (Asiyah), (from) voice to voice (Yetzirah), (from) breath to breath (Beriah), and (from) thought to thought (Atzilus). The words (we utter) fly upward and appear in front of Hashem, and

Hashem turns to observe these ascending words. Life (then) flows through all the worlds, and our Tefilah is answered. All this occurs instantaneously, and it occurs continually..." (*Ohr Torah*, 58b-59a)

This is the way we practice *Ha'ala'as haNitzutzos* / the elevation of the sparks, as well as the elevation of the entire world. Because of the devastating cosmic *Sheviras haKelim* / Shattering of the Vessels, which occurred due to the intensity of the Divine Infinite Light that was unable to be contained in any vessels, resulting in the implosion of the original vessels of creation, scattering sparks of holiness throughout Creation, the world is not yet in a perfected state. In other words: Creation is still in process, and we can contribute to its crystallization through our Davening.

Throughout the world there are broken, exiled and fallen sparks of Divinity which sadly give rise to feelings of fragmentation and suffering. These sparks are in a state of exile, and thus give off alienating vibrations of despair, death, sin, estrangement, and indifference. What the Arizal calls the *Sheviras haKelim*, the Baal Shem calls *Sheviras HaOsyos* / Shattering of the Letters (שברי כלים והם שברי אותיות: *Ohr HaEmes* (1977), p. 48); the breakdown of language and correct and holy communication. The brokenness of the holy Osyos causes brokenness in the world, thus death, sin and so forth. Our task is therefore to elevate the Osyos back to their Source in holiness and wholeness. Through our Tefilah and holy words, we are able to elevate and return the sparks, these broken letters and words, to their Source and create a Tikkun for the entire world. In this way, all of the broken sounds of the universe are recalibrated and reconfigured into a redemptive prayer, singing the song of Hashem's Oneness and thus revealing unity, health, prosperity and goodness throughout all realms.

In vocalizing the words of Davening, we gather all of the broken 'sounds' of the world, from the screams of sin and negativity to the whimpers and sighs of despair and lifelessness, and transform them all into the song of life, holiness, and goodness. By virtue of our interconnection with all of Creation, and through the power of our positive speech, we have the ability to elevate the essence of the entire world in order to sing the Song of the Creator.

When we positively or prayerfully utter the sound of a *Beis* / 'b' or *Gimel* / 'g', for example, all the Beises and Gimels of the entire world, and all of the phenomena enlivened by those Beises and Gimels, are aligned and uplifted. Even the letters and sounds of other languages, as they are the 'back side' of the original sounds in *Lashon HaKodesh* / The Holy Tongue of Biblical Hebrew*, are elevated and healed. For example, the vibrational

---

* As we have been discussing, the Baal Shem Tov's path in Davening clearly places emphasis on the letters of the 'Aleph-Beis', and specifically 'riding' their resonant waves during articulation. Therefore, it is befitting to now explain the uniqueness of Lashon HaKodesh and its distinction among the languages of the world. *Lashon haKodesh* / the Holy Tongue is the root-system and circuit-board that carries the Divine flow into Creation (See Ramban, *Shemos,* 30:13. Although see Rambam, *Moreh Nevuchim*, 3:8). For instance, the word and reality of *Ohr* / light is created through the sound and sequence of the letters Aleph, Vav and Reish. The word 'table' (*Shulchan* in Lashon haKodesh) comprises the letters Shin, Lamed, Ches, Nun. The letters are the spiritual DNA that configure and express the physical manifestation of the table in the world. The same dynamic is true for every phenomenon. Lashon haKodesh is the essence, source and foundation of all languages. (See Rav Yaakov Emden, *Migdal Oz*, Beis Midos, Aliyas haLashon, 2, regarding a child born in the wild. Note *Pirkei d'Rebbe Eliezer*, Chap. 26, which speaks about Avraham learning Lashon HaKodesh on his own.)

Interestingly, according to Chazal, when a child learns to speak, his father should teach him Lashon HaKodesh and Torah — כשהתינוק מתחיל לדבר, אביו מדבר עמו לשון הקודש ומלמדו תורה (*Sifri*, Ekev, 46. See also *Tosefta*, Chagigah, 1:3. Rashi, *Devarim*, 11:19). Although this is not brought down in the *Bavli* (although see *Mordechai*, Sukkah, 763), and therefore there is no such ruling in the Rif, Rambam, Rosh, and thus Shulchan Aruch. It appears that according to the Rambam (although he does not rule this way L'Halachah, in the *Yad*), this is a Mitzvah of the Torah: *Pirush HaMishnayos* (Avos, 2:1. Note also כל מי שהוא קבוע בארץ ישראל, ואוכל חוליו בטהרה, ומדבר בלשון הקודש וקורא את שמע בבוקר ובערב מובטח לו שהוא מחיי העולם הבא: Yerushalmi, *Shabbos*, 1:3).

Originally, everyone spoke Lashon HaKodesh (*Bereishis*, 11:1, Rashi). "They all spoke the language of the One of the world" (*Yerushalmi, Megillah,* 1:9), this is Lashon HaKodesh, which is One (*Zohar* 2, p. 206a). While today, there are 70 archetypal nations of the world and correspondingly, there are 70 archetypal languages, and each nation is deeply influenced by and connected to their own indigenous language (Maharal, *Gur Aryeh*, Devarim 1:23), Lashon HaKodesh is the *Klal* / the general principle, the unified 'one' tongue, and all the other languages are the *Peratim* / the details, derivatives or manifestations that branch out from the Klal. As the root and source of all language, the Torah contains the seeds of the other 70 languages. Aspects and traces of each derivative *Perat* can be found within the Torah, including 'foreign' words and phrases such as *Yagar Sahadusa: Bereishis*, 3:47. Thus the phrase *Shiv'im Leshonos* / seventy languages has the numerical value of the words *Tziruf HaOsyos* / the combinations of the letters (Rav Avraham Abulafia, *Imrei Shefer*, p. 185), as all the seventy languages are reflections and variations of the initial sounds of the universe, generated by the language of Lashon HaKodesh.

Lashon haKodesh reflects the *Panim* / face of reality and projects the *P'nimius* / inner reality of the Creator within Creation. All of the 70 derivative languages express only the *Achorayim* / back side of reality (See Arizal, discussing the language of Aramaic, which resembles Biblical Hebrew in *Eitz Chayim*, Sha'ar haKadish, 4). Perhaps this is what the Ra'avad (1125–1198) hints to when he writes that all other languages are a *Pirush* / commentary on Lashon HaKodesh (Ra'avad, on the Rambam, *Hilchos Krias Shema*, 2:10). Besides the literal meaning, that translation is always just a commentary of the original, perhaps he is also saying that Lashon haKodesh is expressing the thing itself, whereas other languages are expressing a Pirush on the idea of that thing.

In a state of cosmic *Geulah* / redemption, when everything in the world is in perfect harmony, the Panim and the Achorayim, the Klal and the Peratim, will all be integrated and unified. The seventy languages and the One language, the many nations and the One People, will all be revealed as an organic whole. In a state of exile, separation and misalignment, however, these 70 languages and nations are disconnected from their root, from the One Language and One People. Even now, all peoples and all languages are essentially linked, it is only that the essence has not yet been fully revealed.

Again, in Lashon haKodesh, a table is called a *Shulchan* because its letters, Shin, Lamed, Ches, Nun, are the 'DNA' that animates, and sustains the table. There is an inherent connection between the letters and sound-sequence of the word *Shulchan* and an actual table. Not only is there a connection, but the word / sound / letters of *Shulchan* are the spiritual root vibrations from which an actual table arises and is sustained. However, the English word 'table' is not even similar to the word *Shulchan*. They resonate with completely different sounds and frequencies. The reason a table is called 'table' and not 'chair' is, in a sense, arbitrary. In English, there seems to be no inherent correspondence between the word 'table' and an actual table. Rather, there is an unconscious, collective *consensus* among all English speaking people to refer to something that looks like a table as a 'table' (See Ran, *Nedarim*, 2a.). However, from a deeper perspective, even the word 'table' in English, or in any language, is energetically connected to the physical table for the people who see it that way (see *Likutei Sichos*, 26. p, 308, note 1).

The letter sequence and sounds of the word *Shulchan* are what connect both the conceptual table and the actual table to the very same 'essence' and 'source'. This is the *Panim* / the inner face of the table that is expressed in Lashon HaKodesh. The English word 'table' is related to the *Achorayim* / rear dimension of the actual table. While in exile, and as a result of the *Sheviras haKelim* / Shattering of the Vessels, English speaking people relate to the concept and object of a table by means of the word 'table'.

This understanding of the ultimate root connection and redemptive potential of all human languages helps us understand why many *Mekubalim* / Kabbalists chose to employ Greek, Arabic, Aramaic or whatever was their own native tongue, in their esoteric studies and writings. They would look for *Gematriyos* / numerical values, and various other linguistic hints and allusions hidden within the structures of these languages just as they would with Hebrew, in order to access and arrive at deeper wellsprings of meaning (*Chayei Olam HaBa* (Abulafia) p. 148. Or such hints in Yiddish, *Bnei Yissaschar*, Tishrei, Ma'amar 2:21. See also *Regel Yeshara*, Oven (from the Sefer *Dan Yadin. Emek HaMelech*, 20:4). *Pri Haaretz*, Vayigash. *She'eirus Yisrael*, Sha'ar 1:2. *Divrei Torah* (Munkatch), Mahadura, 2:7. Rebbe Rayatz, *Sefer HaSichos*, Tav / Shin / Hei, p. 8). From this deeper perspective it is not arbitrariness or mere unconscious consensus that a table is referred to as a table and not a chair. Rather, there is a real resonance and relationship. However, it is still an indirect relationship, via the 'back' of the spiritual reality of the table.

Every people, every nation, and in fact every individual person sees and experiences reality in their own distinct way. The manner in which objects and subjects are referred to and named reflects the manner in which these objects and subjects are experienced and appreciated. We can glean deeper meanings and gather many holy sparks from the numerous languages people speak and the words people use, even though the process will be indirect.

The emergence of all worlds and all realities — inner and outer, 'face' and 'back', redemption and exile — is made possible by the seemingly infinite permutations of the original Ten Utterances of Creation. All of the particular sounds, vibrations, letters, words and languages of the world are rooted within Lashon HaKodesh. The myriad of possible permutations and re-combinations of the 22 letters is what gives birth to all the languages of the world.

Eventually, the world will be healed from its state of brokenness and exile, and will be whole and harmonious once again. A time will come when the inside and the outside, the 'front' and the 'back', the spiritual and the physical, the soul and the body will be revealed as one. All languages, sounds and expressions will have done *Teshuvah* / realignment and returned to their root in the Language of One. The sound of Lashon HaKodesh in the future will be enhanced by the accumulation and ingathering of all the languages of the entire world, reunited and redeemed, singing and declaring the Oneness of Hashem.

energies of the 'b' in the word / concept of 'bad', is uplifted when we say the words *Baruch Atah* / Blessed are You. The 'g' sound in the word-concept of 'glutton' is healed when we pronounce *Gadol Hashem* / Great is Hashem. Once articulated in prayer, the *Chayus* / energy of the 'b' and 'g' sounds, and all of the negative concepts they enliven, are metaphysically tied to holier words and loftier concepts, causing the roots of the negative qualities of 'badness' or 'gluttony' to be weakened and eventually to wither away.

This is the deeper purpose of Davening: to elevate and uplift the sounds, letters and words, and by extension the entire world, to their Source Above. We collect the broken letters of the world and bring them back to Hashem, where they are reunited in wholeness and purity with their Infinite Source.

Riding the Waves of Tefilah

As we have been exploring, through Davening we gather all the fallen sparks, letters, words, sounds, vibrations, and expressions of the world, and by extension, the world itself, in order to elevate them. By following the *Derech* / path of the Baal Shem Tov, which directs us to let go of all thought and intellection, no matter how lofty, in the moment of articulation, we are able to enter fully into the sounds and vibrations of these

---

"*Az* / then I will cause the nations (to speak) a pure language, that they may all call upon the name of Hashem, to serve Him with one consent" (*Tzephaniyah*, 3:9), says the *Navi* / Prophet. This means that in the times of Moshiach, in a redeemed and perfected world of unity, all Peratim will be re-connected and returned home into the Klal. All the scattered and broken sounds of the universe will be unified into the one great sound of a healed humanity, declaring *Hashem Echad* / Hashem is Oneness. Following the Tower of *Bavel* / Babel there was a splintering of the One language into many languages. There will come a time when everything will return to the One (*Yalkut Shimoni*, Tzephaniyah, 3:567).

Tefilah is the beginning of this redemptive process, the Geulah of all sounds of the world into a unified sound, singing Hashem's praise, unifying the worlds.

sacred letters and words. Once we have embodied and intoned the Tefilah, the sounds ripple out and fly 'upward'. And as the sounds move upward, so do we, as it were. We too can ride the waves of sound, so to speak, ever higher and deeper within.

Within the sounds of our Davening are gathered all the sounds of the universe. Each of these sounds is then equipped with the 'wings' of love and awe as transmitted through our impassioned vocalization. With these 'wings', the sounds surge upward and we are able to ride these waves. Although this is primarily a metaphor for a metaphysical process, there is actually a corresponding visceral sensation of movement when we pronounce the words of Davening in this way. In fact, we can become more deeply aware of the physical phenomena of sound waves, along with their metaphysical impact, even in the 'silent' Amidah, as we must become hyper-sensitive to attune to such subtle vibrations. By investing ourselves in them completely we *Bo El HaTeivah* / "enter into the words of Tefilah," just as we would enter into a vehicle. In this 'vibrational vehicle' we can ride along with these spiritually charged letters all the way up to the root of all creation.

Four Worlds

Before exploring another related teaching from the Baal Shem Tov, a few words about the "Four Worlds" are in order. Here is the most basic synopsis of this idea, relevant to understanding the following teaching of the Baal Shem: There are four inner worlds, one above and within the other. From the higher/deeper level to the lower/more external level, they are as follows:

Atzilus / Closeness or Emanation, the spiritual unified world. This is the world of Thought, the Divine 'attribute' of *Chochmah* / wisdom, pure, undifferentiated consciousness. The world as it exists in the Thought of the Creator is still considered as *Ayin* / no-thing-ness, as it is just a supernal conception of reality, vastly set apart from our physical reality. *Yesh* / the independent existence of Creation begins to manifest in the next inner world: *Beriah* / Creation. This is the world of *Neshimah* / Breath, and the world of Binah / understanding and discernment, and it is where the *Etzem* / essence of things themselves is created. Then comes *Yetzirah* / Formation, the world of *Kol* / Sound, and of Emotions. Finally, the world of *Asiyah* / Actualization is the world of *Dibbur* / Speech, and of Actions. *Similar to our own lives, first we have a thought for an idea. Then we speak the idea; although Divine speech creates and our speech, for the most part, only contextualizes. For a thought to become a word and for words to be actualized, there are three basic stages: breath, sound, then actual speech. Every word we project is rooted in an exhale that becomes a 'sound' that is further defined as a letter and then a word.

In general, the cosmic process of creation (of *Yesh* / existence) begins in Beriah, and ends in Asiyah. After the original Divine Thought to create emerges out of Ayin, the actual creation of a Yesh begins; first within Beriah, the world of breath, which is the inner essence of voice, sound and speech. Then there is a *Kol* / sound in the world of Yetzirah. And then

---

* As the philosophers write, there are four dimensions of any given object — Chomer, Poel, Tzurah and Tachlis (*Moreh Nevuchim*, 1:69. Maharal, *Derush L'Shabbos HaGadol. Pirush HaGra*, Mishlei, 1:1) — and these are the same as the Four Worlds that the Mekubalim speak of: *Poel* / Maker, meaning the Creator, is represented by Atzilus. *Chomer* / Substance, the first emergence of Creation, is Beriah. *Tzurah* / form, where Creation assumes form, is Yetzirah. *Tachlis* / actualization, finalization of an objective, is Asiyah. These four Stages of Creation, Chomer, Tzurah, Poel and Tachlis, correspond to the four letters in the essential Name of Hashem (*Pirush HaGra*, Sifra Detzniusa, Likutim): the Yud-Hei-Vav-Hei. 1) Atzilus/Thought/Unity/Yud. Beriah/Breath/Hei. Yetzirah/Voice/Sound/Vav. Asiyah/Speech/Hei.

there is an actualization, the Divine spoken word, the Dibbur of creation in Asiyah: "Let there be light, and there was [actual] light."

It is thus, through Divine breath, sound, and speech that Divine inspiration becomes a living word, giving rise to a physical vibration of energy, which is then transformed and solidified as matter in a world of duality.

Beyond the expressive worlds of breath, sound and speech, is the world of Unity, the world of Thought, the world of Atzilus. In this world of pure thought, all exists within the mind of the Creator, metaphorically speaking, before being externally articulated and manifested through breath, sound and speech. Atzilus is the "silence' before the vocalization of an actual Yesh, which, again, happens through the process spanning from Beriah to Asiyah.

In Summary: Within the *Ohr Ein Sof* / Infinite Light, a Divine thought arises to create. In the realm of Atzilus, there is an entire 'conceptual' structure of what this 'other' will look like and how it will function. Similarly, before you create something; you have an idea in your mind about what you would like to create, and then you actually go ahead and create it. This is the creative process as encoded in the Four Worlds.

Now for the teaching of the Baal Shem Tov:

"In Tefilah, one must place all his strength in the words he is Davening. In this manner, he shall move (via his chanting and reciting the letters) from letter to letter until he forgets (releases the grip of attention on) his corporeality, which will allow him to notice how the letters are combining with each other (and becoming words), and this (unification of sounds) arouses a degree of pleasure (as the individual syllables of each letter are combined to form words, harmonious sounds are produced by these combinations, which produces an experience of aesthetic pleasure for one sensitive enough to appreciate it).

And just as the combinations of certain sounds, in a pleasant song or melody, for instance, can arouse a sense of physical pleasure, how much more must this be so on an emotional level. This is the world of Yetzirah, the realm of the emotions (first the sounds are physically pleasurable to our ears, and then they register deeper within our hearts as they arouse an emotional response).

And then (as one continues to pray and senses the physical and emotional pleasantness of the sounds and tunes he is producing) he comes to (experience) "letters of thought," in which he no longer hears what he is praying (or chanting). This is the world of Beriah, the world of the intellect and mindfulness (he thus moves from the external world of sound, to the world of aroused emotions, to a subtle world of quietness in which he is still vocalizing the prayers, just in a much more quiet and relaxed manner).

After all this he will come (automatically) to the level of *Ayin* / no-thing-ness, where he will (experientially) lose all of his physical potentials (his body will go limp and he will enter into a trance-like state without movement or speech). This is (experientially) the world of Atzilus, the level of *Chochmah* / pure consciousness." (*Keser Shem Tov*, 2:17b. *Baal Shem Tov Al HaTorah*, Amud HaTefilah, 16)

This technique of gathering individual letters together to form words of Davening, and then to enter the silence of pure consciousness, is a form of *Hispashtus haGashmiyus* / divestment from (entanglement with) physicality and ego, which is the ideal state we need to access in order to really immerse ourselves in Davening, and for our Davening to have a real impact (*Berachos*, 32b. *Tur* and *Shulchan Aruch*, Orach Chayim, 98. Shaloh HaKadosh, *Asarah*

Hilulim, p. 319. *Nefesh Hachayim*, Sha'ar 2:14).

The more we enter into the letters, vibrations and sounds of the Davening, the more the 'rational' content of the words recedes. The words chanted in this state, in effect become a kind of trance inducing drone which provide us with a launch pad into deeper states of consciousness. The sounds themselves marginalize and silence all other sounds and stimuli until the mind is quiet and still, allowing one to go progressively deeper and deeper until one experiences a total Hispashtus HaGashmiyus.

In the teachings of Rav Avraham Abulafia, the practice of 'chanting' the actual letters of the Aleph-Beis as a means to achieve Hispashtus and Deveikus is prominently discussed. A few hundred years later, there were great Tzadikim and Mekubalim who utilized such methods of repetitive 'chanting' to attain deeply transcendent states of consciousness and Hispashtus HaGashmiyus.

For example: The illustrious sage Rebbe Yoseph Caro practiced a form of repetitive recitation specifically using passages from the Mishnah, the essential text of the oral Torah, in order to make contact with the Maggid, or angelic interlocutor of the Mishnah (See *Magid Meisharim*, Hakdamah, by Rav Shlomo Alkabetz. *Shaloh*, Meseches Shavuos, p. 4). During this same period, Rebbe Chayim Vital records a similar practice involving the Mishnah, where through the repetition of certain sounds from the text one enters higher, deeper states of Hishpashtus. In his words:

"...To attain any type of higher awareness and spiritual intuition you need to...isolate yourself...and divest yourself (in your mind) from your physical self...once this is accomplished, begin to read a Mishnah, whichever one you choose. Read it aloud many times over and over again...And when you are overcome with exhaustion from chanting the Mishnah, if you are worthy (refined and inwardly cleansed) it is possible that the spirit of the teacher (of the Mishnah you are chanting) will rest upon your lips… If you are not worthy of this high level… As a result of the rapid movements of the mouth during the repetitions of the Mishnah, your mouth will eventually stop moving on its own, and you will begin to fall into a kind of waking-sleep (a hypnagogic state), and then in this liminal state you will 'see' how you are receiving an answer to your question…" (*Sha'arei Kedushah*, 4, Sha'ar 2, Hakdamah 1).

A similar idea is expressed in the teachings of the holy Baal Shem Tov, as we have been discussing. The more we are able to enter into the sonic and vibrational dimension of the words themselves, rather than getting stuck in their semantic meanings, the more we are able to access an experience beyond even sound: a sentient silence, a state of Hispashtus and Ayin.

This process is as follows: we begin with the letters themselves, as we slowly lose ourselves within their vibrations the primary sounds of the letters morph into words, from here the words take on a kind of musical quality, endlessly resonating and reverberating as instruments in an orchestra. In this way, we are able to move from the world of Asiyah, the physical dimension of letters, into the inner dimension of our emotions, the world of Yetzirah, where letters form words. There, our emotions are aroused by the stringing together of the various sounds of the letters and words, and our heart opens to their Source.

What began as a single letter-sound, becomes a word and then many words and many sounds. There is a subtle inner joy and pleasure generated by slowly moving from one sound into the next, like playing consecutive chords of music. This is the inner experience of Yetzirah. From this moving experience of having our emotions aroused by the music of the letters we are able to move deeper into ourselves as we become more sensitized to the contemplative introspection of the world of Beriah, the dimension of mindfulness. The aroused emotions become subtler and subtler and so too does our chanting of the prayers. Similarly, during Shacharis, we move from singing the 'verses of praise' loudly, to a quieter, more tranquil state when we sit down and recite the Shema and its adjacent blessings.

Finally, there is a complete collapse of all sound and noise, both external and internal. The mind is cleared of all thoughts, feelings and sensations, and we arrive at a motionless state of total oneness, connected with the *Ohr* / Light of the Ein Sof present within the letters. This is the inner world of Atzilus, and within Davening this is the Amidah, although these states can occur on all levels and in all parts of Davening.*

Another way of mapping this, from above to below, is that Atzilus is the Infinite *Ohr* of the letters. Beriah is the *letters* themselves. Yetzirah is the way the letters come together to form *words*, the *Tziruf* / combination of letters. And Asiyah is the outcome of these combinations, the *actuality of the articulation*. In Davening we move from below to above: from the sonic pronunciation of the words in Asiyah to the musical tonalities of Yetzirah, to the letters themselves in Beriah, until we reach the Ohr within and beyond the letters, the Infinite Ohr of the Ein Sof in Atzilus. This is the ladder of prayer that takes us from longing to light, and back again.

---

* This is the deeper reason why we should not skip ahead during Davening. According to strict Halachah, a person may be able to skip ahead if they come late to Minyan and the Minyan is ahead, yet the Mekubalim teach that we should, nonetheless, not skip. Our sages tell us לעולם יסדיר אדם תפלתו ואח״כ יתפלל / "A person should always arrange his prayer (in his mind) and only then pray" (*Rosh Hashanah*, 35a). Says the Ben Ish Chai (*Ben Yehoyada*, ad loc), this means a person must always go through the *Seder* / order of the Davening and Worlds, and only then Daven the Amidah. This is because, normally, you cannot move from your mundane life into the highest realms without passing through the successive stages.

Letters as Modes of Spiritual Transport

Letters are likened to horses; they are a mode of transportation (*Tikunei Zohar*, Hakdamah, 8a. Tikun 5, 20b). If you have an idea in your mind that you want to communicate to another person, you need letters and words to carry it from inside your head out into the world. The words of Davening, when uttered with love and awe, fly and rise upwards, like dancing flames or billowing smoke (*Ohr HaMeir*, Shir Hashirim). We are able to ride on these heaven-bound horses, these waves of sound, these clouds of glory, as they fly ever upward.

Through this method of Davening, not only are we able to experience the rush of emotions of Yetzirah, the subtleness and tranquility of Beriah, and the stillness, no-thingness and Ohr of Atzilus, but we are actually able to enter into in these realms themselves. The letters (the horses) are created via our vocal utterances in the world of Asiyah. From here they move upward (and inward) all the way to Atzilus and beyond — into, and uniting with, the pure Ein Sof. By entering deeply into them we are able to 'catch a ride' and move along with them through each of the Four Worlds (Rebbe Yaakov Yoseph of Ostro (1738–1791), *Sefer Rav Yeivi*, Tehilim, 45). In Davening, we are thus moving through the inner and upper worlds, pulling all of Creation along with us, and elevating everything back to its Source in the Light of Hashem. This process transforms the world of *Tohu* / chaos into a world of *Tikun* / attunement, perfection and unity.

Parenthetically, it should be noted, that even מחשבות זרות / *Mach'shavos Zaros* / distracting or foreign thoughts can (G-d forbid) catch a ride with your words in Davening (*Tzava'as HaRivash*, 71), therefore they must be addressed and dealt with. This particular issue of intruding thoughts requires a lengthy discussion, and will be discussed at the end of the text. However, for our purposes, it is important to mention here that according to the

Baal Shem Tov, sometimes (the positive Sparks within) negative thoughts enter a person's mind because they too wish to be freed from their exile and return to their root in the upper worlds (*Ben Poras Yoseph*, p. 50b-c. *Divrei Moshe*, Lech Lecha). Thus, they seek to hook into our consciousness and catch a ride upwards through our Davening. This topic is explored and explained in much more detail in the appendix of this book.

Movement Towards Unity within Sonic and Visual Dimensions

This movement in Davening that we are describing through the sonic dimension of the Aleph-Beis, from the fullness of sound and emotions to the subtleness and stillness of silence, can also occur within the *visual* dimension of the letters. As the Baal Shem Tov teaches: Just as the sound waves can be ridden as a horse, so to speak, upwards and inwards, from Asiyah to Atzilus and beyond, so can the forms of the letters be harnessed using their visual aspects. Additionally, we can couple the sonic and visual dimensions of the letters in a more multi-sensory approach.

There are two paths in life. The first is represented by the regular order of the letters of the Aleph-Beis, flowing from the first letter Aleph, which is the number 1, toward the final letter, Tav, which is 400. The second path is represented by the reverse order of the Aleph-Beis, called תשר"ק, beginning with Tav, Shin, and Reish, and proceeding to Aleph ("Backwards is the secret of Gevurah": *Zohar* 2, 52a. And Din. *Zohar* 2, 186a. As it requires *Gevurah* / strength to move from the place of duality and multiplicity into a space of unity and oneness. This is also called 'reflective light'). Inwardly, the 'reverse order' means a person is elevating himself and his consciousness from the multiplicity and complexity of Asiyah toward the simple unity of Atzilus, until he reaches (relative to his own level) even beyond the *Tzimtzum* / contraction of the *Ein Sof* / the Infinite Light, to the place of Aleph, perfect oneness. This is the trajectory of Tefilah, transporting us from the plurality of phenomenal existence back to the unity of Hashem. As the Maggid of Mezeritch teaches: "Hashem creates *Yesh m'Ayin* / something from nothing, it is our task to create *Ayin m'Yesh* / nothing from something"; where Ayin represents the Ein Sof, the Infinite Divine.

Beyond the letters of the Aleph-Beis themselves, and at their root, there is *Ohr* / light (see also Ramak, *Shiur Komah*, 7) — the *Ohr Ein Sof* / the Infinite Light prior to all manifestations, revelations and numbers. Thus, as the letters progress from Aleph and the Source of Unity, they become more revealed and multiplied. In this respect, the 'lowest' number in the Aleph-Beis is actually the closest to its Source beyond numbers and forms; Aleph is therefore both the 'lowest' (in terms of quantity) and the 'highest' (in terms of quality) letter, whereas the final letter Tav, which equals four-hundred, is both the 'highest' (in terms of quantity) and the 'lowest' (in terms of quality) letter.

Aleph is the first expression of the One, although it still remains beyond and prior to all forms and letters. Beis, the second letter, is then considered to be two Alephs, Gimel three Alephs, and so on until Tav, which is four hundred Alephs (see *Toldos Yaakov Yoseph*, Bereishis. *Toldos Aaron*, Likutim, p. 493). In essence, there is only One Light. This One Light is first reflected in a single, unified vessel, the Aleph, and then into two such vessels, the Beis, and then three, the Gimel, until the four hundred Alephs of Tav.

In the visual practice of ק"תשר, the reverse flow of the Aleph-Beis, one begins by visualizing the letter Tav, and/or intoning a word that begins with a Tav, 'seeing' it in their mind's eye as an orb of light with 400 refractions. Next, one does the same procedure with the letter Shin or a word beginning with the Shin, shining out with 300 refractions, and then progressing through each letter, ascending through the Aleph-Beis, from the many back to the One. In this practice one visualizes and vividly experiences the metaphysical movement from many lights back to one great, unified orb of light, Aleph, the letter of Oneness.

The letter Aleph (א) is composed of a Yud below, a slanted Vav, and a Yud above. Metaphorically, traveling through the Aleph means moving from the lower Yud through the interface of the Vav to the higher Yud. The 'dot' of the higher Yud is the first point, the 'first manifestation' of form following the Tzimtzum. From there, one pierces through the higher Yud, and goes beyond it, to the pure Infinite Light of Hashem beyond the Tzimtzum. And this is the deeper meaning of the name *Yaakov* spelled in reverse, בקע י / *Boka-Yud* / 'pierce the Yud', and return to the Ein Sof beyond all form.

In this way, one traverses through 'many lights' to one indescribable light, the higher Yud in the Aleph, and finally beyond the Yud, where all imagery implodes into an 'experience' of pure *Ayin* / ineffable formlessness, free from all duality.

This path of riding the letters is visual, and not necessarily part of the path of sound. However, as mentioned, we can join these two paths when Davening for maximum engagement and impact.

Words of Tefilah Create Reality

A major Halachic component of prayer is בקשת צרכיו / *Bakashas Tz'ra-chav* / 'requesting what is needed'. In fact, it is the 'need', and our human desire to reach out for help, that *creates* the positive Mitzvah to pray.*

---

* The Rambam posits that there is a Mitzvah to Daven at least once a day: *Sefer HaMitzvos*, Mitzvah 5. *Hilchos Tefilah*, 1:1. When the verse commands us, "You shall serve Hashem your G-d," which is the Torah source for Tefilah, this can be understood in three ways: a) This Mitzvah is a once in a lifetime Mitzvah — at least once in our lives we shall serve

Hashem in fact puts us into difficult situations and circumstances so that we need to Daven. From this perspective, we are not praying in order to get out of trouble, rather the reverse: trouble and difficulty were created so that we would Daven to Hashem.

How does this idea, that we Daven out of a state of need, mesh with everything spoken about until now? What about presence, awe, love, and divesting from the physical in order to experience *Deveikus* / cleaving to Hashem? How does all of this connect with the Bakashah aspect of prayer?

Davening, as explored above, is all about 'riding' the words of Tefilah to reach deeper levels of selfless Deveikus, while prayers of request seem to be self-centered (Although from Chazal it seems that Tefilah and Bakashah are two

---

Hashem and pray — which is an absurd interpretation, as the Kesef Mishnah, *ad loc*, writes, ועבודה זו צריכה שתהיה בכל יום שאם אינה בכל יום אולי נבא לומר שהיא פעם אחת בכל ימיו וזה ממה שלא יסבלהו הדעת. b) The Mitzvah is a continuous Mitzvah, applicable every moment. c) Although the *Kiyum* / fulfilment of this Mitzvah is anytime we pray, the *Chiyuv* / obligation is to pray at least once a day. This is the opinion of the Rambam.

The Ramban is of the opinion that there is no Mitzvah from the Torah to pray daily, and that one should only pray when in need, and when there is a need then there is a Mitzvah of the Torah to pray: Ramban on *Sefer HaMitzvos*, 5. See also *Sefer HaMitzvos Katan*, 11, quoted in the *Magen Avraham*, Orach Chayim, 106:2. Note, *Sefer HaChinuch*, Mitzvah קריאת שמע וברכת המזון דאורייתא, ותפלה דרבנן: *Berachos*, 21a. 433.

Even according to the Rambam, the source in the Torah where the Mitzvah to Daven each day is derived, is the verse "You shall serve Hashem your G-d (which is Tefilah, *Ta'anis*, 2a) and He shall bless your bread and water" (*Shemos*, 23:25). The Torah is implying that just as water and bread is needed each day, the same is true for prayer: *Kiryas Sefer* beginning of Hilchos Tefilah. See also *Pri Chadash*, Orach Chayim, 89:1. *Mahari Perlo, Sefer HaMitzvos Rasag*, Esei Beis (1973), p.56. The main point, according to all opinions, is that our 'need' is what creates the Torah Mitzvah to pray.

Tefilah is also a Torah-based Mitzvah, according to the Ramban, on Yom Tov: Ramban, *Vayikra*, 23:2 — וטעם מקראי קדש שיהיו ביום הזה כולם קרואים ונאספים לקדש אותו כי מצוה היא על ישראל להקבץ בבית האלקים ביום מועד לקדש היום בפרהסיא בתפלה והלל לקל בכסות נקיה ולעשות אותו יום משתה. This is the way the Beis Yoseph understands the Ramban: *Orach Chayim*, 487.

separate ideas: *Avodah Zarah,* 7b). In other words: While Davening is a path to experience total *Bitul HaYesh* / the negation of ego and self-centeredness (*Torah Ohr,* Megilas Esther, 122c), it seems Bakashah is all about yourself and your needs. Moreover, what does sound and vibration have to do with whether or how your Bakashah is answered? It would seem that these are two completely opposite approaches to prayer.

A grandson of the Baal Shem Tov, Rebbe Moshe Chayim Ephrayim of Sudilkov (1748–1800), known for the book he wrote called *Degel Machaneh Ephrayim,* writes that he heard from his grandfather the following question and answer. On the one hand, the *Zohar* teaches that a person who prays for his selfish needs is likened to a wild dog who runs about barking *Hav, Hav* (woof, woof). *Hav,* in Aramaic, means 'give'. And so, someone who prays for his own selfish needs is like a wild dog barking orders for Hashem to, 'Give, give!' (*Tikkunei Zohar,* Tikkun 6). Yet, on the other hand, one who does not Daven for *Parnasah* / livelihood everyday lacks in faith. So, the question is, which one is it? Should we Daven for Parnasah? Should our Tefilah be inspired or focused on Bakasha? Or should we not care about our selfish needs and Daven in a state of pure Deveikus?*

---

* There are various ways this conflict is resolved in the teachings of the Baal Shem Tov, besides the one that will be explored in this text. For example, as the Degel (*Ibid,* and Bechukosai) writes, when a person has lack in his life he feels pain. Who feels the pain? It is the *Chayus* / aliveness, the vitality of the person that suffers. And the Chayus is from the Shechinah. In this way it is the Shechinah that is really in pain when a person is in pain, and we need to Daven for the Shechinah — our Chayus — in order for the pain to be alleviated. Another way of saying it, is that every lack in this world is analogous to a lack, as it were, in the Light of the Shechinah. The Shechinah is in exile when we are in exile: *Megilah,* 29a. When we do not have what we need in order to maximize our spiritual potential, that is not only a deficiency in us, it is also representative of a lack of Hashem's Presence being expressed in this world. By fulfilling our needs within a spiritual context, the Shechinah can thus be more revealed and manifest within the world and within our lives. See also *Likutei Sichos,* 19, p. 294-297.

In the teachings of the Baal Shem Tov on Tefilah, much is dedicated to the mechanics of Tefilah: how does it actually work, what is Bakashah, how are Tefilos actually answered? On these topics too, there are many profound *Chidushim* / novel ideas that the Baal Shem reveals. Here are a few potent teachings addressing the matter of personal requests.

Davening is a dialogue, a two-way flow. Besides elevating the entire world and ourselves, through the sounds of our Davening, as discussed, the recitation of these sacred sounds creates a corresponding objective reality in this world. In other words, in a 'reverse process', as it were, while our words and sounds are moving 'upward' and 'inward' and dissolving within the Ein Sof, they are also moving 'downward' and 'outward' from the heat of Oneness, as they manifest in the world. When, in Davening, we intone the word *Refa'einu* / "heal us," for example, new healing vibrations are being drawn down into creation.

Simply, our reality is created through our Davening. Normally, Tefilah is understood as a paradigm in which people beseech HaKadosh Baruch Hu Above to grant all of their heart's desires, requesting that their needs may be fulfilled in the most immediate and befitting way. The Baal Shem Tov revealed that the answers to our prayers arrive and materialize in the very manner in which the prayers are formulated. When we say "heal us" with Deveikus, we are maximizing our contribution to the revelation of healing *Chayus* / vitality and *Shefa* / flow. When we Daven 'bless us,' with Deveikus, we are co-creating blessings in our lives in the deepest way.

Our words of Davening, and the way we communicate them and give them context, determine the way our reality actually manifests. This is true on a cosmic, as well as a microcosmic level, and is also true (even if we Daven without deep Deveikus) on a psychological level.

On a psychological level, our words of prayer function as follows. Human speech is a limited reflection of the unlimited potential of Divine speech. Divine speech actually creates reality. "Hashem said, 'Let there be light,' and there was light." Although we do not have the power to 'create' reality in the way that Hashem does, we can shape and influence *our* reality through our speech. In this way, we are co-creators of our life and world; Hashem's words create the objective 'context', while our words create the subjective 'content'.

Another way of phrasing this dynamic is that human communication is dialogic in its very nature. Human speech only arose in the context of an 'other'; it did not exist before the appearance of subjects other than the self. Divine language, on the other hand, is inherently monologic: "Hashem said, 'Let there be light', and [then] there was light." Divine monologue itself *creates* the 'other', and with it the potential for dialogue.

This is one profound distinction between human and Divine language. However, in a state of Deveikus, our words and expressions have a Divine-like quality to them. They are, as it were, imbued with the power to literally and objectively create.

When we Daven with presence, Ahavah, Yirah and Deveikus, this creative power is vested within us. Through Ahavah and Yirah, which are the wings that allow us to fly 'upwards' in Deveikus, we become one with the Source of all Life, as it were, and our speech and Davening become the instruments through which Divine resonance vibrates into Creation. Not that we *personally* have the power to create — rather the converse. It is only when we empty ourselves completely of ego and experience *Hispashtus HaGashmiyus* / divestment of materiality and separate individuality, that the Divine speech can reverberate through us and create new realities on the ground. As the *Navi* / prophet says, "And I placed My words into your mouth, and with the shadow of My hand I covered you, to plant the heavens and to establish the earth" (*Yeshayahu*, 51:16). This means that when a person is in a state of *Bitul* / self-nullification and Deveikus, in total His-pashtus HaGashmiyus, he has the power to "plant heaven and establish earth," not merely to create subjective realities, but to create the context within which objective realities manifest.

In a state of Deveikus, in which the person is connected with the Ohr of Atzilus, one's Davening is vested with the power of ותגזר אומר ויקם לך / "You shall also decree (say) a matter, and it shall be established for you" (*Iyov*, 22:28), as a Tzadik decrees and Hashem fulfills the decree (*Ta'anis*, 23a. *Tana D'vei Eliyahu*, 2). On this level, ישראל ממשלותיו / "Israel is His dominion" (*Tehilim*, 114:2), meaning, *Kaviyachol* / so-to-speak, we have dominion over the decrees from Above. As everyone of Yisrael has a *Nekudah* / point of a Tzadik within, we thus all have the ability to be a *Tzadik Gozer* / "a Tzadik [who] decrees and HaKadosh Baruch Hu fulfills it" (*Likutei Moharan*, Tinyana, 2). Although of course, no one can 'force' the Hand of Heaven, and paradoxically the final and highest level of Davening is total surrender, as mentioned. Yet, the more one aligns with the Divine in such surrender, the more one is granted access to the ultimate power of co-creation, becoming collaborative partners with HaKadosh Baruch Hu in manifesting reality.

In this state of Deveikus, we are not Davening 'to' Hashem, so to speak, rather, Hashem is Davening through us, as just mentioned: ואשים דברי בפיך ובצל ידי כסיתיך לנטע שמים וליסד ארץ / "And I placed My words into your mouth...to plant the heavens and to establish the earth" (*Yeshayahu*, 51:16). When we Daven with Deveikus not only are we a *Shutaf* / partner with HaKadosh Baruch Hu "to plant heavens and found earth" (*Nefesh HaChayim*, Sha'ar 2:10), we become unified with Hashem, as it were, and Hashem thus places His words into our mouth. When we begin the Amidah, the peak of Davening, and say, "Hashem open my mouth," we are deeply becoming aware that not only is Hashem opening up our mouth, but in fact, the

Presence of the Shechinah is now resting upon us and voicing the words of Davening through our lips (*Baal Shem Tov Al HaTorah*, Bereishis, 96. Thus *Safa /* lip and *Shechinah* are numerically 385. *Siddur HaGra b'Nigleh u'bNistar*, p. 106. Also *Lashon* / tongue is 386, Shechinah with the word itself).

Such is the power of Davening in a state of Deveikus.

Sefer Yetzirah correlates the *Bris Milah* / the 'covenant of circumcision' with the *Bris haLashon* / the 'covenant of the tongue' (1:3). The verse, "Death and life are in the power of the tongue" (*Mishlei*, 18:21), can be understood metaphorically, as well as literally, meaning that our words possess the power to hurt or heal, and should thus be wielded consciously. Just as the covenant of circumcision (the procreative organ) creates new life, the same is true with our mouth and power of speech. Our words, when invested and infused with Deveikus, have 'procreative' power.

The well-known magical idiom *Ab'ra keDab'ra* is a Talmudic-like phrase meaning "I will create (*a-Bara*) as I speak (*ke-Dab'ra*)." Our Sages tell us (*Sanhedrin*, 65b) that *Rava Bara Gavra* / "The great sage Rava created a man" — a being referred to as a *Golem*. The classic commentator Rashi writes that Rava did this by employing the techniques of *Sefer Yetzirah* and the art of letter combinations (see also *Maharshal* ad loc. *Sefer haBahir*, 196). While in a state of Deveikus, the sage Rava was able to use his power of speech to transform an inanimate lump of clay into an animate, living being. (A Golem is a being with limited faculties; it has a Nefesh, the lowest level of animating soul, but does not have a Ruach or Neshamah, and thus it does not have the power of speech or free will. See Rav Meir Ben Gabbai, *Avodas HaKodesh*, 2:28.)

In a deep state of Tefilah, reality is not acted upon us, rather reality emanates from us.

The primary form of speech is Divine speech, and as such, it is not merely a revelation or expression *to* another, rather, such speech generates and creates an externality from within an internality, thereby creating an 'other'. Divine Speech is not addressed to someone, rather it initiates the creation *of* a someone or a something. As such, when we Daven and speak the words of Tefilah with Deveikus, unified with the Source of Speech, our words have the power to not only define or contextualize, but to create *Yesh MeAyin* / something from Nothing, Keviyachol.

With Ahavah, Yirah and Deveikus we Can Change Reality

הנסתרת לי-ה-ה-ו-ה אלקינו והנגלת לנו ולבנינו / "The hidden things belong to Hashem (Yud-Hei-Vav-Hei) our G-d, but the things that are revealed belong to us and to our children" (*Devarim*, 29:28). Regarding this verse, the Magid of Mezritch, the primary student of the Baal Shem Tov, teaches, "The hidden," mentioned in this verse, refers to the *inner* world of man, that is, his Ahavah and Yirah, and it is these emotions that connect to the upper, inner worlds Above. "The hidden" is also connected to the Yud and Hei of Hashem's name (and the worlds of Atzilus/Yud, and Beriah/upper Hei). "The hidden things belong to Hashem" — to the Yud-Hei of Hashem. "But the things that are revealed belong to us"; the 'revealed' refers to our outward expressions, our *Kol* / voice and *Dibbur* / speech, which correspond to the Vav and Hei of Hashem's Name (and the worlds of Yetzirah/Vav and Asiyah/Hei). When we sound the words of Tefilah with Kol and Dibbur, revealing our inner feelings outwardly, we affect the lower, outer, revealed worlds. Thus, it "belongs to us and to our children" (*Maggid Devarav leYaakov*, Os 253).

It may appear, from the above teaching, that when our Tefilos are recited with the wings of Ahavah and Yirah, our prayers fly upwards, as it were, and affect the hidden inner worlds, and when our Tefilos are without Ahavah and Yirah, and just spoken plainly with *Kol* / voice and Dibbur, they tend to have a *greater* impact in the lower worlds, rather than only 'flying upward' into the higher worlds, as it were. This would suggest that simple Tefilah, with no inner life of Ahavah and Yirah, has a more permeating effect on the physical properties of this world.

Yet in truth, what the Maggid is teaching is quite the opposite. Everything has both an *Etzem* / essence, the thing itself, and a *Tzurah* / form, the manner in which that essence is expressed. If for example a person named Moshe is sick, there is the Etzem of the sickness and the Tzurah of the sickness. The Etzem of the sickness is the idea of sickness misalignment itself. The Tzurah of the sickness is expressed in the specific symptoms Moshe experiences. And so, when we Daven without the wings of Ahavah and Yirah, our Davening is only connected to the revealed worlds of Kol, which is connected to the world of *Yetzirah* / formation, and Dibbur, which is connected to the world of *Asiyah* / actualization. In these 'lower' revealed worlds the power of Tefilah can only change the *Tzurah* / form of what is currently manifest.

With only the revealed powers of Kol and Dibbur we cannot change the root of *what is*, rather we can alter the expression of its external Tzurah. In the above example of the sick person Moshe, our Davening without Ahavah and Yirah, and only with Kol and Dibbur could effect a change of direction of the symptoms, but not the sickness itself. Then, instead of Moshe being sick, the sickness might manifest in another person, or it might manifest in Moshe's life in the form of another illness, problem or challenge. Instead of having a pain in his stomach, maybe now Moshe experiences hardships with *Parnasah* / livelihood.

However, when a person Davens with the wings of Ahavah and Yirah and 'flies' Above, and deep within, to the World of Beriah,* where the Etzem of existence is created, and his Tefilah is with Deveikus, cleaving to the Source of All Life, the world of Atzilus, then his Tefilos reach the hidden inner worlds Above, the 'place' where the primordial Shefa originates, and he can thus create a new Shefa. When one unites himself with "י-ה-ו-ה אלקינו / Hashem our G-d," the Source of Existence, he can draw down new life.

Normally, without Ahavah, Yirah and Deveikus, we are not able to completely eliminate a specific flow of Divine Shefa that is coming down into the world. What we can do is alter the frequency and trajectory of a flow from negative to positive. We can create a reframing, a new context or vessel to receive that flow. In other words, we can change the Tzurah. Yet, if we Daven with love and awe (the Yud and Hei of Hashem's Name), and with voice and speech (the Vav and Hei), we then fully embody the Name of Hashem and we "can create a new reality"; not just effecting change on the level of Tzurah, but in the actual Etzem, revealing a new essence.

Connecting to the Light of the Letters

Words of Tefilah create new realities. But to do so, we need Ahavah and Yirah to connect us to the World of Beriah, and Deveikus to connect us to the world of Atzilus. Earlier we explored the idea of how, through entering fully into the letters of the Davening with all our *Koach* / strength, with our

---

* Although the world of Beriah is always connected to Binah, which is an intellectual world and not a place of love and awe, in these teachings of the Baal Shem Tov on Tefilah, as explored in great length, the cultivation of Kavanah has to occur 'before' the vocalization of the words, and not while actually saying the words of Davening. Perhaps for this reason, Kavanah is not in the above equation; which includes: Dibbur, Kol, Yirah, Ahavah, Deveikus.

Chayus / vitality and "light," we connect with the *Ohr* / the Divine Infinite Light that rests within the *Osyos* / letters. Now let us go a little deeper into this idea of connecting to the Ohr within the Osyos.

As the Baal Shem Tov teaches, "A person should attach his consciousness to the Ohr Ein Sof within the Osyos, which is the Light of the Face of the Living King. And this is a great principle in Tefilah" (*Keser Shem Tov*, 94). Elsewhere he teaches that "A person has to ask from the letters themselves, which means, from the Ohr of Divinity which is within them, and request from them" (*Degel Machaneh Ephrayim*, Yisro. *Amud HaTefilah*, 21). Therefore, in addition to everything explored above, how we need to fully "enter into" the Osyos of Davening by letting go of any attempt to intellectualize what the Osyos mean (as that causes a limitation to the infinite power of the Osyos and can even be a distraction from pure presence), we also need to connect with the Ohr of the Osyos and ask 'from them'.

It is only when we connect with the Ohr of the Osyos, their dimension of Atzilus and *Ayin* / no-thingness, (the World of Thought), that we can truly tap into a space of pure potential. When we connect with the letters beyond their inner worlds of breath (Beriah), voice (Yetzirah) and speech (Asiyah), while in a state total *Bitul HaYesh* / transcendence of all self-awareness, 'we' can then draw down, through our breath, voice and speech, new vibrations and new possibilities of actual realities.

To contact the Ohr within the Osyos, we need to experience some measure of Atzilus within ourselves. We need to realize 'our own' inner Ayin, a stateless state of non-self-awareness and transcendence of ego. We must connect to our inner Ohr (*Me'or Einayim*, Rimzei Shabbos) in order to tap into the Divine Space of Infinite potential, the Ohr Ein Sof, the Cosmic Ayin, and from that fertile void we may draw a new essence into the actuality of this physical world.

If we are still aware of how intensely we are Davening, we have yet to cross over the boundary of 'self' and reach a point of true Ayin. There can be no self-awareness in this state. In fact, "As long as you can still consciously pronounce the words of Davening," says the Magid of Koznitz, "and do so with your own will and volition, you should know that you have yet to reach the deeper levels of Davening. In the deeper levels of Davening, you are totally non-self-aware and you thus have neither the awareness or power to say at will even one word of Davening."

Being in this state of Ayin and Deveikus, you are connected with the Ohr of the Osyos and can, with the power of the Ohr Ein Sof, create new channels of Shefa by reciting the words of Davening. Yet, paradoxically, in this Ayin state 'you' do not have the awareness or power to say anything. Everything is motionless; all movement collapses, along with your awareness of your mind, body and emotions. For your Tefilah to have an effect in the worlds of Beriah, Yetzirah and Asiyah, they need to be breathed, sounded and spoken. So how can you do this when you cannot even move your toe, let alone say a cohesive statement? In such a mystical state of deep Deveikus, the words of Tefilah come tumbling out of your mouth, as if automatically, with little or no conscious awareness. It is almost as if the words were praying themselves.

From Sickness to Health

Through Davening we may connect to the Light that enlivens the Osyos, their Atzilus, their Ayin, and we may thereby become *Davuk* / glued, as it were, with Hashem. From this place of Deveikus, our Tefilos have the power to call upon a new Shefa of Hashem's blessings to come into this world.

Suppose we Daven for healing, for example, that a loved one should be healed from their illness; the first question must be — what is the inner metaphysical mechanism that gave rise to their sickness? The question is not *why* the person is sick; that is a philosophical question that needs to be dealt with elsewhere. The question is rather, *how* is the person sick? Physically, he may be sick because his heart is not working properly, for example, but what is the metaphysical process through which he became sick?

Creation emerged through the *Asarah Ma'amaros* / Ten Divine Utterances, beginning with, "And Hashem said, 'Let there be light', and there was light." While the Torah recounts just these Asarah Ma'amaros, there is a countless variety of 'Utterances' which create manifest reality. Even two raindrops are distinct from each other, and therefore require their own unique "Utterances." The Ten Utterances are thus the root expressions of Divine creativity, then through the act of *Tzirufim* / letter permutations and combinations, all of the unique, creative 'words' emerge, as they form, enliven and sustain all phenomena. In simple language, say, for instance, that Hashem has a desire to create a tiny worm to exist in a particular region in Africa on the third day of the summer, at 6:48 in the morning, in the year 2021. For this exact worm to be created according to all of the specifications, multiple permutations and combinations of Divine letters are arranged to form the 'code' for its existence, and then it is born.

On a deeper level, creation is continuous and every moment is a new flow of Divine letter combinations animating this little being. Furthermore the worm, moment to moment, has different experiences, so every single moment a new and different Tziruf is being expressed to create the conditions for that new experience.

A Divine 'Utterance' is an expression of a Divine thought and desire. First Hashem has a thought or 'Kavanah' to create something, and then Hashem speaks it into being (Tosefos, *Rosh Hashanah*, 27a). First Hashem has a 'thought' to create the worm, and this is the way the worm exists in the world of Atzilus, in Hashem's mind, *Kaviyachol* / so-to-speak. Then Hashem says, through the various *Tzirufim* / combinations, 'Let there be this worm,' and this specific worm appears. This process is continuous; once this worm is created, Hashem has a thought that it should find food at a particular moment, and Hashem says, 'Let this worm find food,' and it finds food, and so forth.

When someone is sick, let us call this person 'Yitzchak the son of Sarah', the cosmic process is as follows. First there is a Divine thought (in the realm of Atzlius): 'Yitzchak the son of Sarah needs to be sick,' and then there is a Tziruf of Osyos that creates a Divine breath (Beriah), a sound (Yetzirah), and finally an utterance (Asiyah) that says, 'Let Yitzchak the son of Sarah be sick,' and so Yitzchak the son of Sarah, on this physical plane, becomes sick.

In order to secure healing for Yitzchak the son of Sarah, we must Daven, connect and become absorbed in the Divine 'thought' of HaKadosh Baruch Hu, as the Source of this illness originates with Hashem "thinking" this person should be sick.

In order to draw down a new Tziruf that says, 'Let Yitzchak the son of Sarah be healthy,' we must strive to connect with the Ohr in Atzilus, and through that we may connect with Hashem Alone, as it were. Then, we need to Daven for a new thought to be formed in the 'Mind of Hashem', in the world of Atzilus. When the Divine thought, "Let Yitzchak the son of Sarah be healthy," creates a Tziruf of Osyos that flows into a Divine breath (Beriah), sound (Yetzirah), and then utterance (Asiyah) that says, "Let Yitzchak the son of Sarah be healthy," Yitzchak the son of Sarah will become healthy on the physical plane. On a revealed level, this healing could come through a successful medicine or procedure, or through a miracle beyond the normal workings of nature, depending on the Divine thought and particular Tziruf.

In any case, we need to elevate ourselves and our consciousness from Asiyah to Atzilus so that 'we' (although in Atzilus there is no longer any sense of ego or even self-awareness) can experience true Deveikus with Hashem and draw down a new Shefa from Atzilus into the world of Asiyah. It is for this reason that *Chazal* / our sages, divided the morning Davening into four stages, with the fourth stage, known as the Amidah, being the *Ikar* / main idea of Tefilah. Notably, it is during the Amidah that we Daven for our needs, as by this point in the process of Davening we are meant to have entered into the world (or the level) of Atzilus. Then, following the Amidah there are another four stages 'back down' from Atzilus, back into the world of Asiyah. In general, during Davening we begin by moving 'upward' to reach the Ohr Ein Sof, the Ayin, the Ohr, and then we draw the new blessings from there all the way 'down' into our manifest existence. The four ascending steps of the Davening are as such:

1) We begin the process with a strong sense of awareness and appreciation for our body and the miraculous gifts of a new day — *Birchos Ha-Shachar* / the Morning Blessings, in the world of Asiyah, with *Yirah Tata'ah* / lower level Yirah.

2) Then we move on to integrate and elevate our emotions with thanks and praise — *Pesukei D'Zimrah* / the Verses of Praise, in the world of Yetzirah, with *Ahavah Zuta* / lower level Ahavah.

3) Next we focus and direct our intellect towards Hashem — *Kriyas Shema* / the Reading of the Shema, in the world of Beriah, with *Ahavah Rabbah* / higher level of Ahavah

4) Finally, we activate and align our true will with the Will of the Infinite One — the *Amidah* / Silent Standing Prayer, in the world of Atzilus, with *Yirah Ila'ah* / higher level of Yirah and total Bitul.

Following these four ascending steps, we then begin the reverse process, from Atzilus back down to Asiyah. The four descending stages in the structure of *Shachris* / the morning prayers are as follows:

1) *Tachanun* / The Small Confession, in which we view our lives 'from above', so to speak, and seek atonement for ourselves and others, bringing the Light of Atzilus down into the world.

2) *Ashrei* / *Uva leTzion*, in which we refresh and reinforce the *Binah* / deeper understanding cultivated in our Davening, allowing us to bring it into the world and our daily life; the mental world of Beriah, Divine breath.

3) *Shir Shel Yom* / Song of the Day, establishing an elevated emotional resonance within our consciousness; the world of Yetzirah, Divine sound.

4) *Ein K'Elokeinu* and the recital of the *Ketores* / incense ritual, bringing G-d consciousness and purity into the world of Asiyah. This expression of a profoundly simple awareness of Hashem and the recitation of the incense offering represents the elevation of the physical world into the service that is based in the spiritual world of Asiyah. We then conclude the Davening with the *Aleinu* prayer, which seals the entire Davening, and allows us to properly 'bow out' of the posture of Davening, much like a servant would bow before leaving the room of his master.[*]

---

[*] It is beyond the scope of this text to exhaustively explain how each step in the davening represents another 'world'. To delve more deeply, please see the book titled, "Inner Worlds of Jewish Prayer."

This four-step structure is reflected in numerous areas of Davening. For example, not only is the Davening structured in a four-rung progression that facilitates an experience of some form of Ohr, Ayin, and Atzilus when we reach the Amidah, but every single letter and word of Davening contains four levels. The *Chomer* / actual substance and graphic representation of the letters corresponds to the world of Asiyah. As letters are strung together to form (*Yotzer*) words and emotionally pleasant sounds and 'songs', they manifest the world of Yetzirah. As the meanings and deeper understandings of the words are revealed to one's mind, they manifest the world of Beriah. And, ultimately, every letter and word is fundamentally a conduit of HaKadosh Baruch Hu's light — this is the Ohr, the *Elokus* / Divinity within each letter and word, representing the dimension of Atzilus.*

---

* Letters and words in the Torah also have four dimensions (Osyos / Tagin / Nekudos / Taamim) corresponding to the Four Worlds. The lowest dimension, Asiyah, is the *Osyos* / letters themselves without vowels, simply ink on a page. This is the most concrete manifestation of the letters, thus the 'World of Actualization'. Beyond the actual letters, are the *Tagin* / crowns that make the letters more beautiful. This level is revealed upon the letters of Asiyah, as the letters in the Torah scroll have Tagin. While these crowns are not as 'revealed' as the Osyos themselves, they are nonetheless written in the Sefer Torah, corresponding to the 'World of Beauty', Yetzirah. Beyond the Tagin are the *Nekudos* / vowels, which reveal intellectual meaning to the Osyos; without the vowels the words cannot be read and understood. This corresponds to the 'World of the Mind', Beriah. Nekudos do not appear in the letters of a Torah Scroll, yet some of the letters themselves function as Nekudos, showing that in this level there is still some degree of 'revelation' and *relationship* to the written letters. Beyond the Tagin are the *Ta'amim* / cantillations, the melody of the words, beyond how the Osyos are pronounced and intellectually understood. These subtle intentions are so subtle that Ta'amim do not appear in a Sefer Torah at all. This is the hidden level, the 'World of Ayin', Atzilus. A letter or word without vowels, revealed meaning or melody, is somewhat 'dead', without vitality. As an example, the words "You're such a good person" can be sounded as a question, a factual statement, a cutting sarcasm or a loving compliment, and so forth. In this way, the 'song' of the Osyos expresses the fullness of their vitality — their *Ohr*. The Ta'amim are the Ohr of Atzilus within every Os.

Emunah / Ayin / Atzilus / Chochmah / Elokus

Such is the mechanics of Davening: we ascend the rungs of a Divine 'ladder' to connect with the Ohr, and Atzilus within the letters that make up our Tefilos, and through that we connect with Hashem Alone. Then, in this state, revealing our own 'personal' Ohr and Atzilus within, we speak the words of Davening. Speaking is an act composed of breath, voice and words, that draws new Shefa down the rungs of the 'ladder' in a way that can alter physical reality. Still, there is another ingredient for such Davening to have an 'effect'. This element is really included within the above structure, but it is also a Mitzvah on its own, and a fundamental principle of life, so obvious that it is easy to overlook. This is *Emunah* / true, genuine and absolute faith in HaKadosh Baruch Hu.

To connect with the Ohr of the Osyos we need resolute Emunah. Here is a teaching from a student of the Baal Shem Tov, Rebbe Menachem Nochum of Chernobyl (1730–1787), the author of *Me'or Einayim*, in which he explains that it is through connecting with our own inner Ohr that we are able to connect with the Ultimate Ohr, and how ultimately we need Emunah for our prayers to truly be transformational:

"Letters are called *Avanim* / stones, as they build (they are the foundation of) the world...With the words that are spoken (prayed) worlds are created through attaching (ourselves) to the inner Infinite Ohr within the letters. Therefore, if a person is experiencing any form of hardship, G-d forbid, when he Davens or studies Torah he should connect the inner Divine aspect within to the letters and to the inner Light that pulsates through them. And he should Daven to HaKadosh Baruch Hu with truth... and the hardship will fade away. Yet, for this to occur we need complete Emunah, to believe with complete faith in *Hashgacha* / Divine providence, and that there is nothing else besides Hashem, and that Hashem watches over our life to the minutest detail, and all of life is present in front of Hashem" (*Me'or Einayim*, Rimzei Shabbos).

From this we learn that in order for us to connect to the Ohr Ein Sof beyond the letters, we need to connect with our own inner light, our Ayin, our inner Atzilus; as the Me'or Einayim teaches, "He should connect the inner Divine aspect within to the letters and to the inner Light that pulsates through them." Yet, for this connection of "lights" to occur, we need "complete Emunah." Perhaps this is because Emunah allows us to connect with the Ohr 'beyond' the letters through the Ohr that resides 'within' the letters and gives them life.

As explored earlier, an answered Tefilah means that a new Tziruf is formed in the *Mach'shavah* / thought process within Atzilus, within Hashem's mind, K'viyachol. In Atzilus, a new Divine thought gives rise to a new Tziruf, such as 'Yitzchak the son of Sarah should be healthy.' This 'thought' then moves from the realm of Atzilus to the world of Beriah, and from there to the world of Yetzirah, until a new vibration and Tziruf manifests in this world of Asiyah. This new 'word', that vibrates with a frequency that says, 'should be healthy', creates a flow of healing for Yitzchak the son of Sarah until he actually does become healthy.

The foundation of this new Tziruf is created in the inner world of Atzilus, the world of Ohr, but how do we attach ourselves to that level and connect with the Ohr of Atzilus? We accomplish this by connecting the inner Divine aspect within us, to the inner Light that pulsates within the Osyos. But how do we connect with our inner Divine aspect, so that we can connect to the Ohr within the letters? This miraculous connection is made possible only through Emunah.

Emunah is our Atzilus, our Ohr within, the part of us that wants to always be connected with the Ohr Ein Sof. In the words of the Alter Rebbe in *Tanya* (18): "Thus we see that the Light of the blessed Ein Sof is garbed in the faculty of Chochmah (the level of Atzilus) in the human soul, of whatever sort of a Jew he may be. In turn, the soul's faculty of Chochmah, together with the light of the blessed Ein Sof that is garbed in it, suffuses all the levels of the soul in its entirety.... Hence all Jews are מאמינים בה' / believers in Hashem" (see also *Sanhedrin*, 44a. *Kiddushin*, 36a. Rambam, *Hilchos Geirushin*, 2:20. Maharal, *Netzach Yisrael*, 5. Reb Tzadok, *Divrei Sofrim*, p. 152).

We are, as the Medrash says, all מאמינים בני מאמינים / believers, the children of believers (*Medrash Rabbah*, Shemos, 3:12). There is a spark of *Kedushah* / holiness and level of connection with Hashem that is always present deep within us. Even when *Klal Yisrael* / the People of Israel were steeped deeply in the *Tumah* / impurity and idolatry of Egypt (on the 49th level, *Zohar Chadash*, Yisro, *Shaloh* HaKadosh, The *Alshich*, *Siddur Rebbe Shabtai*, *Chayei Adam*, in their respective Hagados, on the verse *Matzah Zu*), Moshe told Hashem at the Burning Bush, and seemingly rightfully so based on their low level of spirituality in Egypt, "They will *not believe* me" (*Shemos*, 4:1). HaKadosh Baruch Hu was upset with Moshe (*Medrash*, ibid), as Klal Yisrael are inherently "believers, the sons of believers," no matter their outer situation. There is a *Nekudah* / point of holiness, transcendence and purity connected to the Ohr of Hashem that resides within each one of us. We need to connect with that Nekudah as we Daven.

To reveal our Nekudah of Emunah in real time, moment to moment, is to sense that Hashem is tangibly present in every situation in life. In the words of the Me'or Einayim, Emunah means "...to believe with complete faith in *Hashgacha* / Divine providence, and that there is nothing else besides Hashem, and that Hashem watches over one's life to the minutest detail, and everything in life is present before Hashem." This implies that our Emunah is more than a Nekudah residing deep within, rather, it is a Nekudah that radiates out into our day to day life. And thus, when we Daven with Emunah, when we connect with the Ohr, the Atzilus, the Elokus within us, we simultaneously connect with the transcendent Ohr Ein Sof, the Infinite Source of all Light that rests within and radiates from the world of Atzilus, whereby a new Tziruf is created and then revealed within our lives. If, however, we do not connect and open ourselves through Emunah to the Ohr within and beyond, nothing can happen; no new Tzirufim can be created and our Tefilah has no real effect on this world.

As we move inward toward the Ohr of Atzilus, the place of Emunah, through the four rungs of Shachris, we also relate to the words in the Siddur on these multiple levels. First we simply observe the actual letters on the page; the world of Asiyah. Second, we observe how the letters interconnect and string together into a harmonious symphony of sounds; the world of Yetzirah. Third, we read the words mentally and have Kavanah in the meaning of the words before vocalizing them; the world of Beriah. And then, sensing that every letter and word is fundamentally a conduit of Hashem's light, we experience the Ohr, the *Elokus* / Divinity within each letter and word; the world of Atzilus.

These four levels are also related to the four levels of Creation and reveal how we interact with the world: 1) the *Olam* / world itself (Asiyah), 2) *Olamos* / worlds, the interconnectedness of all realities (Yetzirah), 3) *Neshamos* / souls (Beriah), and 3) *Elokus* / Divinity present within all of creation (Atzilus). (The exalted transcendence of 'personal awareness' that characterizes Atzilus will be explained shortly).

In the state of Deveikus, of Atzilus, Elokus, we almost automatically speak the words of Davening. We are open vessels, and the words of Tefilah come flowing through us, unobstructed. As discussed, speaking is an act of breath, voice and words that draws new Shefa down into this world, altering physical reality. In this way, it is the actual words of Davening themselves, when said in Deveikus with HaKadosh Baruch Hu, that *create the answer* for our Tefilos. Indeed, this is what the Baal Shem Tov tells us, "A person has to ask from the letters themselves, which means, from the Light of Divinity which is within them, and request from them." The way in which we express our requests *to* Hashem determines the nature of the response we receive *from* Hashem.

Words Create Reality

Such is the power of speech when we are connected with the Ohr of the letters; the Divine Presence speaks through us. This is the highest form of Davening. In this trance-like state the words of Davening spontaneously come tumbling out of our mouth, and these divinely inspired and invested words create new realities. This is the answer to (or 'in') our prayers. In the powerful words of the Baal Shem Tov: שלח דיבורך / *Shelach Dibburcha* / "Send forth your words," ויעשה שליחותך / *veYa'ase Shelichus'cha* / "and they will make (create) your message (request)" (*Ohr HaEmes,* p. 1b. *Baal Shem Tov, Torah,* Bereishis, 94, Haga'ah 78. Note that Tefilah is likened to an arrow: *Bereishis,* 48:22, Targum). In other words, Davening in a state of Deveikus is itself what creates the answer to our prayers.

From this perspective, when we Daven in a state of Deveikus, our prayers are *always* 'answered', as we speak. New Divine vibrations are created in the Ohr of Atzilus, and are then drawn into the world through the words of Tefilah that we are speaking; although sometimes these answers come down into the world *in general* (*Ben Poras Yoseph,* p. 127. *Keser Shem Tov,* 80. *Magid Devarav leYaakov,* 145. *Likutim Yekarim,* 123. *Amud HaTefilah,* 127), not necessarily into our specific, personal world (*Degel Machaneh Ephrayim,* Haftarah of Ki Tetze. *Amud HaTefilah,* 127, note 118. Earlier sources discuss how all Tefilos are effective, although for certain cosmic events such as the coming of Moshiach, every Tefilah brings us one step closer: R. Moshe Metrani, the Mabit, *Beis Elokim*, Sha'ar HaTefilah, 17).

For example, a person Davens for his own healing or for the healing of a friend, and he thus draws down a healing Shefa into the world in general. This Shefa can now potentially be tapped into by anyone who is in need of healing; i.e., another sick person. Maybe one's sick friend will be healed (as this too is for one's 'benefit'), yet because of his Davening other people who are in need of healing will potentially be healed as well. Or perhaps one's Davening inspires new medical breakthroughs or more 'miraculous' healings across the globe, just not for us, specifically. In this sense, we can never be completely certain of the full impact of our prayers. Understanding this reverberatory dynamic radically expands our sense of responsibility, as our "circle of influence" is revealed to be exponentially larger than we ever imagined.

Once the words of Tefilah are spoken, they have a creative power and in the very moment of their articulation their vibrations give rise to new realities. This is the deeper reason for why we need to be very specific regarding what we Daven for.

Our words, when said in Deveikus, have the power to influence and even create the very realities that we are vocalizing in our prayers. We must ensure that we have the appropriate *Mach'shavah* / thought before the *Dibbur* / speech, because the yearnings to which we give voice in our Davening will be the realities we (and others) will have to live with.

Our sages in the Gemara (*Baba Metziya*, 106a) bring the following case: "If the owner said to the tenant farmer, 'Plant the field with *wheat*,' and he went and planted it with *barley*, and most of the valley was wind-blasted and ruined, including his field, what is the law? Do we say that the tenant farmer can say to the owner, 'Even if I had planted it with wheat it would likewise have been wind-blasted, as all the surrounding fields suffered the same fate (so even though I did not do as you asked, I am exempt)?' Or perhaps the owner can say to the farmer, 'Had you planted it with wheat, the following verse would have been fulfilled for me: "And you shall decree a matter and it will be established for you, and the light shall shine upon your ways"' (*Iyov*, 22:28). What is the owner's argument? Says Rashi, the owner can argue, 'I prayed in the beginning of the year that I should be successful with my wheat, but I did not pray for success with barley"' (מה שתבקש מן היוצר יעשה ואני לא בקשתי מן השמים בתחילת השנה שיצליחני בשעורים אלא בחטין). In other words, a person's Tefilos are answered precisely in the way they are worded.

Let us now go even deeper with a story from the Medrash. Once a person was trudging along in the desert, when his legs began to tire, he turned to Heaven and cried out, "Please Hashem, if only I had a donkey." A moment later, he noticed a Roman officer standing nearby. The officer had stopped traveling as his she-donkey had gone into labor. The Roman noticed the man and ordered him to carry the colt on his shoulders. The man sighed, "I asked for a donkey, but did not ask correctly" (*Medrash Rabbah*, Esther, 7:24. *Ohr HaChayim*, Devarim, 3:23). The man Davened for a donkey in the hopes that it would carry him, but he did not specify that and received a donkey that he himself had to carry.

"Hashem sends forth His messages to earth, the word arrives with alacrity" (*Tehilim*, 147:15). Perfected speech, such as Hashem's (Kaviyachol), arrives swiftly, and simultaneously creates that which is spoken. Divine vibrations instantaneously manifest and alter reality. When we redeem and align our own power of speech with the Ultimate Speech of the Creator, meaning when we Daven in a state of Deveikus, our words are vested with this creative power. In this way, it is not so much that we (ego-self) are

Davening, rather the Divine Presence, the Shechinah, is Davening through us. And when Davening occurs in such a state of *Bitul* / nullification of self and Deveikus, healing energy will certainly be created, as 'Hashem spoke, and it came into being.'

Creating a New Tziruf

This is the way Tefilah works in general, and specifically when one is Davening the standard *Nusach HaTefilah* / the codified structure of set prayers. (Although originally כותבי ברכות כשורפי תורה / "Those who write the blessings (such as the *Amidah*: Rashi) are considered as if they were burning the Torah" (*Shabbos*, 115b). This means that the structured Davening was previously done by heart, and even today it should contain a measure of spontaneity.)

Now let us explore a few dynamics from the perspective of individual and spontaneous Tefilah.

As stated, when Davening in a state of Deveikus, we have the power to connect to the Ohr Ein Sof within and beyond the letters, and thereby, transform any harsh Din into something that is actually healing. Any Heavenly decree, whether positive or seemingly negative, is revealed through the letters, sounds, and vibrations of Divine Speech. For example, let's say the Divine speech of Creation is streaming into someone's life as the sequence of the three letters Tzadik, Reish, Hei, which spell the word *Tzarah* / hardship. Because of this Tziruf, the person is experiencing hardship in his life. A Tzadik or even a 'regular' person Davening with pure presence and intention for this person's Tzarah to be eliminated (*Kesones Pasim*, p. 47b. *Amud HaTefilah*, 159), connects with the Source of the letters in the world of Atzilus, and can thus take these very same three letters and rearrange them to read (in his mind's eye) as *Ratzah* / desired.

By rearranging the letters of creation while in a state of Deveikus, the previously harsh decree is transformed into something beneficial, and even pleasurable; a 'desired' reality (See *Toldos Yaakov Yoseph*, Noach, 15d).

When Davening with complete and total Deveikus, not only can we change the *Tzurah* / form of the Shefa from negative to positive, rather, we can eliminate the negative Shefa completely and even create a new Shefa, a new language, a new context. However, even when we are not yet on a peak level of Deveikus, and we are not privy to the power to completely eliminate a specific flow of Divine Shefa coming down into the world, we can still shift a negative *Tzurah* / form, quality and trajectory of that Shefa from negativity to positivity.

Imagine this in terms of a current that is streaming from Above to Below. Divine influx begins as an unformed flow of infinite Shefa rushing down into a person's life. That unformed flow will eventually take shape as a specific expression, most often according to the recipient's moral, psychological and spiritual state. What has a person put out into the world lately? Are they acting with integrity and transparency? If a person has deviated from his inner nature and distanced himself from the Infinite One, the form in which this flow will funnel towards him will be in the letter and sound sequence of *Tzarah* / hardship. In such a case, the person himself can change, do Teshuvah and enter a state of Deveikus. Meaning, he can reestablish a deep connection to his inner light of clarity and faith, and then from there he can connect to the Ohr Ein Sof within the letters themselves. Hence, he re-aligns himself in relation to the Source of the Flow, and thereby elicits a corresponding shift in Divine Speech and Shefa.

It is also possible, as discussed, for the Tzurah of the Shefa to be altered through another person Davening with Deveikus for him, to the point that he experiences a positive influx of Shefa, relief and elation, rather than the previously decreed negative Shefa. The original unformed flow will inevitably reach the person, but instead of receiving that influx through a Tziruf of hardship and suffering, he receives it through a 'desired' form.

The point of all this is that our words, when said in Deveikus, are vested with the power to alter Divine speech or even create new frequencies, which eventually manifest corresponding realities. This process is analogous to the story of the *Mon* / manna in the Desert. At its root, the Mon is 'pure potential'; it could literally taste like anything a person wanted. Yet, according to the Medrash, in order to imbue the Mon with a particular flavor, a person would say, 'If only I could taste this or that food,' and instantaneously the Mon tasted just as he wished (*Medrash Rabbah*, Shemos, 25:3. Although another opinion in the Medrash is that all he needed to do is to 'think' about the particular flavor and it would manifest according to the Osyos of *Mach'shavah* / thought. See also *Yumah*, 75a). In other words, there needed to be an intention and a verbal declaration for the Mon to be transformed from a 'tasteless' object into the exact object that was desired. Somehow, the words one declared shaped their experience of the Mon into a specific form.

Through Davening we connect and align ourselves with the Source of all life and all potentialities. This is the Root of all the *Shefa* / Divine flow that animates the world. This is the Ohr Ein Sof that lies within and beyond the letters. Once we have tapped into this Infinite wellspring while in a state of Deveikus, our 'premeditated' words come pouring forth from our mouths almost involuntarily. The words come through us, rather from us, and they create vessels to receive and channel all the blessings that are needed, for us and for the entire world.

Davening for Others and for the Shechinah's Presence to be Revealed

Obviously, once a person reaches a state of Bitul and Deveikus, he is no longer thinking about himself and his needs, his health or livelihood. He is egoless, as much as humanly possible, and thus transcends his own personal wants, needs and desires. Therefore, the requests that he makes in the Amidah, the peak of Davening, are for the collective: *Refa'einu* / "Heal *us..*," *Bar'cheinu* / "Bless *us....*" He is not asking for himself but for the collective, for all of us. The individual Davening the Amidah in Deveikus, which theoretically we should all be doing, is asking for the healing of all, the blessings for all, and that the entire Klal Yisrael should be complete (*Shenos Eliyahu*, Berachos, 5:1). For instance, when requesting healing, he is requesting that Shefa should come raining down from Heaven in a way that all people should be healed, and healed of all illnesses, maladies and sufferings.

Our sages instruct us in a prerequisite to Davening: "One should not begin to pray before attaining *Koved Rosh* / 'heaviness of the head'" (*Berachos* 30b). Says the Maggid of Mezritch, Koved Rosh refers to the Shechinah. Our prayers should be directed toward lifting up, as it were, the Head, the Presence of Hashem in this world. In this way, our Davening is both *to* and *for* the Shechinah.

When there is a lack within Creation, there is a lack, as it were, of the presence of the Shechinah in this world. If someone is sick, and the world is not yet perfect, this means that Hashem's light is not revealed perfectly in this world. If there is war or poverty in the world, this means that the Shechinah is in 'exile' and the perfect Presence of Hashem cannot yet be fully manifest. When the body/physicality and the soul/spirituality are in complete perfection and alignment, then Hashem's perfection can be perfectly revealed. But, until that time, the Coming of Moshiach, the Shechinah is in exile. When a person Davens with Deveikus he is essentially Davening for Shechinah to be 'healed' and 'uplifted' (*Keser Shem Tov 2*, p. 20d. *Amud HaTefila*, 131). This 'prayer for G-d', as it were, is the deepest level of Davening.

When Davening is performed in a state of Ayin, emptied of personal needs, desires and self-awareness, it is both for the sake of the world at large, as well as for the benefit of the Shechinah. Yet, because this person began Davening with a specific intention and he secured the Mach'shavah and Kavanah before articulating his Tefilah, the blessings that will manifest more generally on account of his Deveikus will impact him as well. This is true even if he is not thinking specifically about himself in the moment of saying the words of Davening.

For example, if a person began Davening focused on a particular healing for one of his relatives, then slipped into a state of Deveikus, and while in the state of Deveikus he was no longer thinking about that relative in need of healing, but rather about the healing of all Creation and the healing, as it were, of the Shechinah Itself, his prayers will still draw down healing for his relative, along with the more general influx of healing Shefa for the world. Ultimately, when the word *Refa'einu* is uttered in a state of Deveikus, a flow of Divine Shefa is initiated and funnels down into the world for all those who need healing.

Revealing Timeless Healing

The *Koach* / power to 'be *Mechadesh*' / to innovate new realities when we are in a state of Deveikus, is the same Koach that allows us to be Mechadesh in Torah. This is because Neshamos Yisrael /souls of Israel are *Mushrash* / sourced in *Atzmus* / the Divine Essence, and this means they are even *Kadam* / prior to Torah. As it says in Medrash, "The Torah and the souls of Israel preceded the creation of the world. Still, I do not know which preceded which. But I (Eliyahu haNavi) say the thought of Israel preceded everything" (*Tana d'Vei Eliyahu Rabba* 14. See also *Medrash Rabbah*, Bereishis, 1:4. *Zohar* 2, 119b).

"Even what a proficient pupil is destined to *Mechadesh* / innovate (*Megilah*, 19b) was already said to Moshe at Sinai" (*Yerushalmi, Pe'ah*, 2:4). The question is, if it's a Chidush then it was not "already said to Moshe," and if it was said to Moshe, it is not really a Chidush? In the process of the unfolding of linear time, there is first a revelation at Matan Torah and then the sages unpack the general principles of Torah to reveal specific details of the oral Torah.

However, the Torah and the Neshamos Yisrael existed before the Creation, beyond the paradigm of unfolding historical time. From this perspective, the Chidushim of Neshamos Yisrael, even if made thousands of years after the Giving of Torah, are rooted in Atzmus, the absolutely timeless Giver of Torah. And when something 'timeless' is revealed within time, paradoxically, it is both a Chidush in historical time, and yet, one that 'was' historically revealed at Sinai. The same is true with Tefilah and the *Ratzon Hashem* / Divine will, *Kaviyachol* / so-to-speak. Through our Tefilos, we are able to create new realities, as discussed, however, these 'new realities' were, on some level, already existent.

In this way, if a person is sick within historical, finite time, through Davening for healing in Deveikus, the individual taps into the essence of his Neshamah, which is pre-Creation and one with HaKadosh Baruch Hu, and a new Chidush of healing is revealed, which is also part of the Ratzon Hashem and therefore already revealed 'before time'.

Creating a Yichud *in the Way of the Baal Shem Tov: Worlds, Souls & Divinity*

In order for the words of our Davening to have a truly creative power they need to be uttered in a state of Deveikus and deep connection with the Light within the letters, as well as with the Light within oneself. To live in a state of *perpetual* Deveikus is a lifelong journey, and very rarely attained. Yet, while much *Avodah* / deep and arduous spiritual work and *Bitul* / self-nullification is required, some measure of Deveikus can be attained through following these progressive steps outlined below, within the practice of Davening.

There is a celebrated epistle of the Baal Shem Tov to his brother-in-law. In the letter, he writes, "On Rosh Hashanah of the year 5507 (1746), I made an oath and elevated my soul in the manner known to you. I saw wondrous things in a vision, the likes of which I had never witnessed since the day my mind first began to awaken.... I ascended from level to level until I entered the Palace of the Moshiach.... I asked Moshiach, "When will you come, Master?" And he replied, "By this you shall know: I will arrive at a time when your teachings have been publicized and revealed to the world, when your wellsprings have overflowed to the outside, [when] that which I have taught you, and that which you have perceived by your own efforts, become known so that others too will be able to perform mystical *Yichudim* / unifications and ascents of the soul like you." I was amazed by this response and greatly troubled, since a long time must pass for this to be possible.... Yet this I can tell you...whenever you pray or study, and in fact with every utterance of your lips, *intend* to bring about the unification of a Divine Name. For every letter contains *Olamos* / worlds, *Neshamos* / souls, and *Elokus* / Divinity.... These are the words of your brother-in-law who longs to see you face-to-face, who prays that length of days be granted to you and your wife and children, and who wishes you peace...."

It is known that one of the ways for a person to create wonderful Yichudim, as the holy Baal Shem Tov revealed, is through the animation of, and
unification with these three dimensions. In another place it is recorded, "In
every word there are *Olamos* / worlds, *Neshamos* / souls, and *Elokus* / Divinity... and a person needs to integrate his soul with each of these levels.
All worlds will then be unified and they will ascend (with the person). This
affects immense joy and delight in both the upper and lower worlds" (*Tzava'as HaRivash*, 75. Amud HaTefilah, 15. In the language of the Arizal, these very same
three dimensions are called *Malachim* / angels, *Neshamos* / souls and *Shechinah* / Divine
Presence: See *Zohar Chai*, Parshas Tetzaveh, 139d. These three dimensions expressed by the
Arizal correspond to the three expressed by the Baal Shem Tov: 'Shechinah' corresponds
to Elokus, 'Neshamos' corresponds to Neshamos, and 'Malachim' corresponds to Olamos.
Perhaps the reason why the Baal Shem Tov uses the language of *Olamos* / worlds and not
Malachim / angels, is because, as explained earlier, in the teachings of the Arizal the 'inner'
quality of creation, the 'angelic' reality is elevated, not the world itself. Whereas the Baal
Shem Tov revealed, today, as we are closer to Moshiach, the Olam itself can be elevated).

What this means is as follows. Every word, which essentially means
every 'thing' and every aspect of this world and all worlds (as everything is
an expression of a Divine word), has three dimensions:

1) The 'letter' or the object, the 'thing' itself. This is its dimension of *Olamos*, also called the *Kli* / vessel or body.

2) The particular quality and distinct vibration of the object. This is its
Neshamah, the soul of the object. It is also the Divine spark or Divine
'word' that animates that object.

3) The highest level of 'meaning' associated with the object, even when
not yet practically manifest. This is the *Elokus*, the Divinity within the
object, and its inner dimension which reveals that there is nothing else
besides Hashem, literally. As the whole world is ultimately part of Elokus,

this is the dimension of the entity that is one with all other entities.[*]

What do these words of the Baal Shem Tov mean — "A person needs to integrate his soul with each (of these three) levels; all worlds will then be unified and ascend (with the person)"? And in what sense would this be or create a *Yichud* / unification?

The ego's sense of reality is called *Olam* / world, singular. Everything and everyone is distinct and separate, each vying for the survival and perpetuation of self. Nothing and nobody is intrinsically connected, in the ego's lens on reality, and all we seek in life is self-survival. The ego is always whispering, 'What could I get out of life and out of this encounter?' This is the world of *Pirud* / separation and *Kelipah* / concealment — the total opposite of the world of *Yichud* / unification and *Kedushah* / holiness. Beyond this self-orientation are three levels of transparency, three progressive stages of integration and unification that a person can experience within themselves and with objects in the outside world:

---

* These three, *Olamos* / worlds, *Neshamos* / souls, and *Elokus* / Divinity, can also be understood as follows. Every letter, and letter combination, is *part* of Olamos. Elokus is the Divinity, the Ohr and power within the letter. Neshamos is the Divine consciousness that animates these letters, and which breathes life into them. We are discussing, in a sense, four dimensions: the world of *Olam* / world, the world of *Olamos*, the world of *Neshamos* and the world of *Elokus*. There is the thing itself, the *Os* / letter itself, and then there is Divine consciousness and human consciousness, as it were, the two perceptions of reality. We, humans, can 'hear' the world (and of course, this is also true regarding 'seeing' the world, although the Baal Shem Tov is talking primarily about the sense of sound), and interact and engage with the world around us with every sound (and sight) that is presented to us as merely a singular sound (or image), without hearing (or seeing) the larger symphony and interconnectivity of life. We, as Neshamos, can hear (see) Olam, or deeper, we can hear the one sound (and one sight) within a larger context of life, and hear the *Olamos* / worlds that are being presented to us, the total interconnectivity of life. As Neshamos, we have the choice to hear (see) the world within its higher purpose, and even deeper, to sense the Elokus within everything.

1) *Olam*, singular, the ego, can become transparent through unification with the *Olamos* (worlds, plural) — connection with all creatures, animals, elements, life forms and indeed all objects. This is the simple sensation that everything, including ourselves, is all part of one vast ecosystem; all life is intimately interconnected, all part of one ecology. The entire planet, ourselves included, is one organism, and nothing exists in isolation from the next. Everything in life is interconnected, and on this level of Olamos consciousness we viscerally sense this truth. This is the first level of *Bitul* / ego transparency, and openness to Deveikus.

2) A higher level of Bitul is experienced through unification with the Neshamos dimension — by connecting your contemplative awareness with the Divine Spark present within every inch and aspect of Creation, you ascend out of limitation and thereby cause a corresponding ascension of the Olamos dimension. This is the more evolved spiritual sensation that you, and every entity, are expressions of specific Divine vibrations. It is the awareness that every person and object in our life is interconnected with our own soul journey. Each of our particular employers, co-workers, neighbors, community and family members, are connected with our Neshamah's path of Tikkun, and that is why these particular people are involved in our life; so that we can attain our maximum potential and Tikkun. Why were you born to these particular parents, with these siblings, in this location, during this time period, having grown up with these friends, working with these people, having met this person today, and so forth? All are necessarily here as parts of the context and content of your life, so that you can attain your full Tikkun and they can attain theirs. In this recognition of soul-connection, we are clearly not an isolated ego floundering in the world of Pirud and Kelipah. Rather, there is a Yichud between ourselves and everything around us on this vibrational level, like notes that make up a great harmonic symphony.

3) Unification with the *Elokus* — by connecting with the Infinite One, the Divinity within everything, you integrate yourself and all the worlds together with the highest sphere, the Crown and Root of every 'word' and every 'thing'. When you attach yourself to the Creative Root of all Creations, you reach the highest and broadest level of *Deveikus* / unity. This is the complete recognition that everything is Elokus. Ascending to this level of transparency and Yichud raises up the dimensions of Olamos and Neshamos, as well.

Practical Yichud with Worlds, Souls and Divinity

Practically speaking, whether you are praying in a field or encompassed by brick and mortar, open yourself to sense and connect to your surroundings. Become aware of the people you are Davening with, and even the particular tree or table you are standing next to, and integrate them within your own mental space. Recognize the interconnectedness between you and everyone and everything around you. This is not merely a mindset, rather the recognition of a fact. Indeed, on a molecular level all organisms are composed of the same material, and there is one biosphere that integrates all of life on earth. This is the first level of awareness, 'Olamos'. No one is an island unto himself and nothing happens in a vacuum, even on an inanimate level.

Consider the 'butterfly effect', whereby even the slightest beat of a butterfly's wing can, to some extent, influence the trajectory of a hurricane on the other side of the globe. Everything in Creation is connected to and affects everything else. The first level of Yichud and integration occurs through the awareness that all of Creation is interconnected. The interconnectivity within Olamos is a fact whether or not we are aware of it. Thus, on this level of Yichud, we are opening ourselves to the awareness, the sensation and experience of what is already the case.

This 'Olamos Yichud' is very visceral and intimately real. It begins as a meditation in the mind, thinking about the interlacing and interwoven reality within which you exist, and then it becomes a literal sensation; you feel this truth in your body.

Now, go deeper and open your mind and heart. Open yourself up completely to the Neshamos, the 'souls' of the people, and even the spiritual vibration and presence of the tree or table next to you. Extend your physical sensation of the interconnectivity of all beings, the Olamos, to the world of Neshamos, of souls, to hear and be open to other people's energy, to the way they are feeling or even thinking. Try to even hear and feel the tree 'tree-ing', the table 'table-ing'. On this level, you are not only connecting yourself to the physical existence and interconnectivity of everything around you, rather, you are connecting consciously to the Neshamah of each creature in Creation.

Everyone we know who exists in our orbit, and everything that we own and everything that exists in our sphere of sight and hearing, is connected and bound up with our own soul in a vast Yichud.

As the Baal Shem teaches: There is a deep Neshamah connection between yourself and the objects in your life (*Keser Shem Tov*, 218, 194. *Tzava'as HaRivash*, 109. *Magid Devarav leYaakov* 101d. *Meor Einayim*, Likutim, p. 166. See *Chulin*, 91a). It is as if our soul expands beyond our body and permeates everything in our sphere and all that we possess. Thus our Sages tell us, "One who steals a penny from his friend, it is as if he robbed his soul" (*Baba Metziya*, 112a). This interconnectivity in the world of Neshamos exists between everything in our lives, including whatever we see, hear, touch, smell or taste. Even if you are praying standing next to a particular person, or sitting on a specific chair, holding a unique *Siddur* / prayer book, it means that your soul gravitated toward this exact situation because you are connected on a soul level. Their vibration, their distinct spark, is connected with yours, in some way. Their narrative, as it is projected to you, the recipient of the situation, is specifically meant for you, and on a deeper level it is part of you, an extension of your own soul, your own narrative.

In this way, step two, the Yichud with Neshamos, is to open yourself to truly sensing the inner nature and Divine spark within the world around you. Feel the 'soul', the rhythm and vibration of the inner life of each thing. Sense the consciousness of everything around you, and notice how that is included within your own consciousness; everything is truly 'part of you'. Things do not happen 'to' you, they are part 'of' you. This second level of Yichud and integration occurs through an awareness that all things are an expression of their deeper soul-consciousness, their subtle root vibration, their inner song.

Now go even deeper. Connect to the level of *Elokus* / Divinity within yourself and within the world around you. Integrate yourself within the highest sphere of existence, even beyond Creation itself. This is the ultimate Source of every word, vibration, movement, object and aspect, both around and within you. On this level, you are acknowledging the G-dly Presence within each and everything in this world, and that *Ein Od Mil'vado* / 'there is nothing else besides Hashem'.

On the level of Olamos, you connect on the physical and vibrational level of all of Creation. On the level of Neshamos, you connect with all on the level of consciousness and spirituality. But on each of these first two levels, you are still connecting as an individual with other individual entities or aspects. On the level of Elokus, you are connecting to that aspect of yourself and of each creation that is truly from the upper worlds, beyond individuality. The level of Elokus is the level on which all independent existences lose their ego-based sense of separation, as this is the wellspring of unlimited and unformed potential from which all things emanate and flow.

Another way of thinking about this is as follows. Everything in this world is a reflection of, and is animated by, the vibration of a particular Sefirah or Divine energy. Understood very broadly, we could say that a lion reflects *Gevurah* / power and might. Rainfall is also Gevurah. Dew, on the other hand reflects *Chesed* / kindness and giving, as does a white sheep. Everything in this world can be traced via its physical or spiritual qualities back to its Sefirah. This is its share of Divinity, which defines its inner life force, and connects it to the upper worlds of limitless potential. This is the wellspring of Divinity that irrigates and enlivens each quality, energy, object and word.

This goes beyond the Yichud with Olamos in which one perceives the interconnectivity of everything in the world and himself as part of and one with all of Creation, and the Yichud with Neshamos in which one unifies with the sense of soul and purpose deep within each creature and creation. Here, again, one unifies and integrates himself with the Divine Creative Potential within the world, until he reaches the highest, deepest level of *Deveikus* / unity with Elokus, as well as the insight and visceral awareness that there is literally nothing else besides Hashem's Light.

Once we have created a Yichud on all these three levels, not only have we expanded beyond our ego, the Olam perception, and entered an inner world of Elokus, but we have also, in the interim, effectively elevated all objects or 'words' to their root in Elokus. These four perspectives of reality, *Olam* / world, *Olamos* / worlds, *Neshamos* / souls and *Elokus* / Divinity, correspond to the Four Inner Worlds that we explored earlier. Olam, which is the prism of the ego, corresponds to the world of *Asiyah* / physical and egoic existence. Olamos is a broader and more expansive perspective, connected to the world of *Yetzirah* / formation. Neshamos is connected to the world of souls and understanding, the world of Beriah / creation, and Elokus is the world of *Atzilus* / nearness, the world of Unity. As we are moving to higher and deeper levels of consciousness, and doing so in a state of Yichud with the world and those around us, we are also pulling along and elevating everything to the level of Elokus, toward the world of Atzilus. Once everything has been elevated, we are vested with the power to reverse the order and draw Divine Shefa back down into the world from Atzilus/Elokus, to the stages of Neshamos/Beriah, to Olamos/Yetzirah, and ultimately back to Olam/Asiyah, thereby enhancing, altering or completely changing the very fabric of reality itself.

Breathing: In Olamos, Neshamos, Elokus

Earlier, we explored the idea of securing your Kavanah during the inhale and then speaking the words of Davening with strength and presence in the exhale. Now, based on this teaching of the Baal Shem Tov we can add a new dimension. In addition to whatever specific Kavanos we are entertaining during our inhale, we can also use that time prior to speaking (and in general the period of time before you begin a prayer session) to perform a Yichud on the levels of Olamos, Neshamos and Elokus.

As you are inhaling and breathing in, in addition to any specific Kavanah you are building, you can gather in, integrate and create a Yichud with yourself and everything around you. You are literally breathing in the world around you. The interconnectivity of life is always present, what you are internalizing, as you breathe in, is this visceral sensation of unity between all Olamos. The same is true with the next level. As you are inhaling the world around you and creating a Yichud with the Olamos, think of how you are also inhaling the Neshamos of everything around you. All Neshamos are connected with your Neshamah; they are all part of your journey, as you are part of theirs. Sparks of your own Neshamah extend beyond your immediate self, weaving into the objects of your life. Breathe that awareness into your body. Create a visceral Yichud with the Neshamos around you. Then gradually slip into the deepest level, and create a Yichud and sense of unity with the Elokus that is within and all around you. All is always already unified in the Divine Oneness; there is no such thing as separation. Breathe this awareness inward consciously until you are no longer 'thinking', rather simply 'being' the Yichud of Elokus.

This breathing exercise transforms the mere conceptual understanding of the intrinsic unity that exists between Creation and Creator into a visceral sensation of Oneness and Deveikus. With every contemplative inhale, you integrate and assimilate the Olamos, Neshamos and Elokus all around and within you. There is no longer any separation between the 'interior self' and the 'exterior reality'. You are one with all of Creation and one with the Source of All Life. Thus you elevate yourself and the world, the Olam around you, to the level of Neshamah and to the Elokus within. You are lifting up the entire Creation to Elokus. And once you have thus gained some level of Deveikus with the Source of All Life during your inhale, the words of Davening that you express with your exhale will be infused and empowered with a Divine-like creative potency.

This breath and Yichud-based practice can be done before Davening or throughout Davening, whether before reciting each word, every two to three words, or before every Brachah. It is even possible to perform one of each of these three Yichudim during the inhale before reciting the first three blessings of the Amidah. For instance, during your inhale before reciting the first Brachah you would focus your intention on connecting with and elevating the level of Olamos. During your inhale right before reciting the second Brachah you would focus your intention on the world of Neshamos, and so on. By the time you begin the *Bakashos* / requests section of the Amidah you would have made a Yichud on, and with, all three levels of Olamos, Neshamos and Elokus, deeply infusing your requests with vitality.

Throughout this process we have cultivated experiential states of genuine Presence, holy Yirah and deep Ahavah. We have connected with our breath and prepared ourselves for Davening by performing a series of *Yichudim* / unifications between ourselves and the three levels of Olamos, Neshamos and Elokus. We have striven to achieve some degree of *Deveikus* / connection, cleaving and unifying with the Source of All Life, with the letters themselves, and with the Light within the letters, the Ohr/Ayin/Atzilus within and beyond ourselves, all in order to Daven with real Deveikus. And yet, the final stage of the Baal Shem Tov's path of Tefilah is to let go of all of these concepts and contents and just — surrender: simply stop and let go. This is the final step in this process, which is paradoxically the simplest to understand yet perhaps the most difficult to perform.

Chapter 10
STEP SIX: SURRENDER

Surrender

ONCE WE HAVE DONE ALL THAT WE CAN TO PREPARE, HAV-ING INVESTED OUR ENTIRE BEING, MIND AND HEART INTO OUR DAVENING, HAVING ATTACHED OURSELVES TO THE OHR WITHIN OURSELVES AND WITHIN THE LETTERS, HAVING ATTAINED SOME MEASURE OF DEVEIKUS WITH THE WORLD AROUND US AND BEYOND US, WE SIMPLY LET GO OF ALL EXPECTATIONS AND BECOME PRESENT.

Certainly we should not allow ourselves to become anxious in antici-pation of seeing the results of our Davening. We should not think, 'I have Davened with such Kavanah! Certainly my Tefilos will be answered. Now

I will wait for the answers to my prayers to materialize' (*Rosh Hashanah*, 16b). This is called *Iyyun Tefilah* / negative delving into (the mechanics of) Davening (according to Rashi and Tosefos, *ad loc.* S'mak, Siman 11. *Shulchan Aruch*, Orach Chayim, 98:5).

"A window/light you shall make for the Ark, ואל־אמה תכלנה מלמעלה / and terminate it within a cubit on high" (*Bereishis,* 6:16). This verse literally means that Noach was asked to build an Ark and to place a window or a glowing stone one cubit from the roof of the Ark, and make a peak or point at the top of the Ark. On a deeper level, this verse teaches us that as soon as a word emerges from your mouth, do not dwell on it, terminate it, as it were, and let it rise on high. In other words: "Once the word has left your mouth there is no need to mind it any longer. Just as one is not able to look at the sun, one does not see it ascend to the higher realms. This is the meaning of "terminate on high"(*Tzava'as HaRivash*, 75, p. 8b. *Amud HaTefilah*, 15).

According to one student of the Baal Shem Tov, "Therefore, good advice for the wise is that he shall Daven for what is needed, and the One Who Desires will do as He feels fit to do, in His good will" (*Toldos Yaakov Yoseph*, Shelach. *Amud HaTefilah*, 128).

This 'letting go' of results, especially after all the hard work that has gone into your Davening, is an act of *Bitul* / nullification of the ego. We need to experience being *Ayin* / no-thing so that a new *Yesh* / something, the new reality co-created through our Davening, has a fertile space to manifest. A full cup cannot be filled.*

---

* Shabbos is Ayin in comparison to the work week, which is Yesh. On Shabbos we let go. And within Shabbos itself, says the Baal Shem Tov, when we recite the Tefilah of Keser, all the Tefilos of the entire week are then elevated (*Baal Shem Tov al HaTorah*, Lech Lecha, 11). What does Keser mean? *Keser Yitnu Lecha* / our Keser we give You. *Keser* refers to the totality of our desires, our yearnings, hopes, dreams, and imaginations. On Shabbos we tell Hashem, "We give everything over to You; all our deepest desires and yearning are surrendered to you."

We need to get out of the way for a new Yesh to be revealed (*Keser Shem Tov* 2, p. 20d. *Amud HaTefilah*, 131). In the context of Davening this means, a) not Davening for ourselves alone, and b) releasing our expectations once we finish Davening, and doing so even while Davening.

This detachment from the outcome of our Davening, even in the midst of Davening, also allows us to enter more deeply into the present moment, which is the infinite wellspring of all existence. It is only in the present moment that we can truly sink into the vibrations of the *Lashon HaKodesh* / sacred sound of our Tefilah. From this place of aural immersion, it is then possible to ride or 'surf' those sonic waves all the way back to their Source — the One Who Spoke the World Into Being — and experience genuine Deveikus.

"Rebbe Levi bar Chiya said (*Berachos*, 64a), 'One who leaves the place of Davening and immediately enters the study hall and engages in Torah study is privileged to receive the Divine Presence,' as it is stated, 'They go from strength to strength, every one of them appears before Hashem in Tzion'" (*Tehilim*, 84:8). May we be *Zocheh* / meritorious to receive the total revelation of Hashem's Presence, with the arrival of Moshiach, speedily in our days.

APPENDIX:

DEALING WITH INTRUDING THOUGHTS DURING DAVENING

AS WE HAVE COMPLETED OUR JOURNEY ALONG THE HOLY BAAL SHEM TOV'S PATH OF TEFILAH, IT BEHOOVES US NOW TO ADDRESS AN IMPORTANT ISSUE, WHICH IS DISCUSSED AND EXPLORED IN GREAT DETAIL BY THE BAAL SHEM AND HIS STUDENTS: THE ISSUE OF *Mach'shavos Zaros* / FOREIGN OR ALIENATING THOUGHTS.[*] ACCORDING TO THE BAAL SHEM TOV, 'BROKEN' OR NEGATIVE THOUGHTS ARE ROOTED IN THE *Sheviras HaKeilim* / BREAKING OF THE VESSELS, AND THEY ARE EXPRESSIONS OF THE 'BROKEN' LETTERS THAT FELL AS A RESULT OF THE COSMIC BROKENNESS, AS EXPLORED EARLIER (SEE ALSO *Ohr Ha-Ganuz LaTzadikim*, BECHUKOSAI).

---

[*] Note that even our sages testify (however we are to understand this): א"ר חייא רובא אנא מן יומי לא כוונית אלא חד זמן... שמואל אמר אנא מנית אפרוחיא. רבי בון בר חייא אמר אנא מנית דימוסיא / "Rav Chiya said, 'I only had full intention once...' Shemuel said, 'I count flowers while Davening.' Rav Bun said, 'I count the beams': *Yerushalmi, Berachos*, 2:4. In the language of Tosefos, שאינו מתכוין בתפלה שאי אפשר ליזהר כדאמרינן בירושלמי מחזיקנא טיבו לרישא דכי מטא למודים מנפשיה כרע: Tosefos, *Shabbos*, 118b. Rebbe Mendel of Vitebsk (1730–1788), who was a prime student of the Magid as well as a teacher of the Alter Rebbe, famously took three hundred of his followers to settle in the Land of Israel. He is recorded as saying that, before he came to Eretz Yisrael, he desired to Daven "at least one Tefilah fully to Hashem" — i.e., to Daven just once with complete Kavanah. However, now that he lives in Eretz Yisrael he understands that he will never Daven a full Tefilah with complete Kavanah, but at least he hopes for one good *Omein* / Amein.

Throughout Chasidic teachings, there is much discussion concerning the approach one should take when intruding or 'negative' thoughts arise in the mind during Davening. Let's say, for example, that your mind keeps wandering off to unrelated thoughts during Davening, such as 'What's for breakfast?' or 'Who do I have to meet today?' Sometimes such thoughts are not only distracting, but actually negative and unholy. (There are Mach'shavos *Zaros*, which means thoughts that are 'foreign' or unrelated to Davening, and then there are actually *Hirhurim Ra'im* / negative, sinful thoughts: Reb Baruch Kosov, *Amud HaAvodah*, Derush HaAhavah v'HaYirah, 168. For the most part these two types of thoughts are considered linked: *ibid*, Kuntreisim l'Chochmas HaEmes, 116).

The path of the Baal Shem Tov in Davening, in seeming contrast to the path of the Arizal, is more about the 'heart space' than the 'mind space'. Presence, Yirah and Ahavah are dominant factors, and the Kavanah is formulated before you pronounce the words of Davening, so that you can fully enter into the sounds and vibrations of the letters, in order to connect with the *Ohr* / light within them. This method of Davening is not a rigorous intellectual exercise like the Arizal's practice of detailed Kavanos, and thus, when the mind becomes less engaged, it is much more likely for 'intruding thoughts' to enter consciousness, making it all the more necessary to address this issue.

It seems clear from the Baal Shem Tov's teachings that a person can know for himself if he really Davened on the level of Atzilus (although perhaps merely Atzilus within the world of Asiyah) by the presence or absence of intruding thoughts during Davening. If he was able to Daven with little or no Mach'shavos Zaros, this is an indication that he Davened effectively, and actually attained some measure of Deveikus through Davening. The Baal Shem and his students also teach that if you Davened without Mach'shavos Zaros, you should know that your Davening was accepted on High (*Toldos Yaakov Yoseph*, Beha'alosecha. *Amud HaTefilah*, 103).

Either way, there is a lot of discussion amongst Chassidic sources about what to do with 'foreign thoughts', including some major *Chidushim* / novel ideas, most notably the notion of *Ha'ala'as HaMidos* / elevating one's thoughts to their spiritual roots. Even a great sage such as Rebbe Nachman of Horodenka testified regarding himself that while he would, for example, immerse himself in a cold Mikvah each morning, he would still struggle with Mach'shavos Zaros, until he became acquainted with the wisdom of the Baal Shem Tov, after which these strange thoughts ceased to be a problem for him (*Shivchei HaBaal Shem Tov*, p. 82). Yet, before delving into this idea, let us begin with the classical ways of dealing with intruding thoughts, taught by the sages and teachers prior to the Baal Shem Tov.

The *Shulchan Aruch* rules that if a foreign thought enters the mind while Davening, you should "wait a moment (be silent) until the thought is nullified" (*Orach Chayim*, 98:1, the Alter Rebbe, *ibid*, rules the same). It is not that you should fight with such thoughts and try to forcefully eject them from your mind, rather, just sit for a moment and let them wash away by themselves. Nor, of course, should you get involved with them and entertain the thoughts, but simply pause and let the thought pass. "Stand still until the thought moves on" (*Bi'ur HaGra*, ibid).

Pausing and waiting for your thoughts to subside is a much more gentle and effective way to clear the mind than actively pushing and fighting with your thoughts. The nature of your subconscious thoughts and fixations is that the more you resist them the more they persist. By pausing for a moment and letting the thought pass, you do not enter into a struggle with the thought; you simply let it dissolve on its own. This technique is more about actively ignoring thoughts than "pushing them aside."

Another option, besides simply ignoring any intruding thoughts, is to push yourself harder to focus on the thoughts you do wish to think about.

Similar to the first approach of 'pausing', this approach of 'focusing' does not entangle us in the intruding thoughts themselves, rather it actively diverts our attention elsewhere. In either case, this is a fundamental principle: avoid a head-on collision with the distracting thoughts; either simply ignore them or actively fill your mind with something else.

It is important to keep in mind that just because you are now struggling with intruding thoughts is not a sign of your weakness or that your Davening is not up to par, rather, quite the opposite, it indicates you are on the verge of attaining a deeper level of Davening. These are the words of the Alter Rebbe in *Tanya* (chap. 28): "Nevertheless (a person who is struggling with intruding thoughts during Davening) must not be downcast and feel dejected and despicable during Davening, as Davening should be done with great joy. On the contrary, he should draw fresh strength and intensify his effort with all his power to concentrate on the Davening with increased joy and gladness, in the realization that the intruding thought that had invaded his heart comes from the *Kelipah* / the negative side in the left part, which, in the case of the average man, wages war with the Divine Soul within him. For it is known that the way of combatants, as of wrestlers, is that when one is gaining the upper hand the other likewise strives to prevail with all the resources of his strength. Therefore, when the Divine soul exerts itself and summons its strength for Davening, Kelipah also gathers strength at such time to confuse and topple it by means of a foreign thought of its own. This refutes the error commonly held by people who mistakenly deduce from the occurrence of the foreign thought that this proves their Davening to be worthless, as if 'when one Davens as is fitting and proper no foreign thoughts will occur to him....'" On the contrary, the appearance of such distraction indicates the potential to attain new heights.

Getting to Know Yourself

Davening is simultaneously an act of expression and reflection. In and through Davening, as we are alone with ourselves and consciously in the presence of the Master of the Universe, our true self becomes more and more transparent. Greater clarity emerges. When standing in a posture of Tefilah, sensing the overwhelming awareness that we are in the presence of our Creator, all the walls of self-delusion come tumbling down. One can no longer fool himself. Rebbe Mendel of Kotzk once quipped, "People call these thoughts 'foreign thoughts' when in truth, these are a person's normal thoughts — and all his thoughts in Davening about Presence, Yirah, Ahavah and Deveikus, are sadly what are truly 'foreign' to him."

Your 'Mach'shavos Zaros' are really *your* thoughts, thoughts that you have most likely thought about many times before, and it is just now, when you are Davening, that you wish to not think these thoughts (שבעמידת האדם בתפלה ורוצה לידבק בקונו נופלים לו מחשבות זרות שלא ברצונו רק כאלו הן באים מן הצד מאליהן וממילא אך מ"מ הן הן מחשבותיו שחשב בהן ברצון שלא בשעת התפלה וכיוצא בהם אלא שבשעת התפלה הם נופלים לו שלא ברצונו: Alter Rebbe, *Likutei Torah*, Bechukosai, 49a. Although there are also other types of even 'stranger' thoughts that enter during Davening, precisely because one is Davening, and the 'opposing' forces within are pushing up such thoughts from the subterranean levels of one's consciousness; although these too are thoughts that were previously entertained: Rebbe Rashab, *Kuntres Avodah*, p. 14. שאנו רואים שבשעת התפלה כשהאדם רוצה לדבק שכלו בגדולת הבורא ית' אזי נופלים לו מחשבות זרות המטרידים ומבלבלים אותו מה שלא היו נופלים לו כלל בכל היום כולו. והענין דדוקא מצד שבשעת התפלה הוא שעת הבירור להפריד הרע מהטוב ולדחותו: *Likutei Torah*, Bamidbar, 3d).

With this in mind, take a moment while pausing and letting these unwanted, intruding thoughts wash away, and be honest with yourself whether or not these are really just your 'natural' involuntary thoughts, meaning they are not so 'strange' after all (although it would be best to simply let go of any negative or distracting thoughts, and not consider them at all, even in this way). These unintentional thoughts can more easily be identified during Davening and indicate to a person what is really going on within his subconscious mind. They can thus be used to point out what areas of his psycho-spiritual life he needs to work on refining, embracing and perfecting. In this sense, these 'normal' thoughts productively reveal what needs *Tikkun* or 'repair'.

Often, the best way to do this type of self-evaluation is to simply notice what grabs the mind as you are trying to concentrate on your Davening. If the mind continually wanders about, observe where it wanders. The mind of course wanders to the areas of our life where our ego is stuck or holding. Clearly, it would be better and more beneficial to let go of these thoughts altogether, since they are intruding on our ability to focus our consciousness on our Davening. Yet, by noticing how these thoughts continue to creep in, you can discover what your inner concerns truly are and work to fix these trouble spots. (Alternatively, the mere act of pushing such thoughts aside is their elevation, as the Alter Rebbe writes, *ibid.*)

Every Thought has a Purpose

Noticing these intruding thoughts alerts us to what we need to work on and what we truly need to Daven for. The Mishnah says, "Do not make your Tefilah set" (*Avos*, 4:4). "Set," says the Baal Shem Tov, means, do not set a fixed agenda for your Tefilah. Before you begin to Daven, do not think, "I need to Daven about this specific idea and nothing else." Rather, we need to be open, fluid, and responsive in our Davening. Whatever pops up or comes to mind while Davening is often a sign of what is deeply troubling you. These are the immediate issues that need attention. In this way, you can welcome them in order to Daven about them; pray for the wisdom and guidance to be able to deal with these very issues that arise during Davening. Such thoughts are thus not distractions, but rather directions, showing us which path will be most productive for our spiritual growth and healing.

It was once asked of the Baal Shem Tov, "What should a person do if he prayed without intention and his mind was occupied with 'foreign thoughts'?" The Baal Shem responded, "It is known that there is nowhere the Divine Presence is not present, even in the midst of foreign thoughts. If one would decide to start over and begin Davening again, it would demonstrate that Hashem's Presence was not present the first time he Davened those words, which would be heresy! Rather, one should have Kavanah in his mind and read with his eyes the words of the Davening that were originally uttered without intention, [but not speak them with his mouth]" (see *Ben Poras Yoseph*, Toldos. *Shulchan HaTahor* (Komarna) 61, 7, 3. This idea of not repeating what was said already seems to apply even when a person did in fact have full Kavanah the first time: *Agra d'Pirka*, 62).

The depth of this principle is that there is nothing random in the universe, and the Divine purpose-driven presence is available everywhere and within everything. Even deeper, not only is Hashem present in an abstract way, but even the 'foreign' thoughts a person has during Davening are for a purpose, and in fact, as discussed, we can actually learn something from them. They are teaching you something about yourself, revealing hidden 'Sparks' that are seeking to be elevated.

'Pause, wait, and notice' are the steps necessary to let go of these thoughts and also to learn from them. Ideally, however, one would Daven with uninterrupted Kavanah and focus, without any distracting thoughts bubbling up. How then can we achieve this type of focus, at least on some level?

Occupying the Mind

An occupied mind is one that does not become distracted, at least not as easily. If, while you are trying to concentrate during Davening, distracting thoughts keep popping up, this shows that your mind and heart are not

fully engaged in the experience (שאין מחשבת עריות מתגברת אלא בלב פנוי מן החכמה:
Rambam, *Hilchos Isurei Bi'ah*, 22:21. This is true with any thoughts. If the mind is empty of chosen thoughts, other unwanted thoughts will enter; the Alter Rebbe uses the analogy of a home without a roof to illustrate this dynamic of consciousness: *Likutei Torah*, Bamidbar, 83d).

When we Daven with full intention and Kavanah, no other thoughts can forcefully enter our minds, as the mind cannot think two separate thoughts simultaneously. In the words of the Ra'avad, וכללו של דבר אין אדם יכול לכוין דעתו לב' דברים כאחד / "The principle is that a person cannot have full intention on two things at the same time" (*Hilchos Parah Adumah*, 7:3).

Maintaining Kavanah and mindful intention is thus one path to ensure that little or no intruding thoughts distract the mind. As being fully engaged in Davening through the mental exertion of applying complex *Kavanos* / intentions leaves no room for other thoughts or even feelings to enter one's consciousness. When Davening with the Kavanos of the Arizal for example, in which intricate, exact Kavanos are prescribed for every detail of the Davening, there is little to no room for extraneous thoughts to take hold. However, with such intensive focus on occupying one's mind during Davening through intricate Kavanos, it makes it less likely that the heart will become inflamed, which is essential to both the foundational root and aspirational fruit of Davening. This is precisely what the Baal Shem Tov's approach to Davening adds, through a redistribution of effort and awareness. The path of the Baal Shem offered a way to integrate the mind (and even the Kavanos of the Arizal) with the rest of one's being, involving and activating their emotions and physical sensations along with their intentions, weaving all of one's faculties into a singular prayerful experience.

By analogy, imagine yourself at your own wedding, or that of your child or very dear friend. At the peak moment of the wedding, maybe when you are standing under or near the *Chuppah* / wedding canopy, you will be completely focused on the immediate present. Such presence is not only the result of one's mental gymnastics in such a moment, but of a true openness and vulnerable sensitivity to the absolute preciousness of the experience. This is true in almost all moments of great joy or, Heaven forbid, times of deep tragedy. It is thus beneficial to attempt to enter into a similar state of immediacy and intensity while Davening, and according to the Baal Shem Tov, this is most fully achieved with one's whole being, not just their mind. For in truth, in the moment of Tefilah you are standing face to face within the Presence of the Infinite Creator, Destroyer and Sustainer of all that is, was and will be. Recognizing this is both terrifying and awe inspiring. This spiritually visceral experience is related directly to the development of the inner qualities of Yirah and Ahavah, as discussed. This is only achieved through a whole-system engagement of all of one's faculties, not through a hyper-focus of all of one's energies on their mental capabilities.

Again, this is the ideal state for Davening, where you are inflamed with such Presence, Yirah and Ahavah that no other thoughts can enter your mind; as a result, you do not need to struggle with intruding thoughts, as there simply are no other thoughts inn this eternal moment.

The question remains, however, what should be done when you are not yet in this deep state of engaged awareness and distracting thoughts do come up? As discussed, one method is to pause and wait until they pass. But what if the thoughts keep coming up in rapid succession, and do not give you even a moment of respite, perhaps even preventing you from speaking a few words of the Davening without distraction? What then?

Emptying the Mind by Using a Chosen Phrase

Rebbe Yeshayah HaLevi Horowitz, otherwise known as the Shaloh HaKodesh, speaks of a practice to clear the mind which involves the repetition of a phrase of Tehilim three times. He writes that if a person is distracted by extraneous thoughts before he begins to Daven and he desires to rid himself of these thoughts to begin Davening, he should gently move his right hand across his forehead three times, and say each time the *Pasuk* / verse, לב טהור ברא־לי אלקים, ורוח נכון חדש בקרבי / *Lev Tahor Bara-Li Elo(h)im, VeRuach Nachon Chadeish B'Kirbi* / "Create in me a pure heart O G-d, and renew within me an upright spirit" (*Tehilim*, 51:12. *Machatzis Hashekel, Shulchan Aruch*. Orach Chayim, 98:1. *Mishnah Berurah*, 98:2). During Davening, when you are in a place in the liturgy that you cannot interrupt, you may utilize this practice by meditating on the passage instead of saying it aloud, thereby not actually 'interrupting' the text of your Davening.

This Pasuk, besides containing innate spiritual powers of its own, serves as an audible focus point. By repeating it three times, the Pasuk fills the mind with its content, sound and light, while simultaneously clearing the mind of all other extraneous thoughts and distractions.

Likewise, the Ramak, Rebbe Moshe Cordovero, records a teaching he heard from the 'old man', Eliyahu haNavi / Elijah the Prophet (*Siddur R. Shabtai*, Sader HaLimud, 16:1. *Avodas Yisrael* (Koznitz), Mishpatim): When you are in the middle of Davening and a negative thought comes to mind, such as jealousy or anger, if it is in a place during Davening where you can make a verbal interruption, repeat the Pasuk, אש תמיד תוקד על־המזבה, לא תכבה / *Eish Tamid Tukad Al HaMizbe'ach, Lo Sichbeh* / "An eternal flame shall be kept burning on the altar, it must not be extinguished" (*Vayikra*, 6:6), and gently wipe your forehead while having the intention to wipe away these extraneous thoughts from your mind (Shaloh, *Sha'ar HaOsyos*, Lev Tov. *Keser Shem*

Tov, p. 16. *Kaf HaChayim*, Orach Chayim 98. The Arizal also teaches a practice of wiping the forehead three times. *Siddur HaAri*, R. Shabsi Rashkaver, p. 16).

The *Poskim* / the codifiers of Halacha speak of a practice in which a person recites the syllable, *Pi* (pronounced 'pea') three times, while moving his hand across his forehead, symbolically erasing the negative thoughts from his mind; the person should then spit lightly three times, symbolically releasing the negative thoughts with the ejected spit (*Shulchan Aruch*, Orach Chayim, *Mishnah Berurah* 98:2. *Beer Heitev* ad loc. The *Magen Avraham* (ad loc) writes that this is not a proven technique).

On the one hand, the sound '*Pi-Pi-Pi*' seems meaningless and irrational. And indeed, while these syllables are in themselves nonsensical and are only meant to clarify the mind by their mere percussive sound and repetition, they do also possess a deeply encoded semantic meaning. *Pi* (Pei-Yud) is an acronym for *Palti* and *Yoseph* (*Sanhedrin*, 19b). Famously, these are two Torah figures who overcame their desire in the face of temptation. In this way, there is an evocation of their memory and merit to help us to overcome our internal struggle with our thoughts, and to focus on our Davening.

Additionally, the *Gematriyah* / numerical value of *Pi* equals 90. Three times 90 is 270, which is equivalent to the word *Ra'* / evil or negativity. In this way, saying *Pi* three times is meant to eradicate any harmful distractions or negative thoughts. *Pi*, on a literal level, means 'mouth' or opening. *Pi* repeated three times refers to the three 'mouths' that 'opened' miraculously in the Desert: the "mouth of the earth," the "mouth of the donkey," and the "mouth of the well" (*Devarim Nechmadim*, Avos). Repeating the word *Pi* three times is also a Tefilah, asking Hashem to help us close the faucet of our 'tempting' or 'negative' invading thoughts, and to 'open' our minds to elevated and holy thoughts.

Breaking Negative Thoughts by Thinking Other Thoughts

One's mind is almost always occupied with thoughts, and if not with chosen, productive, positive and holy thoughts, other thoughts will take hold (In the words of the Rambam, יפנה עצמו ומחשבתו לדברי תורה וירחיב דעתו בחכמה שאין מחשבת עריות מתגברת אלא בלב פנוי מן החכמה: *Hilchos Isurei Bi'ah*, 22:21). And so, if a person is trying to Daven and their mind keeps on slipping into negative thoughts, not only inappropriate thoughts unrelated to their Davening, but actually negative thoughts such as a narrative of anger, hate or jealousy, this means that these thoughts are more intriguing and compelling, sadly, than Davening. What should one do if this is the case? If you merely stop and pause to let the thoughts pass, they may pass for the moment, but if they are compelling, they will probably come back a few seconds or minutes later.

One creative way to negate such persistent thoughts is to pause and think about something that is even more pertinent in your life than the negative narrative, even if it is not directly related to Davening, such as your business or financial situation (*Hachsharas HaAvreichim*, 9. p.125). Now, once the stream of your previous thoughts of anger, hate or jealousy are interrupted, then you can stop choosing to think about your business, and it will be easier for you to re-engage your focus on your Davening.

This practice does not always work for everyone or in all situations. Sometimes, exchanging one set of distracting thoughts with another, even if they are consciously chosen, just exacerbates the predicament and causes more distraction and lack of focus. This can make it even harder to re-engage, as now there are two 'foreign' narratives pulsating through your consciousness. But sometimes it is the perfect antidote and remedy for distracting thoughts. Know yourself, and know what works; whatever method you are using, make sure that it helps you have more Kavanah when you are Davening. Informed flexibility over rigid formulas — that is the essence of the Baal Shem Tov's approach to Davening.

Visualizations

There are also various visualization practices taught by the sages to help you concentrate during Davening and get rid of intruding thoughts. Dovid HaMelech says in *Tehilim*, "I have placed Hashem before me at all times" (16:8). While on a simple level this implies that one should sense Hashem's Presence at all times, this verse can also be understood literally, meaning, 'I have placed the letters of the Name of Hashem (Yud-Hei-Vav-Hei) before myself at all times,' and to actually visualize these four letters in front of you (*Meiras Einayim*, Ekev. 11-22. *Maggid Mesharim*, Vayikra. *Sha'ar Ruach HaKodesh*, Derush 1. *Sha'arei Kedushah*, 3:4. *Be'er Heitiv*, Orach Chayim, 1:3).

This visualization is important at all times throughout the day, not just during Davening. Holding the Four Letter Name of Hashem in one's imaginal field is a most powerful tool to eradicate all manner of unwanted and distracting thoughts (*Noam Elimelech*, Tzetal Katan). This is another method mentioned by the great sages and Tzadikim throughout the generations.

There is also another visualization mentioned by the students of the Baal Shem: If you find that your mind is roaming or drifting during Davening, imagine yourself standing in Gan Eden, in Paradise, in front of the Throne of Glory (*Toldos Yaakov Yoseph*, Tetzaveh. Or visualize yourself standing in the Beis HaMikdash: Rebbe, Rayatz, *Igros Kodesh*, vol. 8, p. 200. *Hach'sharas HaAvreichim* 4. See also *Shulchan Aruch*, Orach Chayim, 95:2 and *Mishnah Berurah*, 94:2). If you can bring this lofty image up into your consciousness and secure a good visualization of it, it will certainly assist you in ridding yourself of all unwanted and intruding thoughts, and allow you to Daven with greater focus and Deveikus.

In general, imagining yourself Davening in Gan Eden can be very helpful to have more Kavanah (*Reishis Chochmah*, Sha'ar HaKedushah, 4). For example: Imagine that you are now Davening in Gan Eden together with and in the presence of all the exalted souls of the Tzadikim or righteous people of the past. Imagine, as you are Davening, that the Baal Shem Tov, or any other Tzadik that you have personally known, physically seen or heard about, is Davening with you (*Yosher Divrei Emes*, Os 33. *Likutim Yekarim,* 129a. See also *Kreina D'Igrata,* 3). Feel the elevated bliss, light and power generated from such a visualization flowing through your Davening.

Submitting One's Thoughts to Hashem

A more subtle approach to dealing with distracting thoughts during Davening is as follows: For one Yesh to disappear and another Yesh to manifest, there needs to first be an emergence of, or immersion in, *Ayin* / no-thing-ness. A seed disintegrates in the soil before it can sprout new life, and if a person wishes to use the wood of a table and make it a chair, he first needs to deconstruct the table (*Likutei Amarim*, Ohr Torah, p. 21). In order for one form to change to another form, it needs to go through a process of shedding its first form; the old Yesh has to become Ayin before a new Yesh can appear. And here is the secret: an object can only become Ayin through our relationship to it. If we are Ayin in our relationship to a certain Yesh, then that object too becomes Ayin, as it were.

Spirituality and physicality mirror each other. Just as changing a silver plate to a cup requires flattening out the old form to alter a spiritual reality, you need to 'elevate' the existing Yesh to a state of open potential in Ayin. This elevation is accomplished primarily by the observer of the spiritual object himself becoming Ayin, including being personally unattached in relation to that object. The observer affects the observed, at least in its relationship to the observer, and thus the observed also becomes Ayin. Then, from this state of Ayin, a new Yesh can become manifest.

Now let us understand this as it relates to changing one's habit of being distracted in Davening, in order to begin experiencing Deveikus. The way your attention is functioning now is the current Yesh, and this needs to be elevated and dissolved in Ayin in order to allow a new level of attention to emerge. For you to be Ayin in relation to your stream of thoughts, one approach is to simply declare that you are above them, unattached and unconcerned. Be nothing and give stray thoughts no landing place. In other words, do not fight the mental distractions, nor show any interest in them; just let them be while calmly ignoring them like an absentminded host. You are not actively avoiding or suppressing your thoughts; you are above them and they cannot touch you. Keep your eyes on the words of the Siddur, and if necessary, keep your finger on the place you are reciting, as thoughts rise and vanish into Ayin.

If this strategy of ignoring thoughts does not seem to help, you may need to submit your thinking to Hashem altogether, both the 'words' of distracting thoughts and the words of the Siddur. Neither the distracting thoughts nor the words of prayer are yours; you are placing them both in Hashem's hands. This way you become the Ayin 'prior to' the Yesh of all thoughts, and before all words you are no more than a silent listener. Before beginning the Shemoneh Esrei, you can contemplate the opening sentence, *Ado-noi Sifasai Tiftach u-Fi Yagid Tehilasecha* / "Hashem, may *You* open my lips and my mouth shall speak *Your* praise." The words and praises of Tefilah are Hashem's own words and praises; you are just a bystander, allowing Hashem to speak through you, as it were. You are a self-empty conduit for Hashem's praise. You might not even *Shukel* / sway or move in the Tefilah, because it is not 'your' Tefilah; there is no more you, Only the One Source of Tefilah, Only Hashem, from which all prayer emerges and to which all prayer is directed.

Either way, once you are nullified along with all of your so-called 'distractions', now you can fill your mind with a new Yesh: the awareness that the words of Davening have profound meanings and intentions, whether you know their details or not. The words of the Siddur are invitations to Deveikus. Listen for, and accept one or more of these invitations. Come back, again and again, to the Ayin above thought, whenever needed. Every word is a doorway to the deepest depths, every letter unlocks infinite reservoirs of Divine light.

Looking in the Siddur, Seeing the Words on the Page

Earlier there was a discussion about whether you should look into the Siddur while Davening or if it would be best to Daven with your eyes closed. It appears from the sources that it really depends on the level of intensity of one's Davening and whether one is Davening in a *Mochin d'Gadlus* / expansive mind state, or *Mochin d'Katnus* / constricted, small mind state. What is also abundantly clear is that for a person struggling with holding intention or being distracted with intruding thoughts, looking into the Siddur will help tremendously. The holy words on the page have the power to break the grip of negative thoughts and empower one's focus. Therefore, if you find your attention drifting away, focus your mind on the words on the page. This, say many sources, is a proven practice to dispel any and all distracting thoughts (Visualize the words on the page in your thoughts to break negative thoughts. This is a proven practice. *Nefesh HaChayim*, Sha'ar 2:13. *Biur HaGra*, Shulchan Aruch, Orach Chayim, 98. The Rebbe, *Igros Kodesh* 22, 8,278. See also Rav Eliyahu Mani (associate and student of the Ben Ish Chai), *Kise Eliyahu*, Sha'ar 3. There is a teaching repeated in the name of the Gra, ובבאה לפני המלך אמר עם־הספר ישוב מחשבתו הרעה / "When (Esther) came in front of the king, he said, "With the book, his negative scheme will recoil": *Megilas Ester* 9:25. Homiletically, this means, 'When we come before the King, with the book (i.e., looking in the Siddur) all negative thoughts will recoil — be nullified: *Divrei Eliyahu*, Inyanei Tefilah).

The holy letters are vessels of light and blessing, they have the Koach to hold our thoughts and dissolve all negative distractions.

The Baal Shem Tov, as well, talks about the power of seeing the letters on the page and how it can help break and eradicate all negativity, *Din* / judgments and concealments, and expand one's consciousness. Here is an example: If a person finds himself in a constricted state of Katnus and isn't able to concentrate on his Davening, or worse, he is being overwhelmed with negative and intruding thoughts, then he should try to pray simply, like a child, and look into the Siddur, Davening word for word. As the Baal Shem Tov testified to his students, when he was traveling abroad in Turkey and was in a relative state of Katnus (however we can understand 'Katnus' in relation to the holy Baal Shem), he cleaved to the simple letters themselves. The letters can anchor you in holiness, even when the winds of distraction are forcefully blowing.

Here is what the Baal Shem Tov says. When a person Davens looking into the *Kesav* / the written letters on the page, and connects himself with them, then he elevates the physical level of reality, as it were. The word *Kesav* consists of three Hebrew letters, Kuf-Tav-Beis. Kuf stands for the word *Keser* / crown. Keser is the essence of all reality. Tav is the final letter of the Aleph-Beis (and numerically is 400) and thus represents Malchus, the vessel, the concretization of Creation. In this way, the letters on the page themselves are the crown, the essence of the 'vessels' of density and physicality. The letter Beis of *Kesav* stands for *Binah* / understanding. When we Daven with even simple mindful understanding and Kavanah, our Binah activates and elevates the vessel, the Malchus, the place of constriction, and gives it life and *Mochin* / intelligence; in this way we crown (Keser) creation (Malchus). In turn, through animating and elevating the Malchus of the letters on the page, we too are elevated out of our own Katnus and experience a higher level of Mochin, *Chayus* / life and animation (*Kesones Pasim*, Balak. *Amud HaTefilah*, 46. See also *Ben Poras Yoseph,* p. 116. *Amud HaTefilah*, 77). Binah (consciousness) is thus the bridge between Malchus (creation) and Keser (Creator).

Before they are read, letters on the page are dead, inanimate and lifeless, in themselves lacking meaning and purpose. They are in a state *Katnus* / constriction, revealing an absence of Chayus and Mochin. It is only when a reader with life and intelligence comes along and reads these words on the page, that they become alive and expressive. The words on the page are 'concealed' until the reader reads and *understands* them. It is thus only through the act of reading, chanting, singing, and understanding their meaning that their *Dinim* / concealments become 'sweetened' and they acquire meaning, purpose, Mochin, Chayus and *Gadlus* / expansiveness.

What's more, even though Hebrew words are read from right to left, most of the letters themselves are written from left to right (note, *Medrash Talpiyo*s, Anaf Geulah). For example, if a person were to write the word אב / *Av* / father, which is spelled with an Aleph and a Beis, they would begin to write the letter Aleph from the furthest top-left corner of the slanted line א and move towards the lower right corner. The same is true for the *Beis* / ב. One would begin with the left side of the upper horizontal line and move rightwards — counter to the right-to-left flow of reading. (This dichotomy is in fact a source of the argument in the Poskim regarding the principle "all turns that you make should be only to the right": *Yuma*, 58b, and how we kindle the Chanukah candles. Does it mean that we begin from the right and move left, as we read words, or does it mean we begin from the left and move towards the right, as we write the letters? The Levush (*Orach Chayim*, 676:5) argues the first way, while *Malbushei Yom Tov,* ad loc, argues the latter.)

Left is Gevurah, Din, constriction, concealment, boundedness. Right is Chesed, giving, openness, revelation. In this way, before the letters on the page are read, they are rooted in Gevurah, constriction and concealment, revealing no information. Reading the letters transforms them into vessels of *Chesed* / loving-kindness, openness, and revelatory expressiveness. Indeed, once a person reads the letters, they become animated and reveal limitless depths of information, ideas, and energy. Even reading with the bare minimum Kavanah, like that of a child, redeems the letters from Katnus to Gadlus.

All of this triggers the same movement within a person's consciousness. The dead letters on the page parallel our own Katnus within our own psyche; our inability to focus, our lifelessness. If we are experiencing a lack of Mochin, weighted down by negative or petty thoughts, if we ourselves feel like we are in a state of constriction, frustration, agitation, or a general sense of 'smallness', then by infusing Mochin, Binah, life, vitality, meaning and Gadlus, into the lifeless letters on the page, we too will be elevated into a state of Gadlus.

This is because there is a psychological feedback loop in what we are doing on the 'outside' and what we are experiencing 'inside'. Actions affect awareness. Reading the letters on the page and having a basic understanding of what they mean, thus infusing them with life and Mochin, is an activity that occurs in our own psyche. Thus, the outer exercise of reading affects our inner experience, and we are pulled out of our Katnus to a relative state of Gadlus.

It is worth noting that sometimes Binah, in relation to the letters, can simply mean just knowing what the words mean, or even just being able to identify the letters themselves A story is told in the book *Shivchei HaBaal Shem Tov* of how, when the Baal Shem was traveling with his daughter and

Reb Hirsh Sofer in hope of reaching Eretz Yisrael, they were captured by bandits who wanted to kill them:

As the bandits were sharpening their knives, Reb Hirsh cried out, "Please, Rebbe, do something." But the Baal Shem Tov remained silent. "Why do you remain quiet?!" screamed Reb Hirsh. Gently, the Baal Shem responded, "I forgot everything." (Because of his travels or reasons beyond our comprehension, the Baal Shem was experiencing a dramatic form of *Katnus HaMochin* / constriction of consciousness.) "I cannot even remember the Aleph-Beis…. Maybe you remember something?" "I also forgot everything," said Reb Hirsh in astonishment, "I only remember the letters of the Aleph-Beis." "Then chant them!" said the Baal Shem Tov. As Reb Hirsh recited each letter, the Baal Shem Tov repeated each letter after him. They went letter by letter, with the bare minimum of 'intention'. Finally, in the middle of the saying of the Aleph-Beis, *Mochin d'Gadlus* / expansive consciousness returned to the Baal Shem and he intuited and said that they would all be saved shortly. Such is the power of the letters themselves.

Body Movement

As an 'external' action can affect our internal experience, a shift of the body can create a corresponding shifting in our deeper consciousness. The human body is a unified organism, every part is interlinked with every other part, forging a deep relationship between our body and our mind. This mind-body relationship can function as a bio-psychic feedback loop, with the activities of our mind affecting the experiences of our bodies, and the activities of our bodies, in turn, affecting or guiding our mental and emotional states.

In *Shushan Sodos*, a medieval text attributed to a student of the Ramban, the author speaks of using physical movements of the head to create shifts in consciousness. He writes that if one wants to elevate his Binah, his 'lower' level of consciousness, and connect it with his Chochmah and Keser, his higher levels of mind and consciousness, "he should lift his head and tilt his head a little backwards" (*Shushan Sodos*, Os 76). The physical movement of the head upwards and backwards propels an inward shift from a lower to a higher state of consciousness.[*]

Within the context of Mach'shavos Zaros, if a person is stuck in negative thought patterns as they are trying to have Daven with Kavanah — for example, if they find themselves continually thinking about what they need to do at work, or about their relationship or finances — they need a shift of consciousness. The mere act of walking around and moving the body may help facilitate this shift. Literally just moving the body, or 'Shukeling' and swaying, can help to inspire the desired shift in one's mind.

Rebbe Pinchas of Koretz, a student of the Baal Shem Tov, teaches that physical movement disperses negative, habitual, self-centered thoughts. This is because a physical shift and movement triggers a mental shift and movement within (*Imrei Pinchas*, p. 136). Therefore, if you find yourself plagued by intruding thoughts as you are trying to Daven, perhaps start Shukeling or walking about, this may help 'move' your mind from one state to another.

A similar idea is found in the teachings of the Baal Shem Tov, which implies that even slight movements of the eyes can shift one's focus and

---

[*] A scientific periodical that explored the various compartments of the brain was once shown to the Mitteler Rebbe, Rebbe DovBer. In the journal it was written that if one desires to recall something, one should tilt the head back with the face up, and if the need arises for contemplation, the head should tilt forward, with the face down. Upon reading this, the Rebbe walked over to his bookshelves, removed an ancient text and pointed out this very same theory, written hundreds of years earlier. Besides the above text of Shushan Sodos, see also Rebbe Meir Ibn Aldavi, the grandson of the Rosh: *Shevilei Emunah* (printed 1990), Nosiv 4, p. 151.

release the 'density' (distractions) of their body. This is perhaps related to the contemporary therapy EMDR, in which eye movement is used to help release trauma from the body. In the words of the Baal Shem, "There are times when a person has to look 'this way and that way' to keep his mind and heart cleaving to Hashem. This is because the density of the body conceals the soul" (*Tzava'as HaRivash*, 80).

The movement of the eyes or head back and forth re-engages a person's ability to focus. It is like a shaking out of negativity, especially if done in rapid movement. When a person is anchored in negative or intruding thoughts, the mere act of refocusing one's attention on something else forces attention away from where it was previously fixated.

Another kind of physical shift can be created though simple relaxation. If distracting thoughts are being produced by inner tensions, then tensely Shukeling or moving around may not help, but bodily relaxation can. When a mental voice is creating inner noise or drawing you away from Kavanah, there is often at that moment a subtle tension in your vocal cords, as if the body is speaking the thoughts that you are 'hearing'. As such, if you can pause to soften and relax the area at the bottom of your throat, along with your tongue and mouth, you may find your mind becomes dramatically quieter and you can return to Davening.

In general, any shift or movement has the power to break ingrained patterns. We may begin with a shift in the body's position and end up affecting a shift of mindset. The movement literally and figuratively takes you to another place. This is one of the inner reasons why the tradition is to *Shukel* or 'sway', moving to and fro during Davening; it is a way of finding stillness in motion. The rhythmic movement can help to focus the mind and maintain the Kavanah. On the other hand, many find that in the Amidah prayer, shifting into stillness and deep calm is what helps them stay present within the Davening. Different moments call for different movements. Staying aware of the subtle shifts, both within ourselves and within the various stages of the Davening, is a fundamental Nekuda / point in the Baal Shem Tov's approach to Tefilah.

Clapping Hands

Clapping your hands to regain focus is another, similar suggestion. In general, clapping the hands while Davening was an early custom among the followers of the Baal Shem Tov and their own disciples (See for example, *Noam Elimelech*, Shemini. מכה כף אל כף: *Degel Machaneh Ephrayim*, Noach). While perhaps the involuntary or non-premeditated clapping of the hands is a demonstration of *Hislahavus* / ecstatic expression, it was also pointed out that the more conscious act of clapping the hands helps break negative patterns of thought (*Meor Einayim*, Likutei Torah, p. 227) and 'cleanses the *Avir* / air' around us (*Likutei Eitzos*, Tefilah, p. 157. *Likutei Moharan*, 1:46). When the air or mental space 'around us' is pure, we are more receptive and open to purer thoughts and influences in our environment and surroundings. Our thoughts tend to be more pure and clear in an environment of purity and clarity; clapping our hands with Kavanah can help clear our minds and 'clear the air'.

Therefore, if you sense yourself wandering from your Davening, give a sharp clap with your hands to bring yourself back into focus. Besides the clearing and cleansing effect of the clap, you will notice that automatically your awareness will be directed to the noise and away from the distracting thoughts. You will thus distract the distraction. Once your attention becomes focused by the sudden noise, you can use that focus to redirect your mind to your Davening.

Using Sound or a Niggun to Cut Away Intruding Thoughts

In addition to clapping or Shukeling, you may find that you can get a strong refocusing effect by using your voice. If you are Davening alone, or in a congregation that is open or accustomed to such expressions, you might try giving a sudden shout, scream, sigh or a cry to shift and sharpen your consciousness. Sometimes a scream or a shout can shock you into refocused presence. On the other hand, if the congregation would not be receptive to this, such a method may startle people, or backfire by increasing your self-consciousness or even subtle arrogance.

A more subtle way to re-engage your attention with Davening, and perhaps equally effective, is humming a *Nigun* / wordless melody. A Nigun has the capacity, says the Rebbe Rayatz, "to eradicate all extraneous thoughts during Davening" (*Sicha Yud Tes Kislev*, 5708). A Nigun has the Koach to clear the mind and empty it from all distracting thoughts. Notably, one of the words for song in Hebrew is *Zimrah*. The root word of *Zimrah* is *Zamer* / to prune (*Yeshayahu*, 25:5. *Sha'arei Orah*, Sha'ar 1). When we sing with intention we are pruning and removing the weeds that crowd the garden of our consciousness. A Nigun serves to refocus our attention and cut away all distracting thoughts.

Elevation of Thoughts

For eliminating distraction, there is another novel approach revealed by the Baal Shem Tov, called *Ha'ala'as HaMidos* / the elevation of attributes, meaning the sublimation and transformation of a 'negative' thought in order to return it to its Source in Kedushah.*

---

* *Keser Shem Tov*, Chap. 171. *Tzava'as HaRivash*, 87. *Magid Devarav LeYakov*, Likutei Amarim, Ohr Torah, 37. *Likutim Yekarim*, 194. *Ohr HaEmes*, p. 2. *Degel Machaneh Ephrayim*, Behaalosecha, p. 177. *Meor Einayim*, Shemos. *Zikhron Zos*, p. 141. Interestingly enough, in the great dynasties of Gur, Tzanz; the Divrei Chayim, the Chidushei Harim and Sefas

Instead of trying to totally nullify Mach'shavos Zaros by either pushing them away or simply ignoring them, which can, at times, also be very effective (see *Meor Einayim*, Likutei Torah, Pesach, p. 117. ואם יראה האדם שמבלבלין אותו this במחשבות זרות, זאת עצתו בוודאי שלא להשיב לו מטוב ועד רע, ולעשות כאלם וחרש לא ישמע: method is much more aligned with the Alter Rebbe's approach), in this approach we actually go deeper into them, and try to get to the spiritual source of these 'negative' or 'random' thoughts.

This practice is predicated on the idea that we can use every emotion for growth in Kedushah, holiness and spiritual Avodah. For example, when feeling sad, it can actually be a good time to Daven (*Mei HaShiloach* 2, Miketz). One can harness a melancholy mood to seriously contemplate our distance from HaKadosh Baruch Hu (*Tanya*, 31: אך שעת הכושר, שהיא שעה המיוחדת וראויה לכך לרוב בני אדם, היא בשעה שהוא עצב בלאו הכי ממילי דעלמא, או כך בלי שום סיבה, אזי היא שעת הכושר להפך העצב להיות ממרי דחושבנא). In relation to specific thoughts, we can attempt to delve beyond their facade, beyond the *Kelipah* / covering shell of the thought itself in order to uncover and reveal the subtle seed of light, the beauty and holiness within it. Once we do this, we can then harness and channel the subsequently aroused emotion or spiritual pleasure for the purpose of Davening and *Deveikus* / attachment and cleaving to Hashem.

HaKadosh Baruch Hu's Presence is everywhere and in everything. Just as every space is filled with Hashem's Presence, and each moment of life is another opportunity to encounter the Divine Presence, the same must also be true with thoughts. Every thought that comes to you (in contrast to thoughts you choose through your free will), although rooted in your subconscious mind, is another opportunity for a deeper encounter with yourself and Hashem.[*]

Emes, there is very little to no conversation regarding what to do with Mach'shavos Zaros.
[*] The Avos established the three Tefilos of the day. אברהם תקן תפלת שחרית, שנאמר: "וישכם אברהם בבקר אל המקום אשר עמד שם", ואין "עמידה" אלא תפלה. יצחק תקן תפלת מנחה, שנאמר "ויצא יצחק לשוח בשדה לפנות ערב", ואין "שיחה" אלא תפלה יעקב תקן תפלת ערבית, שנאמר: "ויפגע

HaKadosh Baruch Hu is always present, even if we are lacking Kavanah and our minds are occupied with other thoughts. Our sages tell us (*Berachos,* 33b-34a), if one says the first sentence of the Shema twice, we silence him, since it may appear as if he is affirming a dualistic heresy. Asks the Gemara, "Perhaps initially he did not focus his attention on the recitation of the Shema, so he repeated it with more focus as he recited it the second time. So why do we silence him?" Answers the Gemara, "Can one have that degree of familiarity with Heaven, to the extent that he can take his words lightly and say them however he likes? If he did not focus his attention initially, we beat him with a blacksmith's hammer until he focuses his attention." In other words, he should have had Kavanah the first time he said the Shema. But what happens, asks the Baal Shem Tov, if he actually

במקום וילן שם", ואין "פגיעה" אלא תפלה / "Avraham instituted the morning prayer, as it is stated, 'And Avraham rose early in the morning to the place where he had stood,' and standing means nothing other than prayer....Yitzchak instituted the afternoon prayer, as it is stated, 'And Yitzchak went out to converse in the field toward evening,' and conversation means nothing other than prayer....Yaakov instituted the evening prayer, as it is stated, 'And he encountered (as if suddenly) the place and he slept there for the sun had set.' The word 'encountered' means nothing other than 'prayed'": *Berachos,* 26b. These three terms that denote Tefilah, "standing," "conversing," and "encountering," represent three forms and postures of Tefilah. There is a 'morning' posture of Tefilah, in which we are standing up, tall, confident and ready to serve Hashem: (כמו (לעיל יח ח) והוא עומד עליהם לשמשם: Rashi, *Bereishis,* 24:30); in this state of mind, we are ready to answer the Divine call and mission with freshness and excitement. There is the 'afternoon', midday posture of Tefilah, when a person who is deeply involved in his day to day life, dialoguing with commerce, pauses for a few moments to reach out and speak to Hashem. Yet, there is also a posture of Tefilah that occurs in the 'evenings', in a place of darkness and uncertainty, the world of suddenness and unexpectation, and even there, in the place of "encounter," where life seems to be merely happening to you almost suddenly, there too one reaches out in prayer. Perhaps for this reason, morning and afternoon prayers are obligatory, but by definition 'night', representing a lack of clarity, cannot be a clear obligation (indeed most time- bound Mitzvos are obligations that need to be performed by day), and it is thus a voluntary act, a Reshus. On an even deeper level, by elevating the unexpected moments, the sudden 'thoughts', the non-premeditated thoughts, we are demonstrating that even in this place of darkness and uncertainty, we reach out in faith and become elevated in Divine union.

did not have Kavanah and he is simply saying the Shema again because he did not have Kavanah the first time? In this case, why not let him say it again and have Kavanah? Why do our sages say that no matter the case, we should silence him? Says the Baal Shem (*Amud HaTefilah*, 116), this is because by repeating the words again he is denying the legitimacy of his first recital of the Shema, and in this way, denying that Hashem was present in the place of his distraction — and that is simply not true. Hashem's Light is always present, even in the place of apparent obscurity and lack of focus (*Heichal HaBrachah*, Otzar HaChayim, Chukas).

Everything, even the most intrusive or distracting thoughts or feelings, is rooted in the Infinite Oneness of HaKadosh Baruch Hu. We can play a proactive role in liberating the Divine from the mundane by cracking open the 'shell' of distraction, an 'externality' of concealment which paradoxically protects the seed of holiness within and prevents it from blossoming before its time. This liberation allows the seed of holiness to realign and return to its Root, and we, in turn, are uplifted to a state of unity and purity within Hashem.

Hashem is always present; even in intruding thoughts the Light of Hashem is there, albeit in a concealed state. Our task is to learn how to peel away the Kelipah to reveal that light.

Sensing Hashem's Presence within All of Life

Life becomes exponentially more meaningful and multi-dimensional when we are able to see that Hashem's Presence is within everything, and that everything has a Divine message for us, just waiting to be revealed. Each and every thought, feeling and experience is there to show us something, to teach us how we can become more fully ourselves. When something comes up, we should always ask, 'Why am I seeing this? Why am I experiencing this?' When a thought enters our mind, we need to ask, 'Why am I having this particular thought and what can I learn from it?'

Within the answer to that question, which often appears in a still small voice from within our deepest self, lies the secret to unlocking our dormant potentials for growth, inner development and connection to HaKadosh Baruch Hu.

In this context, if while you are Davening a foreign thought comes un-invited into your mind, instead of immediately pushing it aside, ignoring it, or pausing and waiting for it to dissolve, take a moment to look directly at it. Listen to it and realize that the reason you are having this particular thought at this particular time is that the inner desire, the inner spark of this thought and feeling wants to return to its Source in Kedushah (The Baal Shem Tov teaches that the reason a person has intruding thoughts during Davening is that the Sparks therein desire elevation: *Ben Poras Yoseph*, p. 50b-c. *Divrei Moshe*, Lech Lecha).

Let's say the intruding thought involves a self-centered physical or emotional desire for pleasure. One can expect that within this desire there is a spiritual Spark that yearns to be released and returned to its Source in holiness. For example, a desire to overindulge in a certain food reflects an inner desire to elevate the energy contained within that food back to its Source. As it says in *Tehilim* (107:5), "Hungry as well as thirsty, my soul withers within me." In other words, my body feels hunger, but more deeply, it is my soul that seeks spiritual replenishment through the elevation of the Divine sparks within the food I am craving (*Keser Shem Tov*, p. 50). The body's hunger is a manifestation of the soul's appetite for elevation.

It is similar with every aspect of life, our thoughts included; there is a symptom and a cause. We are having certain thoughts, but why? In simple terms, these feelings and thoughts are surfacing at this moment in order for us to plant them in the soil of holiness, and discard their shell in order for them to blossom and reveal their inherent beauty. In a sense, we re-root these seeds in their supernal Source in the Infinite Unity of the Creator. When we can do this, even the 'shell', the 'unholy' aspect of the thought or feeling, can be repurposed and redeemed.

But how does one do this? How does one release the negative and reveal the positive quality of a desirous or self-centered thought? How does one actually perform Ha'ala'as HaMidos?

Furthermore, how do we know if the thought that enters our mind is meant to be elevated through some type of engagement with it? Maybe the elevation is meant to occur specifically through pushing it aside or ignoring it. The Toldos Yaakov Yoseph, a prominent student of the Baal Shem, writes that the way to know if engaging the thought can elevate it, is if when you have the thought, it is immediately followed by another thought regarding how you can elevate the first thought. If such a subsequent thought comes to you, it is proof that you can elevate it. If not, the elevation of the thought needs to occur through rejecting it, not by engaging it.

Every Thought and Feeling is Rooted in One of the Divine Sefiros

In this context, it is helpful to know that every thought, feeling and experience is rooted in a pure supernal source and can be traced to its root in one of the Ten Sefiros. Even if a person is experiencing panic, fear or a strong lust or desire, and the mind keeps on burping up thoughts related to these issues, according to the Baal Shem Tov, all these thoughts can be traced to their Divine root. Fear is rooted in Gevurah, the Divine attribute of severity and restriction. Lustful desire is rooted in the Divine attribute of Chesed. The Torah calls the most abominable act of lustful desire "a [form of] Chesed" (*Vayikra*, 20:17). Certainly, such an act is an extremely perverse and negative expression of Chesed, but it is rooted there, nonetheless. In any case, whatever thought enters your mind, it may be possible to trace it back to its Source in one of the Sefiros (although the Alter Rebbe and many other great Tzadikim tell us that this Avodah is only to be performed by Tzadikim — as explained below).

Practically speaking, if a thought or desire for a physically beautiful object or person arises, one should contemplate the source of this desire. One should reflect and consider that the aesthetics and the beauty of this object or person are nothing other than manifestations of the Divine animating force that created it to be this way, and deeper, it is a reflection of the Sefirah of Beauty, the Divine attribute of Tiferes. Therefore, one is able to redirect his desire in service of the Source of Beauty, Hashem (See *Reishis Chochmah*, near the end).

ויברך דויד את ה' לעיני כל־הקהל / "And Dovid blessed Hashem in front of the entire congregation" (*Divrei HaYamim* 1, 29:10). This, says the Baal Shem Tov, means that he showed the people that Hashem's glory fills the world. How did he do so? By showing them that לך ה' הגדלה והגבורה והתפארת והנצח וההוד / "Yours, Hashem, are the greatness and the might, the beauty, the victory and the majesty." He showed them that every emotion of this world, such as "greatness," which is Chesed, or "might," which is Gevurah, or "beauty," which is Tiferes, and so forth — are Yours, Hashem, they are all rooted in and are expressions of You (*Degel Machaneh Ephrayim*, Re'eh. *Baal Shem Tov al HaTorah*, Bereishis, 13).

Three Stage Process

Let us look deeper into the mechanics of Ha'ala'as HaMidos. To do so, it will be helpful to consider a kind of spiritual 'master key' that the Baal Shem Tov identifies in his teachings. The Baal Shem speaks of a three stage process found in every form of rectification or elevation: first there is *Hachna'ah* / submission, then *Havdalah* / separation, and finally *Hamtakah* / sweetening (*Toldos Yaakov Yoseph*, p. 208d. *Amud HaTefilah*, 110). In terms of Avodah and Teshuvah, these three phases can be described as follows.

Hachna'ah is the process of looking honestly at your life up until this present moment and fully acknowledging and embracing all of yourself. This includes not only your body, identity, status, thoughts and feelings, but perhaps also all of your past mistakes and shortcomings. *Hachna'ah* is to humbly accept that you did something wrong; it was your own doing and level of consciousness and is a result of the way you have been manifesting yourself in this world. This is a practice of 'submission to what is'.

Havdalah starts with the understanding that *you* are not what you have done. You are not your thoughts or your emotions; you 'have' emotions, feelings and thoughts, but *you* are not them. You are not even your body, you (your Neshamah) has a body. You may have done something wrong, but you yourself are not wrong. You *did* an Aveirah, for example, but you are not the Aveirah. It is absolutely essential to separate who you *are* from what you *do*, so as not to get shackled and trapped by your own negative misidentifications.

Hamtaka is the rectification and transformation of the Aveirah. From the place of Havdalah you became 'separate' from it. Now you are able to rejoin life and enjoy its 'sweetness', for the seed of holiness within the Aveirah has been elevated and transformed into a means of reconnecting to HaKadosh Baruch Hu from a healthy, wholesome space. From a place of detachment, one can more easily ascertain what the Divine purpose was within a particular thought or action; this in itself is a form of 'sweetening', as even negative experiences are understood within a greater, meaningful context.

In Davening, specifically in terms of Ha'ala'as HaMidos, the three part process unfolds as follows:

1) If and when a negative thought enters your mind, stop and practice Hachna'ah; submit to the reality that you are on the level to have such a thought. Your experience of this distraction is a reflection of where you are currently holding. You will likely feel contrition in the fact that in the middle of your private meeting with the Divine Presence, another part of yourself is pushing you to entertain such trivial or selfish thoughts. Realize that those thoughts hold your attention more than the Davening does, otherwise your mind would not wander into those areas. Be humble and submit to this unfortunate reality. It's not 'bad' to feel humbled at the recognition that you dragged such immature nonsense into your conversation with the King of the Universe; humility is good for us. Swallow this bitter medicine, it is for your own good.

2) Practicing Havdalah in Davening is different from the general practice of severing yourself from a negative trait or action. Here, Havdalah means to separate the narrative of your thoughts from the sensation that you are experiencing in the moment. The narrative is the negative element, and we need to separate it from the related sensations, which are by nature positive. For example, while the narrative of a lustful thought is negative, the sensation of love or yearning for closeness is positive. You can untangle the two and hold on to the sensation of love, while jettisoning the specific narrative you were attaching to it. A fearful narrative is negative, yet the

actual sensation of fear is positive, and can be reflected on and reassociated with awe of the Creator and Hashem's Creation.

3. Once we have practiced Havdalah as stated above, then we can experience Hamtakah, the sweetening of the distraction — as it is now no longer a distraction, but rather an ally in Davening. Having directed and focused the redeemed sensations or emotions of love or fear, etc., towards Hashem, they are now vehicles of Deveikus, carrying us ever-closer to the One.

Sensation & Narrative

Another way of saying this is that every *Midah* / attribute and feeling has both a *Chomer* / essence, which is the sensation, and a *Tzurah* / form, which is the narrative, the mental story that is attached to the sensation, and gives it rise. The actual feeling that we are experiencing is the 'raw data' of warm, cool, open, closed, constricted, expanded, and so forth.

Let's say a person is feeling lust. The Chomer — the sensation of desire to draw closer and connect with an 'other' and thereby experience happiness — is in itself holy and noble and rooted in wanting to get closer to Hashem, the Source of Happiness. The external Tzurah of the feeling of lust is the narrative, the mental story suggesting that connecting with a certain person, or kind of person, will produce the happiness that is sought. Thus, when this type of thought and emotion arises in our consciousness, we should try to go deeper into the raw data of the feeling itself and strip it away from the misdirected desire for the *Kelipah* / negative Tzurah, inspired by the erroneous story and narrative. We should sense the purity of the feeling itself, which can lead us straight to the unlimited happiness of Deveikus.

Again, every feeling or thought that arises carries with it both a Chomer, the sensation, and a Tzurah, the narrative. The issue is, these two different aspects of an experience normally register as one inseparable reality. For example, in the feeling of anger, there are tangible sensations in the body, such as heat in the face, tension in the stomach, and the racing of the heart. And then there is the narrative which prompted the anger — because 'this' or 'that' should not have happened and the situation must be forcefully corrected. In this method of Ha'ala'as HaMidos, the idea would be to separate the sensation, the feelings of anger, from the narrative and mental imagery which drives and magnifies the experience. The sensation of anger itself may be a feeling of being small and powerless. This feeling can be converted into a humbling of the ego, which is an extension of Yiras Hashem, awe of Hashem, which is a valuable element of Davening. In this way we can 'recycle' our sensations and redirect them back to their Source in Hashem.

From Finite Tzurah to the Infinity Beyond Tzurah

In the deepest level of the above practice, one would move from the story, the Tzurah of the thought and emotion, to a space that is beyond Tzurah altogether. For example, in the place of feelings and thoughts of lustful desire that are directed toward a *Murgash* / sensed entity that is finite and embodied in a Tzurah, one can experience an infinite formless love toward Hashem and all of Hashem's Creation.

In this way, the exclusive and finite Midah gives birth to a truly inclusive and infinite sensation directed towards HaKadosh Baruch Hu. A person can burst with holy emotions of infinite, burning love for HaKadosh Baruch Hu by stripping the earthly and finite Tzurah down to its pure Chomer, to its core. The core of lust is a wildly passionate love for the Creator, and thus by extension, for all of Hashem's Creation.

In this way, from the Murgash one comes to the purely *Muskal* / abstract, refined, contemplative love of HaKadosh Baruch Hu (see also *Reishis Chochmah*, Sha'ar HaAhavah in the name of Rebbe Yitzchak of Acco). One transitions from the desire for a finite, potential pleasure to the infinite pleasure of Deveikus, revealing that the initial finite pleasure was merely a tiny fraction of the ultimate infinite pleasure of being close to Hashem (*Degel Machaneh Ephrayim*, Vayigash).

A desire for pleasures of the flesh is an expression of the Sefirah of Chesed in a fallen and exiled *Tzurah* / form. The 'core', the essence of the Midah has become enmeshed in Kelipah and negativity. Through Ha'ala'as HaMidos, we strip away the narrative and Tzurah of this desire. We can even strip away the Tzurah so completely that we are left only with the pure Chomer of the emotion, which is an infinite love for Hashem and all of Hashem's Creation. This same process can be applied not just to lust, as we have demonstrated, but to all of our varied emotions and narratives.

The Spiritual Dangers of this Method

To be clear, there is a real spiritual danger with this method of delving more deeply into Mach'shavos Zaros. If one does not have control over his thoughts, and most people do not, then diving into such thoughts, feelings or desires will only enmesh a person deeper and deeper into their Kelipah. Then, the deeper one goes into them, the lower one will descend, and the more entangled one will become with the 'shell' or Kelipah of these thoughts. Instead of elevating the thoughts to their Source, one will in fact be lowering oneself deeper into the abyss of his own chaotic subconscious. As the Alter Rebbe emphatically states in Tanya with regard to elevating thoughts, איך יעלהו למעלה והוא עצמו מקושר למטה / "How can you elevate these thoughts on high as you yourself are bound below" (*Tanya*, 28. See also, *Derech Pikudecha*, Hakdamah 7. *Maor VaShemesh*, Re'eh. *Komtez HaMinchah*, 16. Note, *Zo-*

har Chai, Vayechi, 217a). As such, the Alter Rebbe, and many later Tzadikim, such as the Bnei Yissaschar and Reb Tzadok, teach that the practice of Ha'ala'as HaMidos is an *Avodah* / a Divine way of service only for Tzadikim, and not for the average man. However, those who are not (yet or never will be) Tzadikim should not become depressed and downcast by intruding thoughts, rather, they should battle them in their Davening in their own way, and with increased joy.

Indeed, honesty is integral for any spiritual practice. For the majority of people, most of the time, their thoughts control them, and attempting Ha'ala'as HaMidos is counter-productive, only submerging them deeper and deeper into the very Kelipah that they wanted to break and elevate. One is 'under' his thoughts insofar as they control him, and, as the Alter Rebbe asks, "How can he elevate these thoughts on high when he himself is bound by below?" The more he allows himself to engage with such thoughts, and does not push them aside or let them dissolve, he will only sink lower and lower.

Yet, it is perhaps also equally true that there are certain areas in life that you have more control over than others. One may be struggling or battling in many aspects of life, and yet within his life there may be certain aspects in which he is 'like a Tzadik', or at least has more control over. For example, it can be assumed that most people reading this text do not struggle with thoughts of, *Chas v'Shalom* / G-d forbid, murdering another human being. They may struggle with jealousy or lust, but they do not, thank G-d, struggle with such destructive urges. These areas or urges that no longer enmesh us in active contention are what teachers of *Musar* / Torah Ethics call 'below the *Nekudas HaBechirah* / the point of choice'. Within our Nekudas HaBechirah we are currently able to, and hopefully do, make good choices day to day. However, there are areas in our life that are 'below' our threshold of free choice — they are thus automatic, healthy and positive choices that we easily make. They have become part of our 'second nature', so to speak. For one person, the choice not to murder is below their Nekudas HaBechirah, it is simply not even a question. For another, telling lies is not a challenge. It could be argued that with issues that are below their Nekudas HaBechirah, a person is, so to speak, on a *Madreigah* / level of a Tzadik, and in these issues Ha'ala'as HaMidos can be practiced, even according to the Alter Rebbe (Or when a person is Davening with tremendous spiritual invigoration, [as a 'Tzadik', see *Tanya*, 13] as Rav Avraham Yitzchak Kaan suggests, *Likutim Yekarim*, Hagaha, p. 58-59). With regards to those particular issues he is at least temporarily a Tzadik, and may thus attempt to practice Ha'ala'as HaMidos. (The idea of Ha'ala'as HaMidos, which is generally reserved as an Avodah for Tzadikim, seems especially more relevant now, in this generation. The (Lubavitcher) Rebbe declared that the Avodah of *Birurim* / sifting and elevating the Sparks has already been completed, certainly on the level of the collective, and thus, what is demanded now is the Avodas Tzadikim, the revealing of Yechidah, a level of Avodas Hashem beyond the place of struggle and strife.)

We all have weaknesses and strengths; we struggle in one area but may be very proficient in another. A person can be a Tzadik in relation to certain issues in their life, a צדיק לאותו דבר / "Tzadik with regards to that thing" (*Tzidkas HaTzadik*, 58), while being the opposite of a Tzadik in other areas. Each person has particular points within himself wherein he may honestly state that with regards to specific thoughts, desires or distractions, they are *like* a Tzadik, beyond struggle, at least most of the time. And therefore, when thoughts, feelings or desires arise to one's consciousness during Davening, one should be honest. Know your state of mind and heart and discern what type of thoughts and feelings these are. Are they truly *Zaros* / 'foreign' to you, or are these your normal thoughts, belonging to the spiritual level where you are currently residing? Also take note whether you feel inspired and awakened enough to attempt to practice the elevation of these thoughts. If not, pause and let the thoughts go, and utilize one of the other practices discussed above.

Interestingly enough, a prime Talmid of the Alter Rebbe, Reb Aharon Strashelye, speaks about another form of Ha'ala'as HaMidos (*Sha'arei Avodah*, Sha'ar Teshuvah, Chap. 3), keeping in line with the *Shitah* / opinion of his Rebbe. Essentially, one should not delve into the negative thoughts that arise, rather, one should push them aside and strip away their *Chayus* / life force and narrative. Then, having removed oneself completely from the Kelipah of the emotion, one can then harness the impartial energy and vitality of the body, the shell itself, to direct the initial passion into a holier and more expansive context.

A Similar Means to Dissipate Negative Thoughts

We will now explore one last idea connected to the practice of Havdalah and learning to separate the core sensation, the Chomer, from the external narrative, the Tzurah. This, perhaps, will be applicable to all people and at all times, and this is the approach suggested by the wise Chasidic Rebbe, Reb Bunim of Peshischa. He taught that one should not push thoughts aside, nor get entangled with them, nor aspire to elevate them. Rather, he advised that we nullify negative thoughts simply through clear and correct observation.

Imagine that you are in the middle of Davening and a foreign thought about a 'horse' enters your mind. This is the actual example that Reb Bunim brings. Of course, a 'horse' is a metaphor, and you can exchange the image of the horse with any more pertinent image. Instead of trying to push the thought and feeling about this horse aside, as the more one resists the more it persists, pause for a moment and mindfully, objectively 'see' the nature of the object you are thinking about or desiring. Realize it is only a horse and nothing more. Such objective acknowledgment helps to deflate the feelings of urgency and immensity often accompanying such distracting thoughts, allowing us to return to what is truly important.

Thinking about a horse in the middle of Davening is certainly distracting, and such a thought needs to be eliminated — but it is not in itself a negative thought, per se. It is not the horse that is the real problem, or even what is holding your attention. Rather, it is everything that you are projecting upon the horse; what you are fantasizing about the horse, what it can do for you, or the feeling you will have owning or possessing the horse. This is the real issue. The narrative you are attaching to the horse is the Kelipah. It is not the horse itself but the 'fantasy', the narrative attached to the horse that traps you like a fly in a web. That is what is devastating and damaging. Whereas the horse is just a horse, and nothing more.

Use your imagination and translate the 'horse' to whatever distracting, negative, materialist, lustful or angry thoughts that enter your mind during Davening, and in fact, during any moment of the day. Whenever such 'horses' gallop through your mind, pause and attempt to separate the objective object or sensation from your subjective, superimposed narrative. Observe the thought, take notice and it will reveal that when you strip away the fantasy, what remains is merely a 'horse'. And a horse, on its own, does not grip your imagination. And so, just as quickly as they appeared, these uninteresting thoughts about 'horses' will disappear and you will be able to go back to your mindful Davening, and in general, your conscious, virtuous life.

May we all be *Zocheh* / meritorious to experience even one real Davening where we Daven with complete, unself-conscious Deveikus and move through the entire Amidah without any interruptions or intrusive thoughts. And then, as the Baal Shem Tov teaches, after we have moved out of the Amidah we will notice that we have truly attained, at least on some *Madreigah* / level, the Ohr, the Ayin, the Atzilus of Hashem; we will have touched (and been touched by) the Ein Sof and can thus rest assured that our Tefilos were *Niskabel* / received and accepted on High.

Among Rav Pinson's published works are:

RECLAIMING THE SELF
The Way of Teshuvah

THE MYSTERY OF KADDISH
Understanding the Mourner's Kaddish

UPSHERNISH:
The First Haircut

A BOND FOR ETERNITY
Understanding the Bris Milah

REINCARNATION AND JUDAISM
The Journey of the Soul

INNER RHYTHMS
The Kabbalah of MUSIC

MEDITATION AND JUDAISM
Exploring the Jewish Meditative Paths

TOWARD THE INFINITE

THIRTY – TWO GATES
Into the Heart of Kabbalah & Chassidus

THE PURIM READER
The Holiday of Purim Explored

EIGHT LIGHTS
8 Meditations for Chanukah

THE IYYUN HAGADAH
An Introduction to the Haggadah

PASSPORT TO KABBALAH
A Journey of Inner Transformation

THE FOUR SPECIES
The Symbolism of the Lulav & Esrog

THE JEWISH BOOK OF
LIFE AFTER LIFE

THE GARDEN OF PARADOX:
The Essence of Non - Dual Kabbalah

THE MEDITATION SERIES:

(1) BREATHING &
    QUIETING THE MIND

(2) VISUALIZATION
    AND IMAGERY:
    Harnessing the Power of our
    Mind's Eye

(3) SOUND AND VIBRATION
    Tuning Into the Echoes of Creation

THE POWER OF CHOICE:
A Practical Guide to Conscious Living

MYSTIC TALES FROM THE EMEK
HAMELECH

INNER WORLDS OF JEWISH
PRAYER

SPIRAL OF TIME SERIES:

(Vol 1) THE SPIRAL OF TIME:
Unraveling the Yearly Cycle &
Rosh Chodesh

(Vol 2) THE MONTH OF NISAN:
Miraculous Awakenings from
Above

(Vol 3) THE MONTH OF IYYAR:
Evolving the Self & The Holiday of
LAG B'OMER

(Vol 4) THE MONTH OF SIVAN:
The Art of Receiving:
Shavuos and Matan Torah

(Vol 5) THE MONTHS OF
TAMUZ/AV:
Embracing Brokenness,
Transforming Darkness

(Vol 6) THE MONTH OF ELUL:
Days of Introspection and
Transformation

(Vol 7) THE MONTH OF TISHREI:
A Time of Rebirth & Upward
Movement

(Vol 8) THE MONTH OF
CHESHVAN:
Navigating Transitions, Elevating
the Fall

(Vol 9) THE MONTH OF KISLEV:
Rekindling Hope, Dreams and
Trust

(Vol 10) THE MONTH OF TEVES:
Refining Relationships: Elevating
the Body

(Vol 11) THE MONTH OF SHEVAT:
Elevating Eating & The Holiday
of Tu b'Shevat

(Vol 12) THE MONTH OF ADAR:
Transformation Through
Laughter & Holy Doubt

THE JEWISH WEDDING:
A Guide to the Rituals and Traditions of
the Wedding Ceremony

WRAPPED IN MAJESTY
Tefillin - Exploring the Mystery

SECRETS OF THE MIKVAH
Waters of Transformation

THE MYSTERY OF SHABBOS
Shabbat Rediscovered

OTHER BOOKS BY RAV PINSON

RECLAIMING THE SELF
The Way of Teshuvah

Teshuvah is one of the great gifts of life. It speaks of a hope for a better today and empowers us to choose a brighter tomorrow. But what exactly is Teshuvah? How does it work? How can we undo our past and how do we deal with guilt? And what is healthy regret without eroding our self-esteem? In this fascinating and empowering book, the path for genuine transformation and a way to include all of our past in the powerful moment of the now, is explored and demonstrated.

THE MYSTERY OF KADDISH
Understanding the Mourner's Kaddish

The Mystery of Kaddish is an in-depth exploration into the Mourner's Prayer. Throughout Jewish history, there have been many rites and rituals associated with loss and mourning, yet none have prevailed quite like the Mourner's Kaddish Prayer, which has become the definitive ritual of mourning. The book explores the source of this prayer and deconstructs the meaning to better understand the grieving process and how the Kaddish prayer supports and uplifts the bereaved through their own personal journey to healing.

UPSHERNISH: The First Haircut
Exploring the Laws, Customs & Meanings of a Boy's First Haircut

What is the meaning of Upsherin, the traditional celebration of a boy's first haircut at the age of three? Why is a boy's hair allowed to grow freely for his first three years? What is the deeper import of hair in all its lengths and varieties? What is the meaning of hair coverings? Includes a guide to conducting an Upsherin ceremony.

A BOND FOR ETERNITY
Understanding the Bris Milah

What is the Bris Milah – the covenant of circumcision? What does it represent, symbolize and signify? This book provides an in depth and sensitive review of this fundamental Mitzvah. In this little masterpiece of wisdom – profound yet accessible —the deeper meaning of this essential rite of passage and its eternal link to the Jewish people, is revealed and explored.

REINCARNATION AND JUDAISM
The Journey of the Soul

A fascinating analysis of the concept of Gilgul / Reincarnation. Dipping into the fountain of ancient wisdom and modern understanding, this book addresses and answers such basic questions as: What is reincarnation? Why does it occur? And how does it affect us personally?

INNER RHYTHMS
The Kabbalah of MUSIC

Exploring the inner dimension of sound and music, and particularly, how music permeates all aspects of life. The topics range from Deveikus/Unity and Yichudim/Unifications, to the more personal issues, such as Simcha/Happiness and Marirus/ sadness.

MEDITATION AND JUDAISM
Exploring the Jewish Meditative Paths

A comprehensive work encompassing the entire spectrum of Jewish thought, from the sages of the Talmud and the early Kabbalists to the modern philosophers and Chassidic masters. This book is both a scholarly, in-depth study of meditative practices, and a practical, easy to follow guide for any person interested in meditating the Jewish way.

TOWARD THE INFINITE

A book focusing exclusively on the Chassidic approach to meditation known as Hisbonenus. Encompassing the entire meditative experience, it takes the reader on a comprehensive and engaging journey through this unique practice. The book explores the various states of consciousness that a person encounters in the course of the meditation, beginning at a level of extreme self-awareness and concluding with a state of total non-awareness.

THIRTY – TWO GATES OF WISDOM
into the Heart of Kabbalah & Chassidus

What is Kabbalah? And what are the differences between the theoretical, meditative, magical and personal Kabbalistic teachings? What are the four paths of interpreting the teachings of the ARIzal? What did Chassidus teach? These are some of the fundamental issues expanded upon in this text. And then, more specifically, why are there so many names of G-d and what do they represent? What are the key concepts of these deeper teachings?

The book explores the grand narrative of the great chain of reality, how there was and is a movement from the Infinite Oneness of Hashem to a world of (apparent) duality and multiplicity.

THE PURIM READER

The Holiday of Purim Explored

———————

With a Persian name, a masquerade dress code and a woman as the heroine, Purim is certainly unusual amongst the Jewish holidays. Most people are very familiar with the costumes, Megilah and revelry, but are mystified by their significance. This book offers a glimpse into the hidden world of Purim, uncovering these mysteries and offering a deeper understanding of this unique holiday.

———————

EIGHT LIGHTS

8 Meditations for Chanukah

What is the meaning and message of Chanukah? What is the spiritual significance of the Lights of the Menorah? What are the Lights telling us? What is the deeper dimension of the Dreidel? Rav Pinson, with his trademark deep learning and spiritual sensitivity guides us through eight meditations relating to the Lights of the Menorah, the eight days of Chanukah, and a fascinating exploration of the symbolism and structure of the Dreidel. Includes a detailed how-to guide for lighting the Chanukah Menorah.

———————

THE IYYUN HAGADAH

An Introduction to the Haggadah

In this beautifully written introduction to Passover and the Haggadah, we are guided through the major themes of Passover and the Seder night. This slim text, addresses the important questions, such as: What is the big deal of Chametz? What are we trying to achieve through conducting a Seder? What's with all that stuff on the Seder Plate? And most importantly, how is this all related to freedom?

PASSPORT TO KABBALAH
A Journey of Inner Transformation

Life is a journey full of ups and downs, inside-outs, and unexpected detours. There are times when we think we know exactly where we want to be headed, and other times when we are so lost we don't even know where we are. This slim book provides readers with a passport of sorts to help them through any obstacles along their path of self-refinement, reflection, and self-transformation.

THE FOUR SPECIES
The Symbolism of the Lulav & Esrog

The Four Species have inspired countless commentaries and traditions and intrigued scholars and mystics alike. In this little masterpiece of wisdom both profound and practical - the deep symbolic roots and nature of the Four Species are explored. The Na'anuim, or ritual of the Lulav movement, is meticulously detailed and Kavanos,, are offered for use with the practice. Includes an illustrated guide to the Lulav Movements.

THE BOOK OF LIFE AFTER LIFE

What is a soul? What happens to us after we physically die?

What is consciousness, and can it survive without a physical brain?

Can we remember our past lives?

Do near-death experiences prove immortality?

What is Gan Eden? Resurrection?

Exploring the possibility of surviving death, the near-death experience and a glimpse into what awaits us after this life.

(This book is an updated and expanded version of the book; Jewish Wisdom of the Afterlife)

THE GARDEN OF PARADOX:

The Essence of Non - Dual Kabbalah

This book is a Primer on the Essential Philosophy of Kabbalah presented as a series of 3 conversations, revealing the mysteries of Creator, Creation and Consciousness. With three representational students, embodying respectively, the philosopher, the activist and the mystic, the book, tackles the larger questions of life. Who is G-d? Who am I? Why do I exist? What is my purpose in this life? Written in clear and concise prose, the text, gently guides the reader towards making sense of life's paradoxes and living meaningfully.

BREATHING & QUIETING THE MIND

Achieving a sense of self-mastery and inner freedom demands that we gain a measure of hegemony over our thoughts. We learn to choose out thoughts so that we are not at the mercy of whatever belches up to the mind. Through quieting the mind and conscious breathing we can slow the onrush of anxious, scattered thinking and come to a deeper awareness of the interconnectedness of all of life.

Source texts are included in translation, with how-to-guides for the various practices.

VISUALIZATION AND IMAGERY:

Harnessing the Power of our Mind's Eye

We assume that what we see with our eyes is absolute. Yet, beyond our ability to choose what we see, we have the ability to choose how we see. This directly translates into how we experience life. In a world saturated with visual imagery, our senses are continuously assaulted with Kelipa/empty/fantasy imagery that we would not necessarily choose. These images can negatively affect our relationship with ourselves, with the world around us, and with the Divine. This volume seeks to show us how we can alter that which we observe through harnessing the power of our mind's eye, the inner sanctum of our imagination. We thus create a new way to see and experience the world. This book teaches us how to utilize visualization and imagery as a way to develop our spiritual sensitivity and higher intuition, and ultimately achieve Deveikus/Unity with Hashem.

————

SOUND AND VIBRATION:
Tuning into the Echoes of Creation

Through our perception of sound and vibration we internalize the world around us. What we hear, and how we process that hearing, has a profound impact on how we experience life. What we hear can empower us or harm us. A defining human capacity is to harness the power sound -- through speech, dialogue, and song, and through listening to others. Hearing is primary dimension of our existence. In fact, as a fetus our ears were the first fully operating sensory organs to develop.

This book will guide you in methods of utilizing the power of sound and vibration to heal and maintain mental, emotional and spiritual health, to fine-tune your Midos and even to guide you into deeper levels of Deveikus / conscious unity with Hashem. The vibratory patterns of the Aleph-Beis are particularly useful portals into our deeper conscious selves. Through chanting and deep listening, we can use the letters and sounds to shift our very mindset, to induce us into a state of presence and spiritual elevation.

————

THE POWER OF CHOICE:
A Practical Guide to Conscious Living

It is the essential premise of this book that we hold the key to unlock many of the gates that seem closed to us and keep us from living our fullest life. That key we all hold is the power to choose. The Power of Choice is the primary tool that we have at our disposal to impact the world and effect change within our own lives. We often give up this power to outside forces such as the market, media, politicians or peer pressure; or to internal forces that often function beyond our conscious control such as ego, anger, lust, greed or jealousy. Making conscious, compassionate and creative decisions is the cornerstone of living a mature and meaningful life.

MYSTIC TALES FROM THE EMEK HAMELECH

Mystic Tales of the Emek HaMelech, is a wondrous and inspiring collection of stories culled from the Emek HaMelech. Emek HaMelech, from which these stories have been taken, (as well as its author) is a bit of a mystery. But like all good mysteries, it is one worth investigating. In this spirit the present volume is being offered to the general public in the merit and memory of its saintly author, as well as in the hopes of introducing a vital voice of deeper Torah teaching and tradition to a contemporary English speaking audience

---

INNER WORLDS OF JEWISH PRAYER
A Guide to Develop and Deepen the Prayer Experience

While much attention has been paid to the poetry, history, theology and contextual meaning of the prayers, the intention of this work is to provide a guide to finding meaning and effecting transformation through the prayer experience itself.

Explore: *What happens when we pray? *How do we enter the mind-state of prayer? *Learning to incorporate the body into the prayers. *Discover techniques to enhance and deepen prayer and make it a transformative experience.

This empowering and inspiring text, demonstrates how through proper mindset, preparation and dedication, the experience of prayer can be deeply transformative and ultimately, life-altering.

WRAPPED IN MAJESTY
Tefillin - Exploring the Mystery

Tefillin, the black boxes and leather straps that are worn during prayer, are curiously powerful and mysterious. Within the inky black boxes lie untold secrets. In this profound, passionate and thought-provoking text, the multi-dimensional perspectives of Tefillin are explored and revealed. Magically weaving together all levels of Torah including the Peshat (literal observation), to Remez (allegorical), to Derush, (homiletic), to Sod (hidden) into one beautiful tapestry. Inspirational and instructive, Wrapped in Majesty: Tefillin, will make putting on the Tefillin more meaningful and inspiring.

SECRETS OF THE MIKVAH:
Waters of Transformation

A Mikvah is a pool of water used for the purpose of ritual immersion; a place where one moves from a state of Tumah; impurity, blockage and death— to a place of Teharah; purity, fluidity and life.

In SECRETS OF THE MIKVAH, Rav Pinson delves into the transformative powers of the Mikvah with his trademark all-encompassing perspective that ranges from the literal, Pshat observation and Halachic implications of the texts, to the allegorical, the philosophical, and finally, to the deep secrets of the Mikvah as revealed by Kabbalah and Chassidus.

This insightful and inspirational text demonstrates how immersion in a Mikvah can be a transformative and life-altering practice, and includes various Kavanos—deep intentions—for all people, through various stages of life, that empower and enrich the immersion experience.

THE MYSTERY OF SHABBOS
Shabbat Rediscovered

Delving into the transformative power of Shabbos. With an all-encompassing perspective that ranges from the literal, Pshat observation and Halachic implications of the texts, to the allegorical, the philosophical, and finally, to the deeper secrets as revealed by Kabbalah and Chassidus, creating an elegant tapestry of thought and experience. THE MYSTERY OF SHABBOS is a profound meditation on the meaning of Shabbos and demonstrates the physical, emotional, mental and spiritual possibilities available and given to us with the gift of Shabbos. Studying and contemplating this inspired text on the depths of Shabbos will unveil a redemptive light in your experience of the Seventh Day -- and by extension, every day of your life.

THE SPIRAL OF TIME:
A 12 Part Series on the Months of the Year

VOL 1: THE SPIRAL OF TIME:
Unraveling the Yearly Cycle

Many centuries ago, the Sages of Israel were the foremost authority in the fields of both astronomical calculation and astrological wisdom, including the deeper interpretations of the cycles and seasons. Over time, this wisdom became hidden within the esoteric teachings of the Torah, and as a result was known only to students and scholars of the deepest depths of the tradition. More recently, the great teachers, from R.Yitzchak Luria (the Arizal) to the Baal Shem Tov, taught that as the world approaches the Era of Redemption, it is a Mitzvah / spiritual obligation to broadly reveal this wisdom.

"The Spiral of Time" is volume 1 is a series of 12 books, and serves as an introductory book to the basic concepts and nature of the Hebrew calendar and explores the special day of Rosh Chodesh.

———————

VOL 2: THE MONTH OF NISAN:
Miraculous Awakenings from Above

The month of NISAN is the first month of the lunar cycle of the year, a month that brings in the spring and a month of redemption. Spring represents a time of plenty, abundance, sunshine, hope, and possibility. Redemption, on whatever level, feels palpable and accessible. In spring, the world is redeemed from the cold winter, the flower is redeemed from the tree, the grass from the earth, and we too feel that redemption is possible. A whole complex of ideas, including newness, redemption, going out of Egypt, and being freed from slavery, is intricately bound with the idea of Aviv / spring and the powerful month of Nisan.

VOL 3: THE MONTH OF IYYAR: EVOLVING THE SELF
& The Holiday of LAG B'OMER

The month of IYYAR is the second month of the spring, a month that connects the Redemption from Egypt in Nissan with the Revelation of Torah in Sivan. The Chai/ Eighteenth day of the Month is the day we celebrate the Rashbi (Rabbi Shimon Bar Yochai) and the revealing of the hidden aspects of the Torah. This is the 'Holiday' of Lag b'Omer. The book explores the unique quality of this special month, a month that has a Mitzvah of counting the Omer every day. In addition, the book explores the roots and significance of the mystical 'holiday' of Lag b'Omer. Including the customs & Practices of Lag b'Omer, such as, bonfires, bows & arrows, parades, Upsherin, and more.

————————

VOL 4: THE MONTH OF SIVAN:
The Art of Receiving: Shavuos and Matan Torah

Sivan is the third month of the lunar cycle. One is a singularity. Two is division. Three is harmony, a unity that synthesizes individuality and multiplicity, Heaven and Earth, Spirituality and Physicality. During this month we celebrate Shavuos and the giving of the Torah, the ultimate expression of the unity of the Above and Below and we aspire to connect with the Keser/Crown of Torah that Transcends and yet includes all Worlds. Learning how to truly receive Higher wisdom in our Lower faculties is the mental, emotional, and spiritual exercise of the month.

————————

VOL 5: THE MONTHS OF TAMUZ AND AV:

Embracing Brokenness -
17th of Tamuz, Tisha B'Av, & Tu B'Av

Each month and season of the year, radiates with distinct Divine qualities and unique opportunities for growth and Tikkun.

The summer month of Tamuz and Av contain the longest and hottest days of the year. The raised temperature is indicative of a corresponding spiritual heat, a time of harsher judgement and potential destruction, such as the destructions of the first and second Beis HaMikdash, which began on the 17th of Tamuz and culminated on the 9th and 10th of Av.

A few days later, on Tu b'Av, the darkness is transformed and reveals the greatest light and possibility for new life. During these summer months of Tamuz and Av we embrace our brokenness so that we can heal and transform darkness into light.

———————

VOL 6: THE MONTH OF ELUL:

Days of Introspection and Transformation

Each month of the year radiates with a distinct quality and provides unique opportunities for growth and personal transformation. Elul, as the final month of the spring/summer season is connected to endings. Elul gives us the strength to be able to finish strong, to end well. Elul also serves as a month of preparation for the New Year/Rosh Hashanah.

We inhale our past year, ending with wisdom and then we also gain the wisdom to begin anew and exhale a positive year into being. The mental, emotional, and spiritual objective of this month is introspection and the reclaiming of our inner purity and wholeness.

———————

VOL 7: THE MONTH OF TISHREI:
A Time of Rebirth & Upward Movement

Each month of the year radiates with distinct Divine qualities and unique opportunities for growth and spiritual illumination. As Tishrei begins the new yearly cycle, it is an appropriate month to introspect, reflect and resolve to move forward and preserve moving forward into the more inward months of the winter. This month creates the space to unburden ourselves from our negativities, and enter a more sacred, grounded sacred space. In Tishrei we are given the gift of forgiveness and then the ability to truly regain our space and inner joy.

VOL 8: THE MONTH OF CHESHVAN:
Navigating Transitions, Elevating the Fall

Directly on the heels of the inspiring and holiday-filled month of Tishrei, Cheshvan is a month that is quiet and devoid of holidays. In the month of Cheshvan we use the stored up energies of the previous months to self-generate our inspiration and creativity and provide ourselves with the strength to rise up after a fall. In Cheshvan we are entering into a stormier, wetter and colder season. It is a month of transition. The mental, emotional and spiritual objective of this month is to weather the transitions, learn to self-generate and stand tall. And if we do fall, we use the quality of this month to get back up and do so with more conviction, strength, wisdom and clarity.

VOL 9: THE MONTH OF KISLEV:
Rekindling Hope, Dreams and Trust

Kislev is the final month of the fall. Throughout this month, daylight progressively shortens, and the temperatures drop. Towards the end of the month, at the darkest hour, the winter solstice arrives and we begin the celebration of Chanukah. We commemorate the miracle of a small jug of oil that burned for eight nights, and as we celebrate, daylight expands. In the month of Kislev-despite the darkness, or perhaps because of it-we have the ability to tap into the Ohr HaGanuz, the hidden light of hope that rekindles our dreams and aspirations.

VOL 10: THE MONTH OF TEVES:
Refining Relationships, Elevating the Body

The quality of Teves is generally harsh—much like its counterpart Tamuz in the summer, thus the tendency for many is to hunker down, retract, curl up and wait for the month to pass by, only to reemerge when the harshness has dissipated. Think for a moment about the 'easier' months of the year, which, like gentle waves in the ocean, carry us where we want to go. We can ride these energies easily and they can propel us forward effortlessly, we just need to go with the overall flow, so to speak. The harsher months, on the other hand, can be compared to the more powerful waves that emanate from the belly of the ocean, which come forcefully crashing down and can easily drown a person before they even realize what has happened. However, those who want to utilize the momentum of the powerful energy that is available during such times can, with caution and creativity, harness these intense waves and ride them higher and farther than other, more gentle circumstances may allow. However, harnessing the power of Tohu, the raw energy of the body, does in fact need to be approached with great care and attention.

VOL 11: THE MONTH OF SHEVAT: ELEVATING EATING
& The Holiday of Tu b'Shevat

Each month of the year radiates with a distinct Divine energy and thus unique opportunities for growth, *Tikkun* and illumination. According to the deeper teachings of the Torah, all of these distinct qualities, opportunities and natural phenomena correspond to a certain data set. That is, the nature of each month is elucidated by a specific letter of the Aleph Beis, a tribe, verse, human sense, and so forth. The month of Shevat is particularly connected to food and our relationship to bodily intake. During this month we celebrate Tu b'Shevat, the New Year of the Tree, and aspire to create a proper and physically/emotionally/spiritually healthy relationship with food.

VOL 12: THE MONTH OF ADAR:

Transformation Through Laughter & Holy Doubt

Each month of the year radiates with distinct Divine qualities and unique opportunities for growth and spiritual illumination. As Adar concludes the monthly cycle of the year, as well as the solar phenomena of the winter, it is an appropriate month to think about our essential identity, before moving out to meet the world come spring. This month we strive to create a healthy relationship with holy humor, unbounded joy, and a general sense of lightness of being. Through the work of Adar we transform negative, crippling doubt and uncertainties into radical wonderment and openness.

www.ingramcontent.com/pod-product-compliance
Lightning Source LLC
Chambersburg PA
CBHW080922100426
42812CB00007B/2347